Russian
Crimes in
Ukraine

Askold S. Lozynskyj

ISBN

Hardcover:978-1-965560-79-2

Paperback:978-1-965560-80-8

Dedicated to
the people of Ukraine

ABOUT THE AUTHOR

ASKOLD STEPHAN LOZYNSKYJ, son of Evhen (an Auschwitz survivor) and Maria (born Safian) Lozynskyj, immigrants from Ukraine, was born in New York City on February 8, 1952.

He graduated from Fordham College with a Bachelor's in classical languages in 1973 and earned a Juris Doctor from Fordham University School of Law in 1976.

He was admitted to the New York State Bar in 1977 and U. S. Federal practice for the Southern and Eastern districts of New York and specialized in commercial and real estate transactions and litigation as well as non-for-profit law. He represented the Ukrainian American community in a legal proceeding against CBS News before the Federal Communications Commission and served as counsel in numerous de-naturalization, deportation, and social security suspension proceedings involving Ukrainian-Americans accused of material misrepresentation of wartime activities. He has devoted many hours of work representing Ukrainian not-for-profit organizations, incorporating and filing for tax-exempt status.

Lozynskyj has served on various non-profit boards, including the Ukrainian Student Organization, the United Ukrainian American Relief Committee, the Ukrainian Congress Committee of America, where he was chair from 1992 to 2000, and on the Board of Directors of CARE (Cooperative for American Relief Everywhere).

He is the author of hundreds of articles (English and Ukrainian) in various print and Internet media, editor of a compilation of writings and biographies of Ukrainian dissidents in English, and author of many books in both Ukrainian and English, many published by University publication houses throughout Ukraine.

He is married to Roksolana Stojko Lozynskyj. They have two children, Maksym and Kyra.

He has received numerous awards and has met with and conferred with numerous world religious, civic, and political leaders.

Table of Contents

INTRODUCTION

This monograph is a collection of essays, articles and reminiscences authored by Askold Lozynskyj, a prominent political activist and public figure, one of the leaders of the Ukrainian diaspora in the United States.

Various topics are dealt with in the publication, but the omnipotent and the ever-present topic is certainly Ukraine. It is present on every page of the monograph. Russia's criminal full-scale invasion and the brutal attack on the Ukrainian nation in blatant violation of International law and multilateral and bilateral agreements are thoroughly analyzed.

The world's condemnation of the aggression and its full solidarity with Ukraine, multilateral assistance from the US and other Western countries to liberate the occupied lands, and the readiness to rebuild Ukraine after the total victory- are the issues on the current agenda. The priority tasks also include the prosecution of the Russian war criminals and their assistants, the full compensation for the inflicted losses and destroyed infrastructure, and the reunification of the broken families. No negotiations with the aggressor state until Ukraine returns to the state borders of 1991!

The author calls for additional vital steps to be taken: the expulsion of the Russian Federation from the UN Security Council and from the United Nations itself, the dismemberment of the RF into the constituent nations, and the complete demilitarization of the country. The nuclear arsenal on its territory should be removed under the UN supervision to Europe's nuclear states, the United Kingdom and France! The economic, political, and financial pressure on the Russian Federation should intensify, and all-round comprehensive sanctions need to remain on top of the agenda.

A surprise visit by President Joe Biden to Kyiv on 20th February 2023 and cordial meetings with President V. Zelensky and his team became yet another vivid manifestation of American unwavering support for Ukraine, "as long as it takes."

The Western diaspora should continue playing an indispensable and important role in assisting Ukraine to restore its sovereignty,

1

independence, and territorial integrity and to occupy a worthy place in the family of democratic nations.

Several essays deal with a very sensitive issue- the status of smaller nations on the territory of the Russian Federation. These are specifically: Erzya Finnu Ugric peoples of the Volga region, the Bashkirs -the ancient civilization of the Southern Urals, and the Mongolian-speaking Buryats living around Lake Baikal. The tragic histories of these peoples are very similar: annexed by the Russian empire a few centuries ago, these entities were forcibly Russified at the expense of their national cultures and traditions and added to the empire. Their semi-colonial status within the RF has remained up till now. Incidentally, thousands of conscripts fighting in the war against Ukraine were mobilized from these regions in spite of numerous protests by local authorities.

The author also stresses the awareness and significance of some important historic events and jubilees to be remembered: Holodomor- a man-made famine of 1932-1933 perpetrated by the Soviet regime against the Ukrainian nation; the Babyn Yar tragedy- mass killings of civilians of Jewish, Ukrainian and other nationalities by the Germans in the occupied Kyiv in 1941-1943.

Askold Lozynskyj enters into polemics with several authors on the issues of the necessity of Ukraine's membership in NATO and the EU, on some religious topics, on the roles of Bohdan Khmelnitsky, Stepan Bandera, and other historic personalities. A lot of precious information is available in these essays.

I would highly recommend this valuable publication to numerous politicians, historians, and all those who are interested in learning more about Ukraine, its history, and its fight against the aggressor for sovereignty, independence, and prosperity. Glory to Ukraine!

Valerii Kuchynskyi
Ambassador Extraordinary and Plenipotentiary
Adjunct Professor, SIPA,
Columbia University in the City of New York

PUTIN'S ALTERNATIVE HISTORY

People may see events differently, but there are certain criteria in the civilized world, and in historiography, in particular, suggested or generally accepted frameworks for respecting sources and interpreting them reasonably by researchers and scholars who work with them. This apparently does not apply to Muscovites or Russians, who have a legacy of disinformation dating back to the czars. Czarina Catherine II, in the XVIII century, commissioned her sycophantic scholars to write a revised history of the empire from the cradle in order to justify the empire's existence and its role. The czarina found herself an empress. The history written to date was adequate for a duchy but certainly not for an empire. Its beginnings had to predate and be more imposing or venerable than that of its subjects or subordinates. So Catherine II, ruler of the Russian Empire, wrote the history of the empire according to Empress Catherine.

Similarly, today, an authoritarian Muscovite leader without a meaningful educational diploma or legacy, nevertheless, this time relying ostensibly on his own or assisted expertise and, certainly, his own imprimatur, has taken on an equally difficult task, this time rewriting or reiterating his own version of the history of the Empire, albeit limiting himself to the relationship between Muscovites and Ukrainians, his most acclaimed subordinates, currently lost as subjects. In essence, the Ukrainian-Muscovite relationship, at least in the mind of Vladimir Putin, spells the history of the empire.

For the sake of clarity, I must reveal that I am reluctant to use the term "Russia or Russians" because that name does not legitimately belong to the descendants of Muscovy but emanates from the words "Kyivan Rus," the cradle of today's Ukraine. I do revert to the terms "Russia and Russians" at times only for the benefit of the readers and to preclude confusion.

Here are some globally generally accepted historical facts in response to Putin's vision and, in particular, his interpretation of the history of Kyiv and Moscow: My aim is to stress that Putin's interpretation of Ukraine-Russia historical events can be acceptable to no one. The Italian Christopher Columbus, on behalf of Spanish monarchs Ferdinand and Isabella, traveled west in three ships and lost his way to the East Indies but came upon America. Some historians have given him credit for discovering America. Other historians insist that the Viking Leaf Erickson did it earlier. However, no American, as well as neither Columbus nor Erickson, had or have the slightest claim to Rome, Madrid, or Stockholm as their cradle, nor does anyone consider Americans, Italians, Spaniards, or Swedes as being brothers except in the Christian human sense. Similarly, the Normans from France invaded and conquered England, but today's English have no claim to Paris as their cradle. Likewise, the French do not stake claim to London.

The son of Grand Prince Volodymyr Monomakh of Kyiv, Prince Yuri Dovgoruky, traveled (actually had to flee) to the East in search of a place and people to rule and founded a settlement-village-town called Muscovy. Today, it is a large capitol city named Moscow in a vast area of land, spanning ten time zones, gained through centuries of invasion, conquest and, bloodshed.

Contrary to all established norms, this empire and its authoritarian ruler of the 21st century claim that Kyiv is the cradle of its people. For the strength of his argument as a nexus, Vladimir Putin mentions Novhorod, conquered by the Muscovites only at the end of the XV century, and its connection with Kyiv. Novhorod did exist as a part of Kievan Rus and later as its own Novhorod State. Putin's argument goes: Novhorod is part of Russia, and the dynasty of the Kyivan grand princes stems from Novhorod. Thus, Kyiv is the cradle of Russia. The real history is that Novhorod from the ninth century was the Varangian settlement of one Prince Rurik. His descendants constituted the Rurik dynasty of princes that traveled south on the Dnipro River and ruled Kievan Rus for four centuries. However, at no time was Kyiv subservient or dependent upon Novhorod. Muscovites trace Novhorod to Alexander Nevsky, who was there in the thirteenth century but never had anything to do with Kyivan Rus. By the way, Novhorod as a settlement was almost four centuries younger than Kyiv and became a state a hundred years after the beginning of the Kyivan Rus state. Putin's argumentation is, at the very least, a stretch and certainly not scholarly or even rational.

Czarina Catherine II, who ruled the Russian Empire in the second half of the XVIII century, was a German. The name "Russian" was misappropriated by her predecessor, Czar Peter, in the early part of the XVIII century, who also moved the capital from Moscow to St. Petersburg, a city built by him and named brazenly after himself. Despite Catherine's German ethnicity, Berlin does not belong to the formerly Muscovites, now Russians, nor does Moscow or St. Petersburg belong to the Germans. In any case, the Muscovites (Russians) and the Germans are not one people. Muscovites are partly Slavs and partly Finno-Ugric. Ukrainians are Slavs, Poles are Slavs, but Ukrainians and Poles are not brothers as well.

A similar contortion of history is manifested in Moscow's claim to be the "Third Rome" (Rome, Constantinople, Moscow). The Orthodox Christian faith came to Moscow from Kyiv. This faith came to Kyiv from Constantinople, today Istanbul. But Kyiv has never claimed to be the seat of Orthodoxy, and, in fact, several years ago, for Canonical sake, appealed to the Patriarch in Istanbul for recognition. Instead, Moscow, whose Orthodoxy is completely dependent on Kyiv, claims to be the seat of Orthodoxy. The irony is astounding, but not to the Russians or Putin as well as many of his predecessors during the times of Muscovy, the Russian Empire, the Union of Soviet Socialist Republics, or now the Russian Federation. Another ironic subject cited by Putin to reinforce the brotherhood argument is the Ukrainian poet bard Taras Shevchenko. Putin writes, "Taras Shevchenko wrote poetry in the Ukrainian language, and prose mainly in Russian." Putin fails to mention that Shevchenko wrote within the Russian empire, that during his period of exile he was prohibited from writing in Ukrainian. My own reluctance to use the term Russia comes from Shevchenko, who never used the term. Shevchenko's political poetry was devoted to expressing his anti-Muscovy sentiments. Shevchenko cursed the Ukrainian Cossack Hetman Bohdan Khmelnytsky for his alliance with the Czar of Moscow, known as the Treaty of Pereyaslav when he sought an ally against the Poles and the Crimean Khanate. The Muscovites used this opportunity, as usual, and began to take over Cossack lands, appoint hetmans, and so on. However, the Cossacks did not become part of Russia in the XVII century, as Putin states, because there was no such state as Russia. Moscow stole the name and history of Kyivan Rus' only in the XVIII century. The abuse by Moscow was not foreseen by Khmelnytsky, and there was resistance, which ended at the battle of Poltava in 1709 under Hetman Ivan Mazepa, where the Muscovy Czar Peter was victorious. The battlefield was on the territory of the Cossacks, and thus, it was yet another invasion of the Cossack lands by Moscow. Czar Peter reinforced his military victory by taking as his own the name Rus, thus Russian empire.

On the subject of Crimea, Putin is entirely off base. Moscow had nothing to do with Crimea until it conquered it as late as in the second half of the XVIII century (1783). Well before then, Kyiv had existed for over a thousand years and had a history of trade with the Crimea, and even more, Prince Volodymyr of Kyiv was baptized there. Crimea is Ukraine by virtue of the fact that at the time of the Helsinki Accords, it was a part of the Ukrainian Soviet Socialist Republic. Helsinki was quite specific on the inviolability of borders. The Soviet Union signed the accords. The Russian Federation has stressed in international relations that it is the successor in interest to the USSR.

Crimea was colonized by the Russians after 1944 when Josef Stalin perpetrated genocide against the Indigenous peoples, thereby deporting the Crimean Tatars and replacing them with Russians. The above represents some of the more egregious historical distortions by pseudo-historian Putin. There are also minor inaccuracies resulting either from the fact that Putin is not a historian but a dictator or from poor fact-checking, for which someone will be punished. The Ems Decree was proclaimed by Czar Alexander II in 1876, not 1872.

In the list of historical events, it is advantageous for Putin to omit the following historical events: the declaration of independence of Kuban (from the territory of Russia) in 1918 and the appeal of the population of Kuban to join the Ukrainian People's Republic; the Holodomor of 1932-33 and the 7-10 million number of Ukrainian victims not only in the Ukrainian SSR but throughout the Russian SSR, where Ukrainians were concentrated, an alarming decline of some 20% and at the same time an increase of almost 25% of the Russian population; the colonization of Ukrainian lands by Russians where Ukrainians starved to death; a referendum in independent Ukraine in December of 1991, when even regions colonized by Russians in the Donbas and the autonomous republic of Crimea voted overwhelmingly for independence; the invasion of Russian troops, weapons, tanks and missiles, and even nuclear weapons into the Crimea and the Donbas region. Volodymyr Serhijchuk, a professor at Kyiv State University, wrote in response to my inquiry about Putin's article: "Putin's main mistake is that he preaches the unity of Ukrainians and Russians - this cannot be "a priori" because they were created in different climatic conditions with different levels of material production. Alexander Nevsky had nothing to do with the creation of Russia, and Novhorod in the IX century was a West Slavic settlement of Ilmen-Slovenes captured by the Vikings, which had nothing to do with the Finno-Ugric peoples... By the way, Putin does not mention the "fraternal" destruction of Baturyn in 1708 and Kyiv in 1918 for the Ukrainian language.

It is very difficult to convince an uninformed person and impossible to convince a bad intention-ed one. So let Putin tell the story in his own way and let the whole world see him as the murderer he is. If a Muscovite is the brother of a Ukrainian, he is the biblical Cain. The problem, however, is not in the alternative version of history but in the fact that this grossly false information may be read by the uninformed and accepted or used. There is no shortage of uninformed or bad-intentioned people.

The main reason, I suspect, why this alternative history appeared now rather than sooner or later is that Putin is closing in on 69 years. He must realize his own mortality. People in Russia naturally do not live that long, let alone men. True, Putin is not a drinker, but a killer's stress must be severe even in the absence of a conscience or soul, as President Biden suggested about Putin. Putin is killing people, women, and children, not only in Ukraine, Russia, Britain, and even Syria, with chemical weapons. His historical legacy is now that of a murderer and a pariah. Russia needs to expend its own people because it is necessary to colonize Transdnister, Crimea, and Donbas. Russian couples do not have many children in comparison to the Islamic population of the Russian Federation. Putin needs to become an emperor like Empress Catherine II. For that, there must be a Russian Empire.

August 1, 2021

APPEASEMENT IS MORALLY WRONG AND POLITICALLY SHORTSIGHTED.

Ambassador Kurt Volcker was the U.S. Ambassador to NATO and U.S. Special Representative to Ukraine on a voluntary basis. He recently commented on Ukraine's accession to NATO membership. According to him, the Membership Action Plan, which he was instrumental in formulating in 1999, is essentially irrelevant for Ukraine since Ukraine has, to date, complied with all reforms required under MAP.

This is a most significant comment since Ambassador Volcker knows better than President Joe Biden or, President Emmanuel Macron or Chancellor Angela Merkel whether Ukraine is a legitimate and ready candidate for NATO membership. Unfortunately, it also means that President Biden's comment in response to a reporter's question following the recent NATO Summit about Ukraine having to reform in order to qualify for NATO was, at best, an example of President Biden being unformed and, at worst Joe Biden simply took a cue from his predecessor and lying.

It is important to consider the comments of Ambassador Volcker given the upcoming Biden-Zelensky Summit. There is no justification for declining Ukraine's accession to NATO except perhaps the specious "redline" argument. At the Biden-Putin Summit, President Biden drew several red lines mostly regarding cyber hacking by the Russians of American industries. President Putin drew at least one redline as well - Ukraine may not become a member of NATO. While President Biden's redlines were customary and rational under international law, Putin contravened every concept of international law. He brazenly addressed an issue of the sovereignty of another country and violated that sovereignty egregiously. President Biden should have declined to consider Putin's proposal out of hand and voiced his displeasure loudly. That did not happen.

It did not happen because of old policy, defined in the XX century as appeasement. Adolf Hitler and Josef Stalin, including the latter's numerous successors, were appeased, which resulted in the murder of millions. Only presidents Jimmy Carter and Ronald Reagan manifested a backbone and refused to appease. President Biden, who often not only falls back on his political tenure and experience but also his alleged moral compass, insisting that this is not "who we are," unfortunately vis a vis Ukraine, has been a poster child for appeasement. This must change.

The Ukrainian community in the United States should be instrumental in this regard. Frankly, even if America becomes an honest broker and world leader, other Ukrainian communities throughout the world should lobby their own governments. Unfortunately, while manifestly opposed to appeasement, many in these communities have enabled and even facilitated that form of behavior of their own countries by advancing conflated and obsequious arguments about Ukraine's need to reform as a precondition to NATO membership, the current war with Russia being somehow a statutory or legal obstacle to NATO membership and other ridiculous arguments, thereby supplying justification for their governments to appear and feel, albeit disingenuously, morally correct in withholding Ukraine's NATO membership.

My plea to Ukrainian leaders in the diaspora is- stop trying to soften the approach. There are no obstacles or bars to Ukraine's NATO accession except an immoral and politically shortsighted, albeit historical policy on the part of the West known as appeasement. Ukrainian Americans need to remember that U.S. Democratic President Franklin D. Roosevelt recognized the USSR as millions of Ukrainians were dying in the Holodomor and then gave away Eastern Europe to Uncle Joe at Yalta, that Republican President Gerald Ford tried to convince the American voters that there was no Soviet influence in Eastern Europe, that Republican President George H.W. Bush warned Ukrainians about suicidal nationalism and took four months to recognize Ukrainian independence. I could go on. Democrats and Republicans were similar in appeasing.

The Biden-Zelensky Summit is a great opportunity for America and , specifically, President Biden to show the world and Ukraine precisely "who we are." Do we Americans have a backbone, a moral compass, or are we simply inveterate appeasers? This summit is very significant for Ukraine. But it is no less important for Americans to show the world "who we are."

August 7, 2021

NEW YEAR'S HOPES AND GREETINGS

As I look back upon the Old Year and look to the New, I realize that I need to expand my horizons of hope but, nevertheless, keep them within the limits of what is possible because otherwise, my hopes turn into fantasies. This obviously limits a person and, in particular, his imagination or creativity. One must hope. Otherwise, there is no success, no change, and no progress; everything remains as disappointing or simply mundane as it was. Despite the fact that a person does not control his dreams or often his circumstances, he needs the help or participation of others and much luck; he must reach for the stars in thehope of at least some success.

Dreamers can be political animals and vice versa. More often, dreamers achieve more than those who are easily satisfied. Therefore, one should not be satisfied with the status quo, especially when it is not very fortuitous.

Ukraine is an independent democracy with serious problems, the biggest in East, Moscow, and its own crippling disease, Little Russians, excessive courtesy, and caution. On the other hand, our successes are also the result of the indefatigability and invincibility of our people. Today, as historically, all our difficulties are largely the work of our own hands. Even Moscow is the result in part of Ukrainians. Monomakh's teaching bypassed his sons, and his cap sits on the head of our grief to this day in Moscow.

Today, Ukraine is on the verge of preparing for an extension of war again, again with Moscow. New recruits are being trained. This is an extremely alarming phenomenon, especially since no one wins wars today. There will be victims. Moscow does not recognize tears. She does not care for victims.

I envision that Ukraine will remain a state not only on the basis of its preparedness to defend itself but also on the basis of diplomatic pressure. There is obviously a question of its territorial integrity. I have real hope that pressure from the United States and Europe on Moscow will make it clear to Putin that he will not be able to win the war against Ukraine and that it will be a war against the entire Western world.

Why am I more optimistic than the history of Ukraine-Moscow justifies? Because today, the world is different, far more transparent, and therefore able to resist Moscow's disinformation. Today, Moscow is not only a political outcast, but also not competitive with the world in economic terms. Today's Vladimir the Terrible is like Ivan the Terrible, who lost no less than he won because he made too many enemies.

Today, more so than during the First Cold War, the influence of the Ukrainian diaspora can have concrete results because Ukraine is a subject of international law, even with the current inaction of Ukrainian diplomacy. Today, European traditional conservatives have wasted themselves and have been replaced by new ones that once seemed unfriendly to Ukraine but may prove better for Ukraine than the so-called traditional partners of the past. Ukraine may or may not understand this because its leading cadres are not prepared for a political game.

We have before us a very interesting version of a new political phenomenon of international relations. The Social Democrats of Germany, the DeGaulists of France, and the Democrats of the United States, traditionally not the greatest friends of Ukraine, come with diplomatic assistance and more to Ukraine. They have already been joined by leftists, including the Greens, who are revolutionary and persistent in pursuing the "sacred mission" of saving the planet. Conservatives like Merkel, Macron, and the odious Trump turned out to be the worst option for Ukraine. They were more aligned with the enemy. If the unfortunate politician and talented writer Volodymyr Vynnychenko had at least a primitive understanding of international relations and ideological concepts, he would have been more useful for our statehood only a hundred years later. But chronically, Vynnychenko, the writer and the communist, on ideology was out of place in 1918 to lead the liberation struggle and the state.

Life and the world are dynamic. Change is the essence of political processes. The concept of an independent democratic Ukrainian state is not part of conservative thinking. An independent democratic Ukraine is a revolutionary idea. Ukraine needs not only nationalist revolutionaries but also strategic ideological allies, not opportunistic would-be friends. It is important that the international community understand not our tragic history and, therefore, mercifully come to our aid but recognize the key importance of the strategic geographic position and the necessity of a symbiotic partnership with Ukraine.

For this, Ukraine needs not only wise but also competent people. Writers should not be involved in finance, and financiers should not write literature. The most important component of wisdom is recognizing one's deficiencies. Everyone should be in their place because they can help with their abilities, not because that position will serve their life's ambitions or financial wherewithal. Historically, we Ukrainians have not practiced this. It is true that such anomalies sometimes appear in other nations, but in our country, they seem to be a historical malignancy.

This is not about anyone in particular. Actually, my remarks are about many, and therefore I do not want to criticize the present with specificity, but to consider the future. The New Year is a beginning. Our determination should be not to repeat previous mistakes because, obviously, then we cannot hope for the best. To achieve more, critical and sometimes revolutionary decisions must be made. Happy New Year and to a new, even revolutionary agenda, dear Ukrainians!

December 31, 2021

CHRISTMAS REFLECTIONS

During this Christmas week, I reflected upon basic religious and even ecclesiastical topics with some passion, resulting in indignation, and then decided to write them down to gauge the reaction of other Ukrainian Catholics. Here they are, meant constructively and hoping to garner a response, in particular from our bishops. Silence on their part would be noted as well.

About a week ago, Pope Francis held a business meeting with Hilarion, who is charged with the Moscow Church's foreign affairs. The essence of the meeting was to discuss the next meeting in 2022 between the Pope and Cyril, the head of that church. The last such 'summit" took place in 2016 in communist Havana.

It seems that Pope Francis is concerned with all things except the appropriate affairs of his flock. No press release reported that the Pope had voiced his concern over the imminent invasion of the Muscovites into Christian Ukraine. Pope Francis appears to have forgotten about his Ukrainian flock. Furthermore, not only the essence of the conversation but the meeting itself was a disgrace to the Catholic Church, if not to Pope Francis. Granted his socialist biography from Argentina and the first years at the helm of the Church, some bizarre behavior can be expected.

The problem is not only with the person of Pope Francis, who is probably too old to change, but the fault of the Church's Council of Cardinals which does not react to his peculiar behavior.

At least to the average Catholic, the myriad deeds of this Pope reflect a lack of understanding on his part that he is simply an ordinary, erroneous, and even sinful person when he acts in matters other than of the faith, including politics. Equally important, the church leadership does not see that the Catholic Church, in general, is falling precipitously in terms of numbers. Pope Francis, with his mysterious leadership, only exacerbates this decline.

The church needs reform because we seem to be going back to the abuses of the medieval leadership of the church, perhaps not as egregious. One thing we can predict is that in 2022, another meeting between the Pope and a surrogate of the Kremlin will further embarrass the Church. Maybe Putin will join the meeting. I think that Pope Francis will not object.

As to our Christian churches in Ukraine, the one and the other, here there is a genuine need for a summit. I do not refer to the evangelicals of a significant number because it's hard to cope with the Catholics and Orthodox. I fervently believe that Ukraine is a fundamentally Christian country despite the assertion of Ukraine's Permanent clown at the UN. We have celebrated 30 years of independence and so I and many observed the Christmas of Jesus on December 25, while the vast majority of Ukraine and part of our diaspora will celebrate on January 7. Are we incapable of celebrating together? By the way, the Ecumenical Orthodox Church, to which the Orthodox Church of Ukraine belongs, observes December 25. There are no obstacles here except the inactivity and lack of initiative by our church leadership. A consensus about Easter will have to be addressed with Patriarch Bartholomew. However, when you consider that the OCU is numerically the largest in his jurisdiction, Patriarch Bartholomew will make concessions.

The third theme is the outright humiliation of women in our churches. This conversation begins with such very ordinary privileges as serving at church altars. This is even allowed in the Roman Catholic Church. In other Christian churches, much more is allowed, including consecration and leadership. There is no doubt that our Catholic and Orthodox Churches are living in the mores of two thousand years ago, referring to the gospel written then by ordinary men. They wrote their version of events, and because their predominant characteristic, like that of every human being, was to err, they could only write subjectively. The Church, even today, justifies its male chauvinism with a little-understood presence of the

Holy Spirit. The Church must not only be Christian but must think Christian, and such thinking dare not allow gender discrimination. Imagine if we opened the Church equally to both genders; we would be enriched spiritually and numerically. Numbers are important because the Church is an assembly of its faithful and has a mission to bring human beings closer to God.

Finally, I assume, importantly, there remains a seemingly dormant issue regarding establishing a Ukrainian Catholic Patriarchate. This was one of the most volatile Ukrainian Catholic issues in the latter half of the XX century. With the death of the martyr of the Church, Patriarch Josef Slipyj this issue has been relegated. The naysayers, including some in the Ukrainian Catholic hierarchy such as Metropolitan Senyshyn, Bishop Horniak, and Bishop Marusyn, then argued the position of the Vatican that territory was required for the Ukrainian Catholic Church to be recognized as a Patriarchate. Well, that requirement appears to have been met thirty years ago, yet no progress. I am not sure whether there has been no action on the part of the Ukrainian Catholic Synod of Bishops or there has been yet another denial by the Vatican. This thirty-year period of dormancy and silence implies a dysfunctionality of the Ukrainian Synod or blatant and very political disingenuity by the Vatican. This matter is of great significance even if a Patriarchate of the Ukrainian Catholic Church would not address any of the aforesaid real issues. At least the faithful of our Catholic Church would know to whom to address their concerns.

The life of a Christian requires a fundamental and constant renewal. That is why every year, we celebrate the birth, death on the cross, and resurrection of the Son of God according to the church calendar. Why do we do this as Christians? To renew our faith and spirituality. Unfortunately, today's church leaders like Pope Francis do not understand this.

In the end, as a Christian in my heart, I feel committed to my Christian faith and duty with the audacity to pass on my ruminations to Pope Francis himself, although many may consider him the infallible head of the Church. To be a worthy and good follower of Jesus Christ means to distinguish between good and evil and to stand on the side of good. Voluntarily meeting the devil means approving his activities. Jesus Christ said, "Get away, Satan!". In contemporary terminology, that means, "Get away from my Church, Hilarion, Cyril, and Putin!"

December 30, 2021

"ONCE THEY ARE IN YOUR HOUSE, THEY DO NOT LEAVE."

US Secretary of State Anthony Blinken recently spoke about the arrival of RUSSIAN paratroopers into Kazakhstan at the alleged invitation of the President of that country. These are the kind of people that when they are in your house, they do not leave, Blinken said. History shows that this has been the methodology of the Muscovite and Russian imperialists.

I recently was reading the history of the Ottoman Empire. In the conflict with the Ottoman Empire and the Crimean Khanate, in the early 1770s, Russians invaded Crimea. In the conflict with the Ottoman Empire, the Crimean Khanate did not oppose the Russian invasion. Some ten years later, in 1783, Crimea was annexed to the Russian Empire. Catherine wanted to capture Constantinople as well, but she did not succeed. There was no invitation, and there was serious opposition.

I do not predict when Kazakhstan, which is between a rock and a hard place, neighboring Moscow to the north and Beijing to the southeast, will be annexed by Moscow because today it is not profitable for Putin, and Kazakhstan has some substantial land mass. What is certain is that the Russian troops will remain in Almaty as they remained in Transnistria, South Ossetia, Abkhazia, Crimea, and East Ukraine. Perhaps we Ukrainians understand the words of the US Secretary of State best, despite different interpretations of Pereyaslav. Ukraine's naive hetman Bogdan invited Muscovites to our house in 1654 for the sake of protection. They have not left. Recently, 600,000 Russians were settled in the Crimea without invitation.

Questions arise. Why are Russians invited when conflicts arise? Are they genuinely invited, or does Moscow arrange conflicts? The answer is that very often, Russians organize conflicts in order to "settle" them with their presence. But there are also cases of naivety of conflicted leaders and even unconflicted ones.

Separate talks are underway with the Russians and representatives of the United States, NATO, and the OSCE. The West needs to recognize seriously that the Russians understand only strength. The main weapon against the Russians is the fear of losing personal material well-being, the fear of Russian kleptocrats, from Putin to his chief tycoon, of personal financial losses. The Russian leaders are totally amoral in that they do not care about the economic consequences for the population because the Russian people require only vodka and pig fat. A popular revolution in Russia even if it happened, would be suppressed mercilessly and very expeditiously.

Furthermore, Moscow is not fearful of war because human casualties, as in Stalin's time, are just statistics, which, incidentally, can be purged and new ones fabricated. So, what hope can there be for successful negotiations?

Is complete isolation of Moscow by the world community a possibility? Neighboring states that are afraid of Moscow will not join this. This includes Belarus, Kazakhstan, Uzbekistan, Kyrgyzstan, and Armenia. Isolation will not include Syria, Iran, China, Vietnam, North Korea, Venezuela, Cuba, India, or even Pakistan because such strongmen regimes, abusive of human and civil rights themselves, share the protection of other thugs. Most notable among them is China with the second largest economy in the world. Therefore, in the best case, these negotiations will not settle issues but may postpone conflagrations for a while.

The President of the United States expressed in very general but strong terms the nature of US action in the event of a further Russian invasion of Ukraine. Strengthening NATO's presence on the border with Russia, providing Ukraine with more weapons, and seriously targeted economic sanctions against Russia, which include the "nuclear economic sanction" of excluding Moscow from the international financial transit SWIFT. Are these just words, threats, and nothing more? And what will be the consequences of introducing and implementing even such a regime?

We sometimes forget that "democratic and independent" Russia has been invading the territory of its neighbors throughout its thirty-year existence, that is, in fact, since the 1990s in Transnister, in 2008 in Georgia, and in 2014 in Ukraine. Sanctions imposed so far have weakened Moscow economically but not deterred it. Since then, Moscow has been so bold as to allow itself to murder 298 civilians, including women and children, by blowing up civilian aircraft, together with its ally Syria, participating in the use of chemical weapons against innocent civilians in Syria. This happened without sanctions at all.

Therefore, it is important to conduct negotiations but negotiations with evidence of consequences. We must demand the withdrawal of half of the Russian troops from the Ukrainian border during the negotiations. Otherwise, serious economic sanctions against Moscow's kleptocrats, including Putin, his family, and friends, should commence, but with the so-called SWIFT nuclear option in temporary abeyance.

In the meantime, also let us arm Ukraine to the teeth and locate a greater number of troops on the borders of NATO and Russia. Negotiating with Moscow from a position of weakness when the Russians are on the border, and our threats are promissory in nature, will not be influential in the success of negotiations. Would immediate partial implementation infuriate Putin to the point of withdrawing from the talks? I think Putin understands only power, personal financial loss, and weapons. If it were not for his own peril, he would have devoured Ukraine a long time ago.

Unfortunately, world politics and diplomacy is a deadly game of the strong. Weakness or procrastination that shows weakness does not portend victory or result in peace and justice in accordance with international norms of respect for state sovereignty and the inviolability of territorial integrity. There will be no lasting victory here. Our best hope is a temporary Spring.

January 7, 2022

DAMN GERMANS

The recent behavior of Germany adds new meaning to the axiom that politics is the art of the possible, meaning bringing the Germans into the community of civilized nations.

First, the Germans compelled the Brits to fly over Denmark rather than Germany in transporting arms to Ukraine, and then they specifically forbade Estonia from supplying Ukraine with, I suspect, antiquated German Democratic Republic Soviet weaponry.

The political significance is questionable, yet it does lead one to exclaim, "Damn Germans."

The exclamation is relevant since President Biden several months ago waived certain sanctions on Nord Stream 2, which he attempted to justify quite incongruously "in order to appease the Germans" who, after Russia, stand most to gain from NS2. Angela Merkel may be gone, but she appears not forgotten, even if the Germans themselves are forgetful of American appeasement. German pro-Russian policy remains business as usual. This has been the case for 250 years except for 4 when a conflict between their imperial aspirations resulted in the loss of millions of lives, many not affiliated with either side.

At the end of the week, I sent an email to Germany's Permanent Representative to the United Nations advising her that those pesky Ukrainian Americans were considering staging protests at her doorstep on First Avenue in New York City, given that Germany stands so close to the dreaded Russians that it has become enemy number 2 on the Ukrainian list.

From 1941 to 1944, the Germans ravaged Ukraine, killing millions in the process. In 2008, at the NATO Summit in Bucharest, Germany blocked Ukraine's Membership Action Plan. There may be scores to settle, but Ukrainians are hopeful that at long last, Germany will pursue policies based on moral principles and respect, at the very least, for the territorial inviolability and sovereignty of its neighbors in Europe.

President Biden himself did not have a particularly good week in foreign policy as well as domestic matters. At his year-end press conference, he rambled and offered conflicting and confusing replies to many questions, leading to a statement by many of his supporters that no president, and in particular one who is 79 years old, should hold two-hour press conferences. His statement inferring allowing Putin a minor incursion into Ukraine compelled the White House and the President himself to walk back some of his language immediately. If we add the German behavior representing a slap in the President's face, then President Biden's week was quite forgettable.

Nevertheless, over the last year, the United States has been an active actor in its support for Ukraine. Secretary Blinken traveled throughout Europe, including stops only last week in Kyiv to meet with President Zelensky and in Geneva to meet with Russian Foreign Minister Lavrov. Lavrov mendaciously assured the U.S. Secretary that Russia had no plans to invade Ukraine. Unfortunately, whatever happens, Lavrov's credibility is very much suspect. Threats are acts of aggression as well and punishment has to be meted out. If Russia withdraws but new sanctions are not imposed, Russia will have been rewarded for its bad behavior nonetheless.

To effectively support Ukraine, NATO members must continue supplying military aid. President Biden has clearly stated that the United States alone has provided over $600 million in military assistance during his first year in office. Additionally, NATO should reinforce troops and resources along its Eastern borders. It's essential to implement new, targeted sanctions—while we may not fully cut off the SWIFT system just yet, we should start taking steps in that direction.

This opinion has been given by more than one retired United States and NATO military general and at least one former U.S. Ambassador to Ukraine. Frankly, commencing the termination of Russia's access to SWIFT is not a simple procedure and not an overnight process. This would sound an alarm in Moscow very persuasively, sending a message that its current behavior, even short of invasion, is unacceptable.

Finally, for reasons known only to Ukraine's Foreign Ministry and its Permanent Mission to the UN, that international forum has been entirely inactive in this matter. The UN has to be involved. Russian aggression at Ukraine's border is not simply a Ukrainian or European matter but a global one.

January 22, 2022

AN UNHOLY ALLIANCE

The recently forged alliance between two thugs is somewhat reminiscent of 1939. Then Hitler and Stalin agreed to cooperate in a land grab. And so it ensued. Hitler took Poland and Czechoslovakia, and Stalin extended the Soviet Empire to Western Ukraine and then took the Baltic states. The biggest Nazi collaborators were Stalin and the Kremlin.

Similarly, brutality and mendacity are the hallmarks and strategies of this new alliance of global thugs. As recently as January 31, 2022, at the UN Security Council, the Russian Permanent Representative al stated with a straight face that Russian troops are not massed at Ukraine's border. He said this despite all the technological evidence. Russian credibility is no longer an issue. American Ambassador Greenfield was forceful and to the point. Ukraine's Ambassador was the opposite. He decided to reference the British children's lyricist Lewis Carroll. That is an approach rarely used before at the UN, however not very effective.

The island of Taiwan has been quite appetizing to the Chinese Communists for a very long time. Even more endearing has been killing. Today, a genocide of the Uyghur people in Xinjiang is taking place with only minimal global attention. China is very fierce in its police powers; not only is Chinese Indigenous dissent repressed, but other nationalities and religions within China are slaughtered in the nature of genocide with all UN Convention attributes yet protected by a Chinese veto at the UN Security Council.

How dangerous is this new alliance? The answer is more dangerous than Hitler and Stalin. Putin and Xi are not only birds of a feather, but they have different territorial interests, although they may be neighbors and subject to conflict. This is not a play for time as Molotov-Ribbentrop was. This is more foreboding. China needs to take over Taiwan for the sake of Chinese hegemony. Russia needs to invade Ukraine for the sake of history. Without Ukraine, Russia is only Russia with a history of less than a millennium. There will not be a 1941 fallout and confrontation.

The US and the Europeans have been remarkable in the current crisis. Thank God that FDR is not the Commander in Chief. There has been no sighting of Neville Chamberlain. Joe Biden, with all of his near octogenarian frailties, has been staunch and unyielding. Boris Johnson has been magnificent even if disheveled and criticized at home. One has to be optimistic despite the fact that the thug morbid alliance consists of the world's second-largest economy and the second-largest nuclear power. With that in mind, heavily targeted sanctions, corporate and personal, including economic and financial isolation, have to be imposed sooner rather than later.

Deterrence does remain an option. Russia has not been stymied. It simply has essentially placed the entire world at peril, which means that Putin has achieved his goal even if Russia is a total pariah. Putin is somewhat appeased by his global attention. He is the world's most famous thug. Xi is a close second. Together, they will address deterrence. Russia will supply gas to China, which needs it. Activation of Nord Stream 2 may no longer serve as a deterrent. Germany may have to find a moral backbone.

China has become more newsworthy of hosting the Olympic Games. Frankly, how bizarre is that? China hosts games participated in by all countries as it conducts a genocide and represses millions within its own borders. The world diplomatically protests through partial political absence at opening ceremonies, but the games go on. Talk about rewarding bad behavior. Xi and Putin brazenly issued an incomprehensible joint statement on the occasion, essentially telling the world that what they do is a matter of their own sovereignty. How bizarre is that!

This is the world we live in. It's immoral, much like in the past. Civilization? Democracy? Human rights? The quintessential alleged symbol of goodness and what is right, the Pope himself is confused and thus behaves immorally, having met the devil on a multitude of occasions and decided to sit down and talk.

We need to consider what the future of humanity forecasts. Global warming is important and has been addressed in part, even though China and Russia remain outliers. There are other issues, such as global security and human rights, the prevention and punishment of genocide, and the development of civil societies, including freedom of the press. What exactly is the civilized world we live in? Yes, we no longer feed Christians to the lions. But we continue almost everything else, perhaps with somewhat refined trappings.

The world and its atrocities are being exposed. The democratic, civilized community has to act forcefully and immediately. We cannot wait for irredeemable events to unfold.

February 6, 2022

AN ANTIQUATED CONCEPT FROM AN OUT-OF-TOUCH COMMENTATOR

A friend of mine from Tennessee recently sent me an Opinion published in the local newspaper "The Daily Times" by the elderly Patrick Buchanan on the subject of the Monroe Doctrine as it relates to Putin's positioning troops on Ukraine's border. Talk about waking the dormant both Buchanan and the Monroe Doctrine! In his commentary Buchanan essentially justifies historically Putin's contemporary behavior without condoning an actual invasion. He suggests that:

A powerful army on a nation's border can send a message and dictate terms without going in and without going to war...the message being sent by the Russian army is clear: Putin wants his own Monroe Doctrine. Putin wants Ukraine outside of NATO permanently.

My friend asked me to respond to the well-known albeit long-misguided commentator. I wrote the following:

Dear Editor:

Pat Buchanan appears to be getting old. While displaying a knowledge of American history, he manifests almost total ignorance of world history. His treatise on the Monroe Doctrine is wasted effort since so much has transpired since the Monroe Doctrine. Most important are two world wars and the Helsinki Accords, not to mention the formation of the United Nations and a plethora of international accords. The Monroe Doctrine is dormant, aside from the fact that it was never applicable to Russia. The United States, while influential in global politics, is not a menace to its immediate neighbors. Just ask Mexico and Canada how much they fear the United States. Then, ask Russia's immediate neighbors in Europe. You may even ask a non-governmental Belarusan. The comparison is ridiculous. Kindly convey my suggestion to Mr. Buchanan that he familiarize himself with such concepts as the territorial integrity and sovereignty of independent states. Thank you.

Respectfully,

Buchanan did not exhort or incite an invasion. However, his commentary was very dangerous and out of touch. America is a country of average people very much influenced by others whom they admire for their notoriety. In this age of Proud Boys and Oath Keepers, the paleo-conservative Pat Buchanan maintains a respected, if not prominent, place. After all, surprisingly, Donald Trump is still the most influential person in the Republican Party. Buchanan speaks to a portion of those people even if age prevented him from participating in the January 6, 20201 riot at the Capital.

These people are not friends of Ukraine. They lean very much towards authoritarianism. A thug like Putin represents a symbol of power. The intricacies of global issues, the territorial integrity, and the sovereignty of independent countries are not an issue. Power is more important. In fact, Donald Trump once said that he loves the uneducated. He also said that he admired Putin for his staying power. The uneducated with a voice and with weapons are exceedingly powerful (dangerous-AL).

Right or left-wing fringe groups are not indigenous to America. They are pervasive in Europe as well. Threats and the use of force cannot be acceptable on the level of societal or governmental behavior. People like Buchanan suggest that such behavior is acceptable. Buchanan may be irrelevant today except for the fringe, but even a small group can be very dangerous because of the methodology it espouses.

Russia is a perfect example. Many contend that the problem is

Putin, but these people are shortsighted or simply ignorant of history. It is not xenophobic to fear Russians in general, allowing for the few and far between exceptions. I often repeat myself when I point out that Ukraine proclaimed independence on a Saturday, and by Monday, the allegedly democratic Russian Boris Yeltsin made territorial claims against Ukraine. One of Russia's best dissidents was Alexander Solzhenitsyn, a Russian chauvinist. Today's Russian opposition leader, Alexei Navalny, has often lauded Russian history, certainly as it pertains to Ukraine. In the short and long term, long after Putin, Russia will continue to be a threat to Ukraine and a menace to the world.

February 10, 2022

RUSSIAN FACTS

The recent United Nations Security Council meeting convened by the Russian Federation under its own chairmanship was more eye-popping than normal, and that says much. Russia routinely distorts and misinforms. The UNSC is mostly an exercise in futility since five permanent members have veto power, including Russia, which is essentially a rogue state.

At the risk of lending credence to yet another Russian farce, the discussion that ensued offers an opportunity to point out that Russian interpretation of legal documents and its representation of reality differs diametrically with that of the entire world, including even China, Gabon, Ghana, India and the rest of the world.

Russia brought representatives to the event, one Tatyana Montyan, an alleged Ukrainian attorney born in Crimea, trained in Moscow as a Police officer and known for her prowess as an MMA fighter. She apparently is the female version of Vladimir Putin, who was trained as a KGB agent and known for his prowess in judo. Ms. Montyan's problems with credibility lie in her bombastic nature. Here is one of her quotes:

> *"...bombing and killing civilians, including children, has always been the United States' favorite pastime. More than 400 children in Yugoslavia alone were killed by the US and its NATO allies, in Iraq and Afghanistan without an account at all."*

Earlier, she had commented on a statement of President Alexander Lukashenka of Belarus about plans to return Ukraine to the "bosom of Slavism." She stressed, "The head of the republic knows how to say the right thing." Aside from the legal and political incongruity of questionable ancestry determining modern political relations, her antiquated subjectivity was exposed as she referred to independent Belarus as "the republic" reminiscent of the Belorussian

Soviet Socialist Republic.

No matter the intent, Ms. Montyan was a circus sideshow. She was loud and outrageous, making no legitimate legal or political points. Frankly, I wondered why Russia brought her in. She did not help Russia's questionable cause.

On a more serious note, Russia brought in Deputy Foreign Minister Sergeii Viroshin to run the show and present Russia's main case. Viroshin is a graduate of the notorious Moscow School of International Relations, often misrepresented as a law school. It is a school for Russian intelligence and diplomacy with little difference between the two.

Viroshin stressed Ukraine's lack of respect for and non-compliance with Minsk 2, the agreement of February 12, 2015. The fact that he was not legally trained became obvious when he stated that Russia is not a part of the Agreement, thereby jeopardizing his own standing to bring this matter before the Security Council.

The facts are entirely different, as explained later by Ukraine's Permanent Representative to the UN. The February 2015 Minsk Agreement, as well as previous and subsequent documents in connection with Minsk, were executed by Yu. Zurabov, the Ambassador of the RF to Ukraine.

In any event, Viroshin, clearly overmatched in the legal framework, relied on two main arguments: Ukraine is in violation of the Minsk Agreement because it refuses to negotiate with the alleged separatists in Donbas and has not provided special status to the region with a veto power. He insisted that he had read the Agreement, yet similarly to missing the Russian signature on the Agreement, he failed to note that the word veto was nowhere to be found therein.

The very first provision of the Minsk Agreement refers to a ceasefire. Since then, on a daily basis, almost without exception, Russia and her surrogates violate that provision some ten times daily and, most recently, more than fifty times daily.

Most recently, Russia violated the Agreement by firing at a kindergarten on Ukraine's side. The remaining 12 provisions are contingent upon Russian compliance, with the first as a sine qua non. How does Ukraine address the other provisions when it is constantly under fire? Moreover, Russian violation of the first provision has been barbaric, irrespective of and even targeting civilians, including children.

No one at the Security Council, not even China, took Russia seriously. China did defend Russia. It simply attacked the US for expanding NATO as a segue to attacking the US for expanding its alliances in the Southeast. China does want Taiwan.

Finally, and most egregiously, the Revolution of Dignity 2013-14 was referred to by the Russian speakers as a bloody coup d'etat. The reality is that there were some ten government casualties, all as a result of the return fire. The number of casualties on the side of the revolutionaries was in the hundreds. The initiators of the deadly fire were the government forces. The Russian surrogate fled before he could be captured.

One cannot argue with Russian facts. They are unassailable by a reasonable person if only because they are so ridiculous that one cannot even consider how to address them. Everything is admissible at the UN Security Council, no matter how outrageous. There are no rules of evidence. Nonetheless, it is a forum for diplomacy, and so it has extrinsic value.

Russia abuses the UNSC all the time. Russia does not respect rules or diplomacy. Gary Kasparov, the Russian chess grandmaster, was asked whether Putin was playing a chess game. He replied that Putin does not play chess because chess is based on rules and Putin is a criminal. Perhaps it was appropriate for an MMA proponent to appear on behalf of Russia. MMA has a few rules, i.e., no eye gouging. Even that does not apply to Putin. Consider the chemical bombing of civilians in tandem with the Syrian Assad. While publicly, the West needs to exploit all diplomatic channels for peace, in reality, Russia should be treated as a rogue state and Putin as an international terrorist with all available remedies at our disposal.

February 19, 2022

DARWINIAN WORLD ORDER AND LESSONS LEARNED

Here are some of the lessons of the current Ukraine crisis: a Darwinian global order prevails, POTUS does not comprehend the primary purpose for sanctions, and aggression is often emboldened by unwitting accomplices.

Despite strenuous efforts to establish international organizations to secure peace, the global order is determined by survival of the fittest even today. The United Nations and NATO are at least two most prominent international structures that have proven to be essentially worthless in deterring aggression. The supreme irony appeared on screens all over the world as an aggressor presided over a session of the UN Security Council convened to preclude that very aggression. An exchange of poetry between victim and perpetrator only added to the absurdity of the exercise.

NATO's rhetoric has been strong, but in each case, any statement has concluded with the words, "We will not be going into Ukraine." Irrespective of Article 5, it is not necessary to stress that point. This repetition has only served Russia and Putin, proving assurances that they have nothing to fear from NATO's military might as they embark on their imperialistic adventure into Ukraine. Frankly, NATO spokespeople do not seem to understand the purpose of NATO or its charter. The Preamble reads:

> *The Parties to this Treaty reaffirm their faith in the purposes and principles of the Charter of the United Nations and their desire to live in peace with all peoples and all governments. They are determined to safeguard the freedom, common heritage, and civilization of their peoples, founded on the principles of democracy, individual liberty, and the rule of law. They seek to promote stability and well-being in the*

North Atlantic area. They are resolved to unite their
efforts for collective defense and for the preservation of
peace and security.

If NATO members seek to promote stability and well-being in the North Atlantic area and to preserve peace and security, certainly the place to start would have been to preclude a Russian invasion of Ukraine. NATO countries made it very clear, even stressing the fact that they would not send troops to Ukraine. The Russians came perhaps even emboldened by NATO's gratuitous proclamations. Now, should Russia prevail in its aggression and Ukraine either ceases to exist or becomes like Belarus, the world's biggest aggressor will become NATO's immediate neighbor. That's like waiting for the cancer to metastasize before opting for surgery.

President Joe Biden, essentially a good Christian man and one steeped in politics for many years, has manifested a lack of understanding of the purpose of sanctions, specifically emphasizing on more than one occasion that his sanctions will not deter aggression. Sanctions, in law and legal definition, are penalties or other means of enforcement used to provide incentives for obedience to the law or rules and regulations. It would stand to reason that sanctions should be imposed to deter or provide incentives for obedience to the law, such as not invading a sovereign country. In this case, the invasion has taken place, so deterrence is no longer an option. Punishing Russia is good, but it does not help Ukraine fight a war where it is somewhat overmatched.

The list of unwitting accomplices is long and includes both the bad and the very good. The very bad include a former American President who lauded dictators, emphasizing his feelings for the Russian thug in an effort to become the most famous man in the world. This fracturing of America emboldened Putin because America could not be expected to lead the world since it could not put its own house in order. And then there was the very good, the leader of the Catholic Church who, in an effort to ostensibly unite the world's Christians, reached out to the devil himself and met with one thug after another from Moscow.

In a recent effort to do penance, he went to the Russian Embassy in Rome with great remorse. But the damage had been done.

In a Darwinian world, only the fittest survive. Morals and rules, just as treaties and legal documents, mean nothing. The law of the jungle prevails. We live by these rules because man is either inherently evil or simply unfit. The very invasion of Ukraine by Moscow is evidence of our collective failure as a global civilized community.

February 25, 2022

AN ACTION PLAN FOR THE WESTERN DIASPORA TO HELP UKRAINE

The first days of the war were not as the Russians had anticipated. Becoming even more unhinged by this setback, Putin has increased not only the numbers of the Russian military but also the variety of weapons and methods of warfare. The latter should be most alarming. A missile was fired indiscriminately at the very center of the City of Kharkiv, not in the direction of the Ukrainian military, but directly at the innocent population. Sixty kilometers of Russian military convoy is expected to bring a new blow to the capital, Kyiv. All this can be seen on the screen. There can be no further reasonable debate as to the intentions and manner of operation of the enemy. Can Ukraine survive such a large-scale military and even a nuclear arsenal operating without regard to civilian life? Ukrainians want to believe in our own strength and will, but we need serious help. This is a threat to the world. Putin is the XXI century's Hitler and Stalin and with nuclear weapons.

For Ukraine, the Western world, led by America, has so far responded extremely forcefully. It seems everyone is helping us. Most recently, Europe has spoken out in favor of Ukraine's accession to their Community, and most European countries supply weapons for Ukraine's defense.

What Ukraine needs now is the protection of its airspace by a NATO air force operation. Why are NATO and the United States slow to respond to this request? This question is difficult. Because actually doing that means physically entering a war where there could be a clash of Russian missiles, planes, and similar NATO weapons. It is one thing to declare Ukraine's air closed and another far more difficult to defend such a reality. So, it is incumbent today to convince the Western world that Moscow's choice is on the side of indiscriminate aggression. This aggression begins in Ukraine, but if Ukraine is defeated, it encompasses the entire North Atlantic region.

What should be the approach of our communities? We must learn from the President of Ukraine. Even his greatest opponents must acknowledge his proper and heroic approach. It is an approach not to give up; it is an approach to thank and not to scold the West and to ask for additional help, including participation in the defense effort not only in the supply of weapons but eventually, if needed, joining Ukrainians on the battlefield, whether on the ground or in the air. Today, the battlefield is Ukraine. For NATO and EU member states, facing the enemy of mankind in Ukraine is better than later at the doors of Warsaw, Bucharest, Berlin, or Paris.

Dear Ukrainians! Reprimanding our friends and allies for not loving us enough is not helpful in consolidating long-term friendships. It should not be a mystery to any Ukrainian that we are cursed by geographical location. Our rich soil and beautiful nature are bestowed upon us but at a geostrategic cost. The defense of our territory and our people will be long-term.

At the same time, it is necessary to bring the war to the enemy here in the Western Diaspora. This is a war against the Russians. This war must be waged at every turn. Russian agents, aka diplomats, must leave America. Russian planes must not be allowed to fly or land in America. Russian products, Stolichnaya, Lukoil, and the like, cannot be sold in America.

The war with the Russians should also be brought to international forums, conferences, and even educational institutions. There are good Russians, but they are few and far between. Our enemy is not only Putin but every Russian who believes or works for Putin's "Russian world." Please remember that American institutions, universities, and seemingly innocent and non-political forums are replete with Russian agents of disinformation. Naturally, I use America here as an example. This applies to Australia, Germany, Brazil, etc.

Our victims and refugees are obviously in need of humanitarian assistance. The number of refugees will soon reach one million, mostly children and women, as men under the age of 60 take part in the war. The United Ukrainian American Relief Committee (UUARC) has opened a separate fund for this purpose. The UUARC has a history of assistance and community accountability. Donate through UUARC. Other funds, I can not guarantee.

We also need legal assistance from our lawyers, who specialize in immigration law, to procure immigration status and various assistance for our migrants. I urge Ukrainian lawyers around the world to inform their Ukrainian communities about the availability of assistance in this matter by providing their contact information for services "pro bono" or at a reduced war emergency rate. To this end, you have been given the opportunity to receive higher education in the West.

We are a good and undaunted people. Unfortunately, we have experience with war and suffering. Today, we are united in our goal, probably more than ever. Today, perhaps for the first time in history, the whole world, except the Russians, is on our side. A stressful time always evokes emotions. During such an emotional phase, it is difficult to think lucidly, although it is necessary to act. We need to adopt a single simple strategy - a strategy to fight the Russian enemy and to express gratitude while asking for further help from our friends, the Americans, the British, the French, the Canadians, even the Germans, and in particular, the Lord God and the Mother of God. We have seen at least two miracles already. We stopped the first invasion, and even the Germans began to help us.

Glory to Ukraine! Glory to her heroes! Glory to our people! Thanks to our friends! Death to the Russian enemy!

March 1, 2022

FURTHER ACTION PLAN

The Russian invasion has been ruthless and inhuman. Moscow's war crimes are carried out almost every day in front of the eyes of the whole world. A few days ago, there was a threat of a nuclear disaster, and apparently, this threat is still imminent because the nuclear power plant in Zaporozhye is in the irresponsible and criminal hands of the enemy. The employees of the station are being held at gunpoint and have become hostages. Who can predict the future behavior of the enemy with a mentally ill leader who, incidentally, had threatened a nuclear response earlier? The matter of securing nuclear power plants in Ukraine has been addressed with the International Atomic Energy Agency. A war crimes complaint has been filed with the International Criminal Court in The Hague.

These appeals to international bodies may be ineffective because Moscow does not pay attention to international law and international institutions. We must recognize that the decision to condemn Moscow by the UN General Assembly with an overwhelming majority of 141 votes and only 5 against it was a great but only symbolic victory. All this is not only frustrating but very dangerous. We live in a lawless international community.

The most important thing for Ukraine today is establishing peace in the Ukrainian sky, a no-fly zone. America and NATO have declined to do so, citing the possibility of a NATO-Moscow conflict that could end in World War III. This caution is a bit confusing in light of Moscow's nuclear threats and war crimes. Respected military experts point out that if the sky is closed, victory in the war may be on Ukraine's side. Moscow has a great advantage over Ukraine in the sky, but Ukraine, because of its territory and indefatigable population, has an advantage on land. Therefore, we must insist and not abandon this position, pointing out that a possible but not certain clash between Moscow and NATO can bring victory and the defense of all of Europe. On the other hand, Ukraine's loss could end not only in the spillage of Ukrainian blood but also that of soldiers and civilians of Europe. Ultimately, In the end, Moscow's missiles fired from the territory of occupied Ukraine can reach Washington. Therefore, caution should be rational and far-sighted. Let's not fool ourselves once again with arguments of appeasement. Currently, an immediate delivery to Ukraine of more Javelins, Stingers, and finally, Warthogs, the latter intended to shoot down Moscow planes, is necessary.

There are also some still unclear neglected matters: why aren't Moscow's diplomatic agents expelled from all our allied countries, firstly from the United States? Why don't we Ukrainians find opportunities to confront these criminals? Why do we still purchase and use oil and gasoline from Moscow? A dear friend from Canada drew my attention to this. A discussion and mutual information amongst people across the globe are very useful, but it has to be constructive as in this case. The Arab world of allies must be involved in this in order to increase production and maintain a price balance. A single local city government (Newark, New Jersey) in the United States is suspending the licensing of Russian Lukoil. It needs to be done throughout. Protests should be held against American and other companies that continue to do business in Russia. The most striking example is the Coca-Cola Company. I would suggest an avalanche of letters to this company from consumers as well as physical protests in front of the head office in Atlanta, Georgia. There is a Ukrainian-organized community in Atlanta, and it must act.

These suggestions are very real and easy. They should be applied as soon as possible. We need to understand that every day of war and resistance on the part of Ukraine is a defeat for Moscow, but we must remember that Putin is not a normal person but a mentally ill despot and criminal capable of anything, even a nuclear strike in one form or another.

All activity is useful. However, the demand to remove Russia from the UN Security Council will simply not be according to the UN Charter. It should also be borne in mind that sometimes it is better to have a diplomatic forum that includes Russia because, indeed, Russia is the greatest threat to world security, and a dangerous Russia is why the UN was formed. The formation of the UN is a good thing in spite of its inefficacy. Unfortunately, even the introduction of a UN no-fly zone in the Ukrainian sky requires a decision by the UN Security Council, where Russia has a veto. And then there is the issue of implementation. The UN does not have an air force.

In a previous writing, I referred to a metaphor of us being like ants, which I borrowed from a Ukrainian in southern Ukraine under constant fire. If we follow that paradigm and each work tirelessly, doing simply what we are meant to do, we will prevail. And Ukraine and the world will be saved. That is not hyperbole.

March 5, 2022

WE AMERICANS ARE NOT BLAMELESS

Putin's declaration of war on Ukraine was a long-winded, spoken rumination about the glory of the Czarist Russian empire. Many Americans did not understand this psychosis and interpreted it to be a hearkening to the Soviet Union. Putin had on previous occasions noted his heartfelt affection for the USSR, but in this most recent instance, Putin was quite clear. He longed for the Russia of long ago; he wanted to be a Czar. In his alternative version of history, he even blamed Lenin, the commissar, for the formation of the Ukrainian state and the Ukrainian nation. Kyiv was founded in the V century, and Ukraine existed as the Kyivan state from the IX century. Moscow was founded in the XII century and became an independent state only in the XV century.

For a long time, most Americans knew not and cared even less about Russia. In fact, during the 2012 presidential campaign, when Governor Mitt Romney stressed that Russia poses the greatest global security challenge, he was ridiculed by President Obama. Earlier, President George W. Bush had managed to look into Putin's soul and naively saw something human. Let's not address the criminality of President Trump; let's call it naivete. The American elite, which recognized the Soviet Union as an evil empire very late, continued to see Russia as a cultural inspiration and its newest Czar as a business and political option.

In September 2015, one such elite columnist for The New York Times, David Brooks, bemoaned how much he misses old (Czarist and Soviet) Russia. He wrote:

People who came of age after the end of the Cold War may not realize how powerfully Russia influenced Western culture for 150 years. For more than a century, intellectuals, writers, artists, and activists were partly defined by the stances they took toward certain things Russian: Did they see the world like Tolstoy or like Dostoyevsky? Were they inspired by Lenin and/or Trotsky? Were they alarmed by Sputnik, awed by Solzhenitsyn, or cheering on Yeltsin or Gorbachev? That was because Russian culture had an unmatched intensity. It was often said that Russian thinkers addressed universal questions in their most extreme and illuminating forms.

This romanticized version of Russian culture certainly had an effect on America's elite. Without disparaging some or all of the personages Brooks mentioned, it should be stressed that Lenin and Trotsky were killers and terrorists. Solzhenitsyn was a Russian chauvinist. Yeltsin, three days after Ukraine proclaimed independence, made claims against Ukrainian territory and then put Putin at the helm of the empire to succeed and protect him. While some may argue that they did not know Putin, Yeltsin certainly did – a KGB colonel trained to kill.

Fyodor Dostoyevsky wrote in Crime and Punishment:

> *"Yes...I'm covered with blood", Raskolnokov said with a peculiar air; then he smiled, nodded and went downstairs. He walked down slowly and deliberately, feverish but not conscious of it, entirely absorbed in a new overwhelming sensation of life and strength that surged up suddenly within him."*

This captures the essence of the Russian soul – covered with blood, feverish with killing to the point of not being conscious and acquiring a newfound strength from that killing.

Unfortunately, this excerpt from *The New York Times* represents the naivete of our American elite society. Today, Ukrainians are paying the price. Putin was emboldened by such "useful idiots." Is there a lesson here?

Josef Zissels, a Ukrainian Jewish leader and former Soviet prisoner of conscience, has stated on many occasions that Putin did not make Russia what it is today; Russia made Putin.

Russian history from the XII through the XXI centuries is replete with the oppression of its own people and the persecution of those peoples whose lands Russia invaded. This is the basis for that Russian soul.

If there were any delusions about the Russian soul, they would have been dispelled by the ongoing Russian war crimes in Ukraine. But how we failed the Ukrainian people and humanity is astonishing. Naivete may be an excuse, but certainly not justification. Let's look into our own souls, fellow Americans. There must be more that we can do to right the wrong! The Ukrainian people need our help.

March 7, 2022

PLAN OF ACTION AGAINST COMPANIES DOING BUSINESS IN RUSSIA

In the course of his ongoing psychosis and attacks against the United States and the West, Vladimir Putin recently asserted that the economic sanctions imposed were a declaration of war against Russia. What that means is that the sanctions are beginning to hurt. In essence, this should serve as an impetus for all to ratchet up sanctions and apply even more pressure.

The United States of America today banned the import of Russian oil, liquid gas, and coal.

> *I, JOSEPH R. BIDEN JR., President of the United States of America, hereby expand the scope of the national emergency... Accordingly, I hereby order: Section 1. (a) The following are prohibited: (i) the importation into the United States of the following products of Russian Federation origin: crude oil; petroleum; petroleum fuels, oils, and products of their distillation; liquefied natural gas; coal; and coal products;*

> *This was done with the approval of America's allies. It would appear that Western governments are doing their part. We need to continue doing ours.*

This is a follow-up with pragmatic suggestions to a list compiled by the Yale School of Management of companies that remain in Russia with significant exposure compiled by Jeffrey Sonnenfeld. Since this list was compiled, Coca-Cola, McDonald's, Pepsi, and Starbucks have left Russia. This list for the moment includes such titans as Bridgestone, Caterpillar, Citi, Deere, Hilton, Honeywell, Hyatt, Intercontinental, Kellogg, Kraft Heinz, Marriott, Mars,

Nestle, Otis, Papa John's, Philip Morris, Pirelli. Some do more business in Russia than others. Intercontinental has only one location, but that is one too many and can be easily eliminated.

It has been suggested the approach to accomplish our goal should be two prongs. The first is to pressure investment giants such as Blackrock, Vanguard, State Street, Fidelity, etc., urging them (& their clients) to sell their portfolio positions in these companies still operating in Russia. This can be done by directly contacting these firms or by reaching out to their clients (which include large pension funds private and government, endowments of not-for-profits, and the like) to divest themselves from companies with Russian exposure. This should compel the companies doing business in Russia to consider a moral compass or the bottom line.

The second prong is relatively easy to initiate, but it does require widespread and even global response, cooperation and adherence. Initiating a boycott of a company's products is as easy as presenting it on social media and having it go viral. What makes it viral are its recipients and actors. No company in Russia wants to see its sales worldwide diminish because it insists on doing business in Russia.

Most companies on the list accrue less than 10% of their gross global income from Russia. With only 10% or less of its business revenue coming from Russia, the loss of Russian income would be more than compensated by its business elsewhere as a result of good publicity or, in reverse, a decrease elsewhere (around the globe) amounting to more than 10% of its gross income under adequate pressure and a boycott would make its Russian venture not cost-effective. Thus, the leverage is greatly on our side.

Every individual can become a part of this effort from the comfort of his/her own home. We have witnessed the limits of diplomacy - both in speed and scope of action. Civil society is not bound by the same set of rules and this is how we can play an active and effective role.

The war in Ukraine, aside from the civilian casualties on our side, is going better than was to be expected. The aerial attacks are very troubling, and the lack of protected sky is frustrating. Naturally, the lack of a NATO no-fly zone over Ukraine's sky will not be compensated for by Polish Mig 29s, but they are familiar to Ukraine's pilots, and Ukraine will be that much more competitive in the air. We need to carry on, work with our Western governments and on our own, and with God's help, good will triumph over evil. We in the diaspora can do a lot as long as we remember the metaphor that we are a great nation, like ants, with each member scurrying and doing his/her part.

March 8, 2022

NONSENSE RHETORIC

The issue of supplying Ukraine with air firepower has reached a level of nonsensical rhetoric. Vice President Harris left this morning for Poland to address this issue. Aside from the fact that VP Harris has little if any, experience in foreign policy or military logistics, her trip may be simple grandstanding, raising more questions than providing answers. On Sunday Secretary Blinken asserted that the US had given the green light for such a transaction. When Poland responded that it would send Migs to the US airfield in Germany, the US demurred, stating it was caught off guard and expressing grave concern that this would viewed by the Russians as participation of NATO in the war effort.

Certainly, there are questions for both the US and Poland. Why fly the Migs to Germany when the distance between Poland and a Ukrainian airfield is less than one hour away? Secondly, how is supplying Migs, in terms of war participation, different from supplying Stingers and Javelins? The Migs would never be used in an offensive manner. Ukraine has no intention of flying over Russian skies and bombing the Kremlin. The Migs would be used to defend Ukrainian skies.

In any event, this matter is taking entirely too much time, and there is blatant dis-ingenuity on the part of both the US and Poland. In the meantime, civilians, women, and children are being slaughtered. Migs are not a panacea, but they make Ukraine's air defense more competitive and its civilians safer.

The New York Times recently published an opinion piece by one of its most respected longtime columnists and multiple Pulitzer prize winner. Thomas Friedman wrote:

> *Because there is only one thing worse than a strong Russia under Putin — and that's a weak, humiliated, disorderly Russia that could fracture or be in a prolonged internal leadership turmoil, with different*

factions wrestling for power and with all of those nuclear warheads, cybercriminals and oil and gas wells lying around.

With all due respect, Mr. Friedman fails to consider many factors in this conclusion. Firstly, while Putin is a product of the Russian soul rather than Russia being the product of Putin's psychosis, Russia is not a monolith and hardly a homogeneous society. There are at least 150 nationalities that make up the Russian Federation. Almost all, in one way or another, have been maltreated by the Kremlin.

Russia's census as to determining nationalities within its borders is grossly misleading. The customary approach of Russian census takers is entering the home of a family, asking questions in Russian, receiving responses in Russian, and upon leaving, telling that family that since it does speak Russian, all members will be counted as Russians. Very few object for obvious reasons.

At a recent rally of Ukrainian Americans at Lafayette Park in front of The White House, one of the speakers was a representative of *Free Russia.* She spoke on behalf of Russians who oppose Putin. When she concluded, I approached her and said, *You do not look Russian. Are you a Buryat?* She acknowledged that I was correct. Many similar non-Russians in Russia have picked up the mantra of Russians opposed to Putin.

The ethnic Russian population in the RF is declining even if the census does not indicate so. Ethnic Russians average significantly fewer children than other ethnicities, in particular those of the Islamic faith, i.e., Chechen, Buryat, Yakut, etc.

Consideration should be given to the fact that Putin is relatively isolated. While in the United States, a war declaration is within the purview of Congress, in Russia, there is no real parliament or congress. In any event, the Russian *Duma* did not declare this war against Ukraine. Putin declared himself and called it a military operation.

Finding Putin a pathway to end this war and save face is an academic discourse. The better approach is to find a way to eliminate Putin. Discord in Russia and a struggle for power would be a welcome sight. This is a project for all humanity. I am certain that as I write this there are many who are considering this option as the only viable solution. A Russia without Putin, where 150 ethnic groups would be deciding its future, would be a Russian Spring. When was the last time there was a Spring in Russia?

March 9, 2022

A MORAL DILEMMA

Some companies that have left Russia have simply released their employees. Others continue paying them. Is this a moral issue and is there political benefit in not paying them? Similarly a discussion n has ensued since Big Pharma has been largely carved out from the sanctions regime as they continue doing business in Russia. The moral argument is that people with various illnesses need drugs to survive. However, in both examples, the allegedly moral argument fails to consider numerous other moral underpinnings. The issue then becomes moral equivalence.

Civilians and even children are being murdered indiscriminately in Ukraine. Numerous attempts at establishing previously agreed-upon human corridors have been violated by the Russians. This war has become a glaring showcase for war crimes. The West has been supportive short of becoming involved in preventing the carnage. Additionally, no one has come close to suggesting what has been termed an off-ramp for Vladimir Putin.

The following is indisputable: Vladimir Putin is a war criminal (in addition to being simply a criminal in the past, and yet enjoying Western collegiality), a terrorist, and the one person in control in Russia and responsible for everything. Russia is a rogue state by any standard. The Russian people are not simply misinformed victims or unwitting accomplices. Putin has ruled for more than twenty years. His rating, accurate or not, hovers in the 70%. We often hear that the Russian population is a victim as well. That is what the United States Department of State argued erroneously throughout the existence of the USSR, that the Russians were a captive nation. There are think tanks in the United States even today that argue in favor of the Russian people as victims.

Frankly, I would argue that the Russian mindset and culture are an acquired characteristic, one based on a longing for empire. The Russian soul is that of Dostoevsky's Raskolnikov with no remorse. Many Russian human rights activities, such as the preeminent Solzhenitsyn, were chauvinist. Apologists argue that he was a great writer, but so what? Sakharov was not a chauvinist, but there was a non-Russian ethnic element in Sakharov. Besides, there are exceptions. Sakharov and his wife were outliers. Russians are not born oppressors, but very often, they are reared sociologically to become imperialists and chauvinists. It is simply a part of Russian history and culture. Mass murderers are revered as being great leaders.

The discussion today centers on the war and the way to end it. Even the average American in Nebraska has to be concerned and not simply because of sympathy for Ukrainians. Europeans are genuinely scared. Germany is contributing to NATO at its peril. Still, I have yet to hear a pathway for peace from a Western analyst. Even a Putin victory over Ukraine would not mark an end to hostilities. Ukrainian resistance would continue. Putin, perhaps emboldened by victory, would look towards other parts of Europe.

Putin's psychosis is predicated on a legacy, that of yet another great Russian czar. Most czars of Russia were evil. Putin does not have moral dilemmas. He also does not care for human life.

There are two pathways. One is a victory for Ukraine, which, in all likelihood, would require more than the West is doing today. It certainly would require Ukrainian Migs, Patriots and other weapons so far missing. The other pathway is turmoil in Russia. With the current sanctions, mass unemployment, and lack of Western drugs, even the Russian people may arise.

I recently spoke with Professor Jeffrey Sonnenfeld from Yale. He has and continues to compile a list of American companies that did or are continuing to do business in Russia. He concurs that companies leaving Russia should not continue paying their employees. He also feels that America's Big Pharma should not be carved out from the sanctions list. He sees Russian popular revolt against the Putin regime as a very viable pathway to ending the suffering of Ukrainians.

The moral dilemma boils down to allowing the slaughter of innocent children by continuing to pay the salaries of Russians for no work and providing drugs to Russians who are ill, all of whom are willing to stand by and watch the indiscriminate carnage in Ukraine. Anyone who believes that average Russians are not aware of what is happening in Ukraine and who is carrying out the war crimes is delusional. Russia has been banned from sporting events. Even that should raise an eyebrow or two with the Russian populace about Russian malfeasance. St. Petersburg has been removed as a venue for the European football club championship. Even sports fans know that Putin is pure evil.

There are Russian protests, and there are severe laws against them with heavy penalties, so it appears that the opposition is deterred. Russian protest has to be raised to the level of a revolution against the criminality of Russia's latest czar because popular life in Russia has become unbearable. We need to spur on that revolution.

March 12, 2022

CONVERSATION WITH A FRIEND

Yesterday, I talked on the phone with a longtime friend in Kyiv. I have known him for many years. Our conversation relaxed me, and more importantly, it seemed to be good for him. He is extremely proud of our boys and girls who are defending Ukraine. However, there were moments of multiple day or night sirens when he needed to go to the basement for cover. There is also a very colorful red sky in Kyiv proper, especially at night. He told me that our people have grown very much in these four weeks. Now, no one will say that Ukraine is not militarily ready for NATO. If NATO joins us against Russia, we will lead NATO together with America.

My friend is a big fan of America. Today, he is extremely grateful that America is helping Ukraine so much, but he prays that it will continue to help.

He told me that all of Kyiv now speaks only Ukrainian. It was a mystery to me when I visited Kyiv only last summer. I went to restaurants and experienced my normal Russian language confrontations. I am not a passive observer. The war actually started in 2014. During the presidential election, I went to Kharkiv. A Russian-speaking village council head told me the Russians have made him a banderite.

It was so nice to hear my friend's voice. However, the war and the physical destruction of Ukraine will require a lot of physical reconstruction of the infrastructure. And even more rebuilding of human life.

So, we have already started talking about the future, but the war is not over. Prospects for human development will be limited. My friend has high hopes for reconstruction through the American Blinken Plan similar to that of Marshall.

Ukraine, albeit somewhat physically diminished, is growing before our eyes as not only a European but Ukrainian country, known all over the world for its spirituality, perseverance, and even military prowess. That is why we say that we are of Cossack descent.

We have jumped forward a bit ahead of ourselves. Firstly, we must defeat the enemy, an enemy unlike any the world has seen since Hitler. There are so many war crimes here, missiles aimed at civilians, children, and homes. And what's next? Like a mad beast, a Muscovite, whether Putin or Kyril (a so-called religious patriarch), their purpose is to wipe the Ukrainian nation off the face of the earth. Muscovite shortcomings on the battlefield and great human losses, i.e., military losses, are like a fire burning inside that beast, which is then capable of anything, biological, chemical, and even nuclear weapons. Human life, that is, the civilian population and innocent children, do not matter.

At a recent press conference in Brussels, President Biden answered questions about Russia's use of chemical weapons. There would be an appropriate response from the United States and NATO. In a speech in Warsaw the following day, for the first time, President Biden revealed what needs to be done - to remove Putin. How this should happen and by whom are the second and third questions.

In fact, what should the end of the war look like? Victory for Ukraine, the retreat of the enemy beyond all borders of Ukraine, surrender of Donbas and Crimea, integral parts of Ukrainian territory in favor of Ukraine. Economic sanctions must continue. Moscow is an outcast. The Muscovites themselves will either kill or arrest their mentally ill leader. Muscovites don't care whether they kill or arrest. No man, no problem was the mantra of the old Soviet Russia. This has survived. Sanctions and complete isolation will do their thing, and the empire will fall. The nations within the empire will strive for at least autonomy. Russia will never be a normal country. Her church is abnormal; it is Stalin's church. Its people are a creation that grew up in the swamps of Moscow and St. Petersburg on Cossack bones and fed on lard and moonshine. May they live, and if they do not change, they will rot. The good ones will leave this hell.

There is a young generation of extremely capable people in Ukraine. I am not closing the curtain upon the older people. All Ukrainians can have and deserve a normal, fruitful European life in their beloved Ukraine. They themselves will rebuild it with our Western help.

For now, we must continue to fight. All of our ants, because we are a nation of ants, must go in one direction, first to victory and then to reconstruction. Each of us has a job to do. Let's not forget Shevchenko, "There is no other Ukraine in the world, there is no other Dnipro."

March 26, 2022

INTELLIGENCE OR DISINFORMATION

United States Intelligence recently came up with a very special piece - alleged information that is so blatantly incredible that it shames even that not-so-principled sector of our government – his close advisers are misinforming Vladimir Putin as to the war situation in Ukraine and the consequences of American and European imposed sanctions. This came on the heels of President Biden speaking from the heart in Warsaw, insisting that Russian thug Putin had to be taken out. Regime change was never on the agenda and had never been expressed before since such rhetoric might precipitate the use of nuclear weapons by Putin, asserted the apologist. The message was transmitted to President Biden and he quite clumsily walked back his assertion.

Nonetheless, very few people in the world believe that Putin is being misinformed by his own top people. Putin does not have advisers. He has sycophants. They come and go at his will.

The need for this piece of disinformation by Intelligence was too obvious - to cover up President Biden's sentiments even though they were spot on. Misleading intelligence is often used by governments to explain away impolitic statements and incongruous policies. Consider some such duds: during the Cold War, American Intelligence insisted that the Russians were a captive nation as well, in this way attempting to bring together a stronger and larger alliance of people opposed to the Communist regime to enable the invasion of Iraq in 2001 in order to take out Saddam Hussein, a long time thorn in America's side, American Intelligence insisted that Hussein was in possession of chemical weapons; more recently in order to appease Putin without appearing to do his bidding American Intelligence insisted that Ukraine militarily was not ready for NATO. In each instance, retrospectively, the United States has looked foolish and probably much more than that.

Aside from appearances of poor intelligence, serious ramifications ensued in each case. As the Soviet Union disintegrated, the United States accepted without reservation that there would be a democratic, non-aggressive Russia. Both Presidents Bush and Clinton played up that unlikely scenario. There was no reason to expect Russia to become democratic and tolerant of its neighbors who once made up the Russian empire. Boris Yeltsin may have added to the obvious fiction with his tomfoolery and drunkenness, but when sober, he knew exactly what he was doing to ensure a future Russian empire. He named a thug as his successor. He had to know or the very least, have vetted KGB Colonel Vladimir Putin. The KGB chose a certain type of individual for its hierarchy. American Intelligence could have paid attention to Yeltsin himself and noted that only a few days after Ukraine proclaimed its independence, the democratic Yeltsin leveled claims to Ukrainian territory.

While no one bemoans the removal of Saddam Hussein, the Middle East has been a mess since his demise. No one would argue for a return to the stability of Saddam Hussein. Still, a more carefully calculated and surgical approach may have resulted in fewer casualties and less spending.

Finally, there is no doubt that had Ukraine been admitted to NATO membership with a MAP at Bucharest in 2008, there would be no Russian invasion of Ukraine today. Regarding that military readiness canard, American Ambassador Volcker, who drafted the guidelines for NATO membership, has argued many times over the years since 2008 that Ukraine is more than ready for NATO. One striking indisputable fact of the current war is that Ukraine is more than ready and that if Ukraine were in NATO, it would be NATO's second most serious military member, Turkey, notwithstanding. Ukraine would be a reliable democratic member. Turkey is neither democratic nor reliable.

The lesson learned is not a new one. Appeasement does not work on thugs and criminals. It only emboldens them. Exculpating Putin! What a concept! Another lesson is that American intelligence should stick to the facts and, perhaps, if it's not too far-fetched at all times, retain a moral compass. America does so much good. But it seems intent on neutralizing that good with its own bad behavior. As Americans, we cannot be proud of that. Today, we are trying to exculpate Vladimir Putin or enable him to save face. Give me a break! There are children dying because of Putin, and we are looking to give him a break. That is so contrary to what we believe.

April 1, 2022

RE-BRANDING

I am a Ukrainian American and quite proud of my heritage. Practically, I am intrusive and prone to quick action rather than lengthy deliberation. My friends say I'm effective; others insist that I'm annoying. Since I am no longer young, I have become even more stubborn because of experience, irrespective of many mistakes. When I am told that you are wrong, I laugh because I have been wrong so many times. As long as no one gets seriously hurt, being wrong is neither a crime nor a sin.

No one will say that I am calm or at ease and that is why I sometimes avail myself of natural calming aids. My method of choice involves moderate imbibing of what I call Ukrainian white, cold as ice. This choice is one's own taste preference and is honed with patriotism. Another drink does not suit me, and I will debate with anyone that there is a finer drink than Ukrainian horilka.

The war imposed upon me several tasks to help Ukraine, providing vests, helmets, bedding, and ambulances for the Ukrainian fighters, monitoring compliance with economic sanctions, including my own version of compliance, by making sure that people in America do not have the opportunity to buy Russian vodka. In my free so-called leisure time, and I have much since I am retired and spend my time mostly reading and writing, I frequented five liquor outlets in my neighborhood, essentially persuading or persecuting the proprietors to stop the sale of Russian vodka.

In this instance, my approach was relatively provocative. I arrived at each store, asked to see their stock of Cognac XO, picked up the most expensive bottle, and as I approached the cash register, alerted the person assisting me that I wanted to see their stock of Vodka. Invariably, I noticed more than one brand of Russian vodka. Thereupon, I stammered and stated that I would not be comfortable purchasing the XO because they were selling vodka manufactured by a country that is murdering innocent civilians, including children, in

Ukraine. At that point, I left the store.

I returned to each store a week later. I don't know how many prospective customers made similar remarks while refusing to complete their purchase, but in three of the five stores, the policy had changed. On the shelves of three outlets, there were no Russian products, except Stolichnaya, but with a conspicuous sign that it was distilled and bottled in Latvia.

Obviously, as per the above description of myself, my predilection is not to trust anyone. I had to investigate on my own. Indeed Stolichnaya is now the property of a private firm, distilled and bottled in Latvia. Soon, it will be renamed simply Stoli, as it has been called in the West for many years.

Additionally, in one of the outlets, there was yet another conspicuous sign. Next to a vodka named Rusalka, the sign read, distilled and bottled in Ukraine. Hastily, I picked up the larger 1.75-litre bottle since we were expecting guests for Easter and made it to the cash register. Only later, at home, when I put on my glasses, I read the back of the bottle. To my dismay, it read, distilled and bottled in Belarus. Well, I was livid as I had no intention of supporting Putin's ally.

The first thing the following morning (there was an annoying wait as I rise at 5 AM, but liquor outlets in New Jersey open at 9 AM), I took the Rusalka and stormed into the liquor outlet. Fortunately, I do not use obscenities, so my attack upon the manager was somewhat subdued. He took my best shot and the bottle, calmly walked over to the Vodka section, and pointed out that the sign was next to the Rusalka liter bottles, not the 1.75 liter. He handed the liter to me; I put on my glasses as this time I came equipped and read the inscription on the back: distilled and bottled in Ukraine. I was shocked but filled with gratitude that this outlet had sympathized with the Ukrainian cause; I picked up a second liter immediately, and the manager and I walked to the cash register and made the appropriate financial adjustment.

As I was leaving, I asked whether he could explain this bizarre situation. He replied that he could not but promised to remove the bottles from Belarus. I cannot figure it out.

It has been surmised that Russia's main weapon, aside from its weapons of mass destruction, is propaganda and disinformation. One has to marvel at how many people and nations Russia fools with its disinformation. But its most supportive ally is greed, including that of Western companies. As the war drags on it is anticipated that German automobile companies may return to Russia as early as May. The Irish professional service firm Accenture has left Russia, but in fact, it has simply sold its Russian operations to its Russian affiliate. We need to be reminded that in the past, Google and Apple have worked closely with Putin against his opposition in Russia in the election to the Russian Duma. Russian intelligence has a nefarious history of spying on people. This was done by the Finnish company Nokia, which has removed itself from Russia but has left its equipment both hard and soft. Russia continues to spy via Nokia. Finland wants to join NATO now because it fears Russia. How's that for irony?

Politicians are equally duplicitous. When Russian opposition leader Alexei Navalny was recuperating in Germany after his poisoning by Putin, Chancellor Angela Merkel visited him in the hospital. At the same time, she was conspiring with Putin to construct Nord Stream 2. During the current war, Europe has imposed economic sanctions against Russia but continues to feed the Russian economy by purchasing Russian energy in the amount of 35-50 billion euros over that span. European sanctions have been reduced to zero, and in effect, the Europeans have been paying the cost of Russia's war.

Ukraine is grateful to the West for its rhetoric, economic sanctions, and military assistance. However, what is really needed is some sincerity. Sincerity in politics and business – what a concept!

April 14, 2022

GREAT RUSSIAN CHAUVINISM – AN INCONVENIENT EXAMPLE

In the May 12, 2022 edition of "The New York Review of Books," Gary Saul Morson reviewed two recent translations of Alexander Solzhenitsyn's novels, "The Red Wheel/Node III (8 March- 31 March): Book 3" and "Between Two Milestones: Book 2, Exile in America, 1978-1994." Under normal circumstances, I would not have raised an eyebrow, nor would I have read the review. But there is a war going on, an egregious manifestation of Russian imperialism. Solzhenitsyn, while a renowned dissident, was seldom identified as the Russian chauvinist and imperialist that he was.

Mr. Morson, anticipating the contemporary calumny of Russian imperialists, chose to write the following:

"Foreseeing the conflicts likely to arise eventually if Ukraine, with its large Russian-speaking population and its close cultural ties to Russia, chose to secede, Solzhenitsyn, who considered himself both Russian and Ukrainian, hoped to preclude the devastating conflict we see today."

In an apparent attempt to further mislead, Morson informs the reader that Solzhenitsyn's mother's maiden name was Scherbak, a Ukrainian name.

In fact, Solzhenitsyn was far removed from dual loyalty or democratic circumspection. He wrote after Ukraine's independence:

"Not the whole of Ukraine in its current formal Soviet borders is indeed Ukraine. Some regions ... clearly lean more towards Russia. As for Crimea, Khrushchev's decision to hand it over to Ukraine was totally arbitrary."

Morson is an equal opportunity denier or apologist. Many Jewish scholars have accused Solzhenitzyn of antisemitism. Morson does address the scourge of Russian antisemitism of which Solzhenitsyn was aware and sensitive. Morson points to Solzhenitsyn defending himself against that charge but never quite doing so successfully. Morson wrote, "The charge of anti-Semitism particularly offended Solzhenitsyn, who, as some critics conceded, defended Jewish dissidents and the right of Jews to emigrate in order to avoid religious and other persecution in the USSR."

However, Solzhenitsyn was enamored of the czarist empire. He firmly believed in the reforms of the Russian czarist prime minister Stolypin, who was assassinated in Kyiv and whose assassin happened to be Jewish - Dmitry Bogrov. It is noteworthy that Bogrov claimed his assassination of Stolypin was motivated by revenge for the antisemitism of the Russian Empire.

Solzhenitsyn's Russian chauvinism and pro-czarist politics are largely responsible for accusations against him of being an anti-Semite. This issue was addressed by Morson in his review. What was not addressed was Solzhenitsyn's view that Russia had to be Russian.

For Solzhenitsyn, the fact that Jews constituted a disproportionate number of the Bolsheviks and their secret services underscored its non-Russian, internationalist nature. In fact, Jews made up a disproportionate number of communists in America in the 1930s and 1940s as well. Does noting this fact make one an anti-Semite? No, it does not. However, stressing that fact and repeating it over and over in order to stir up animosity is a form of antisemitism. Indeed, in his "Two Hundred Years Together," Solzhenitsyn stressed that fact.

Why take on Solzhenitsyn? Because he was a very traditional, typical Russian, and that made him very dangerous. He was and remains respected highly in the West as the author of "The Gulag Archipelago" and other literary and dissident works. Together with

Andrei Sakharov, he was the quintessential Russian Soviet dissident. But, unlike Solzhenitsyn, Sakharov was not a Russian imperialist.

Solzhenitsyn's legacy of being a Russian anti-Ukrainian and anti-Semitic voice is as important as that of being a dissident and literary figure. Once the world recognizes the dark Russian soul of Solzhenitsyn, it will recognize, or at least begin to recognize, this fundamental feature of Russian nature. These chauvinistic pronouncements of Solzhenitsyn are of special import today. As such, it's time to concede that Solzhenitsyn is to literature what Putin is to international relations, Morson's apologies notwithstanding.

If President George W. Bush looked into Putin's soul and came away, at least initially, with a favorable impression, only to be severely disillusioned, then a deeper look into a typical Russian soul such as that of Solzhenitsyn is crucial for global security.

A persistent nuclear Russian menace is not the world we want. It is equal to, if not more dangerous than, global warming. The lesson to be learned is that most Russians, in terms of chauvinism and imperialism, rise to the level at least of Alexander Solzhenitsyn, however much he is admired in the West. Thus, the demise of Vladimir Putin would be only a temporary reprieve.

Russian society is replete with chauvinists and imperialists. This requires much more than regime change. Persistent vigilance and a carrot-and-stick approach must be our mandate. Over the last fifteen years, from Russia's invasion of Georgia, the invasion of Crimea and the Donbas, the MH17 killing of almost 300 innocents, and the atrocities in Syria, Russia has not been held responsible for its grievous crimes. Lack of punishment emboldens criminals. My conclusion is that every Russian potentially has that criminal mentality, which may manifest itself when unchecked. It's time to check Russian criminality and do so with such force that it makes a difference.

April 28, 2022

CATHOLIC CORRESPONDENCE

"One" is a quarterly publication of the CNEWA (Catholic Near East Welfare Association) based in New York founded according to the publication page by the Holy Father with its mission printed on the publication page: "CNEWA shares the love of Christ with the churches and peoples of the East, working for, through and with the Eastern Catholic churches."

Its March 2022 issue carried an article about the war in Ukraine. The following correspondence should be easy to understand. I wrote the following letter to the Editor:

> "There are two major problems with The Tragedyedof Russia and Ukraine by Michael J.L. La Civita. The most serious is the last sentence Russia and Ukraine, whose people rightly claim Kievan Rus as their own.
>
> Christianity came to Ukraine from Constantinople. Christianity came to Moscow from Kyiv. Following the above logic, Ukrainians may rightfully claim Istanbul as their own. How ridiculous is that? Moscow has no relation to Kyiv or Ukraine other than being its oppressor for centuries.
>
> The second problem is that Mr. La Civita seems to go out of his way to dis-inform about the current Russian aggression. He describes the the Russian onslaught as missiles targeting key military and communications posts near Ukraine's principal cities: Kyiv, Kharkiv, Odessa, even as far west as Lviv. Nowhere a word about Russia targeting civilians, women, children, maternity hospitals, orphanages. The entire world is condemning Russian war crimes and considering invoking the UN Genocide Convention.
>
> Being Christian may suggest forgiving, but Mr. La

Civita is not the victim here. That right of forgiving belongs to the victims. In any event forgiving does not mean intentionally misinforming.

The underlying error is that many religious people in the West view Muscovite or Russian Orthodoxy as a religion in our sense. Orthodoxy in the Duchy of Muscovy, the Russian Empire, the USSR, or today's aberration was never separated from the state. Vladimir Lenin, one of the most evil men in history whose idea of governance was predicated on the indiscriminate use of terror, called religion the opiate of the people because Orthodoxy was used by the state to brainwash the population. Unfortunately, Mr. La Civita is too charitable or simply naive."

The editors apparently brought my letter to the attention of the author, who was kind enough to answer:

"Dear Mr. Lozynsky,

Thank you for your email.

The magazine article in question was written and published in the earliest days of the Russian invasion of Ukraine – before the military began its targeted shelling of civilian centers, as you note. Who knew Putin and his war machine would target the very people he seeks to "save" from the clutches of Western civilization – I wish I had the powers of a seer, but alas, I do not.

Regarding the last sentence, my history of Russia and Ukraine was written from an ecclesial perspective. This perspective transcends nation-states, nationalism, and the politics that ultimately divide and destroy.

Thank you for taking the time to read the piece. I appreciate the criticism.

Sincerely,

Michael La Civita"

I then replied to Mr. La Civita's answer:

"Dear Mr. La Civita:

Thank you for your expeditious response. Your first point is well taken. However, your second is troubling since we are not discussing an ecclesiastical conflict but a very real political and military one in which people, including hundreds of children, are dying. It seems like this was an off-the-cuff retort totally unresponsive to a serious flaw in your perspective of Ukrainian-Russian relations.

More importantly, however, I am concerned about your silence on my third point. This is not entirely your personal issue. The Holy Father, in my view, shares the blame for emboldening Putin, Kirill, and the Russians. After all, he met with those two and Hilarion, thereby giving the impression that somehow he was treating them as equal spiritual partners. I would suggest that you pursue the study of the relationship between church and state first in Muscovy, then in the Russian empire and under Soviet rule. This is the crux of the problem, and the Roman Catholic Church has been complicit in perpetuating the charade. This charade is nothing less than Russian propaganda and disinformation.

I am eager to continue this dialogue with the purpose of showing you and others in the Roman Church how unfair you have been to Ukrainian Catholics by, in essence, siding with their oppressor at the expense of Ukrainian martyrs. Such a sincere dialogue would go a long way toward improving relations between

*Ukrainian Catholics and the Roman Church. While
many do not express their feelings openly, Ukrainian
Catholics are deeply offended by the Pope and the
Roman Church.*

*Thank you for being at least receptive to hearing the
views of a dismayed Ukrainian Catholic.*

Respectfully,

Askold Lozynskyj"

No further communication was received from Mr. La Civita or
"One." My only conclusion is that the Roman Catholic Church's
concern for Ukraine and Ukrainian Catholics is strictly "pro forma"
or, perhaps, simply mercenary.

May 2, 2022

PALIANYTSIA

The *New York Review of Books* recently published a review of two new publications on language that read:

> *"There are recent reports that Ukrainian defense forces are making their prisoners pronounce the word palianytsia (a kind of bread) as a reliable indicator of Russian or Ukrainian upbringing." It seems that the Russians cannot pronounce the "lia," instead pronouncing it as "la."*

This little bit is already well known in my house because when my wife Roksoliana went to Ukraine for the first time, much to her irritation, most Russified her name, and she suddenly became Roksolana.

This seemingly trivial difference in pronunciation simply underscores that contrary to Putin's claims, Ukrainians and Russians are different people, even in language and even more so in behavior.

Recently, a Ukrainian court sentenced a young Russian soldier to life in prison for not only killing Ukrainian civilians (killing more than ten) but doing so execution style. The killer is very young. He is deeply disturbed, clearly a degenerate, but not an aberration in the Russian military or society.

In the same issue of *The New York Review of Books,* there is an article by American journalist Tim Judah entitled *The Russian Terror.* The essence of his analysis is that the killing of civilians is carried out by Russian soldiers mostly in the form of executions, the deliberate destruction of civilians, including women and children, with specific intent and much cruelty.

The question is, "Who are these Russians?"

American society has suffered two major tragedies in the past week, the first, a racist shooting spree by a mentally ill teenager in Buffalo and the subsequent murder of nineteen young children and two teachers at a school in Texas. The first murderer, a white supremacist, justified his crime with a nearly two-hundred-page manifesto. In addition to his illness, the morbidity and influence of American white racist groups played a role.

The second case was the result of the application of a sick Texas society as espoused by its governor, Abbott, who at a news conference chose to defend the position that Texas licenses 18-year-olds to buy weapons, and former President Bush's adviser Carl Rove, defending semi-automatic weapons by distinguishing them from automatic. The additional irony was provided just a few days later and 100 miles further when the often disparaged National Rifle Association held its convention with Donald Trump as the main speaker.

Society can be sick, and adding the vagaries and passions of personal mental illness leads to tragic events. Even more so during wartime and especially when one side is devoid entirely of morality. The above military convict is probably not mentally ill in the traditional medical sense. He is a result of his society – Russian. This society is not only scarred by Putin and the Kremlin. A soldier is also a consequence of the upbringing of his home, and that stereotypical Russian home is degenerate as well, imbued with lust for power and empire.

Back in 2012, US presidential candidate Mitt Romney claimed that the biggest threat to the world today was Russia. He was ridiculed by US President Barack Obama. The last two US presidents before President Biden reflected (hopefully, this is an important past tense use of the verb) two prevailing views in American society about Russia – an immoral one in the persons of Trump and Kissinger and primitively naive in the person of Obama. The war in Ukraine has hopefully educated America.

Russians are not a homogeneous nation in the traditional sense. They are a mixture that took shape on wild terrain and under the captivity of being a vassal state of the Golden Horde and the Khanate. Alexander Nevsky, much revered by the Moscow Church, was simply a conqueror of land, not a martyr for any faith. The

Western world, starting with America, has never understood this. Very few American presidents saw Russia as the personification of evil. Now, the Western world has joined at least indirectly in the defense against this evil pseudo-nation. Were it not for the heroism of the Ukrainian people who understood best that Russia was evil, today, the world would look completely different. Ukraine saved the world and seemingly against great odds.

What will have to be done at the end of the war? There has to be an ending and a victorious one for good. Reconstruction must ensue similarly to what was done with Germany and Europe. It is little understood by us even today how much of Europe was destroyed or scorched not only by the Nazis but by the Red Army as well. Ukraine will have to be rebuilt as the European country that it is and similarly accorded a comparable Marshall Plan.

However, it will be necessary not to pacify but rather to reconstitute Russia and its society, starting with the Kremlin and ending with Russian mothers who instruct their sons to rape and murder women and children. The Moscow Church, as a fifth column, a pillar of the evil regime, must be eliminated, starting with its parishes in Ukraine. All international institutions, including the United Nations (rescinding Russian succession to the USSR, especially in the Security Council, which was never voted upon), should at least begin the process of neutralizing Moscow and dismantling it into, at the very least, its constituent federated republics and perhaps to its national minorities. Russian access to international sports competitions individual and country should be suspended for an indefinite time. The gradual release of some of the most basic sanctions must depend on progress in the liberalization of Russian society and its demilitarization.

Obviously, there will be great resistance not only from the Kremlin but from Russia's imperial mothers. This is where the program of psychological treatment of those who do not want it should be pursued. Western culture, as culture in general, cannot have a strictly political bent, but it can and should have a moral basis of at least good over evil, equality of people, justice, and basic human rights. These should not be major undertakings for cultural figures because this direction should be the basis of their craft anyway.

These are broad, ambitious, and clearly wishful plans, but the thrust must be a consensus of the good, that we must not go back to business as usual the time before February 24. While we cannot take lightly the danger of global warming, in fact, a nuclear and sick Russia is the greatest threat to our world. This is the most important lesson of the current war.

May 31, 2022

RUSSIAN CHAUVINISTS

The current war, the Russian invasion of Ukraine, planned by Putin and the Kremlin and enthusiastically supported by not only Kirill, so-called patriarch and his so-called Orthodox (Christian) church of Moscow, but also by ordinary Russian soldiers and their mothers, has revealed much, perhaps most importantly the true face of the barbaric and brutal Russian aggressor. However, there are still many naive even Ukrainians, Americans and others, including world leaders such as French President Macron, who believe that in Russia, Putin is a fluke, an aberration, an outlier. I address this article to the blind and those unwilling to see. Paraphrasing the well-known Ukrainian Jewish Soviet dissident Josef Zissels, Putin did not make Russia; Russia made Putin. This article is about Russian hatred of Ukraine and Ukrainians, based on its need to be an empire and lacking the history and culture for that designation. This is quite important because Putin is seventy years old and a mortal, but the son or daughter of every Russian mother is potentially a Putin.

In the first years of the Cold War after World War II, having recognized the mistakes made by President Franklin Delano Roosevelt, infiltrated by Soviet agents at State and Treasury (Hiss, White), nevertheless naive but deliberate American government officials began to understand the need to contain at the very least the Soviets while defending the enslaved peoples. Still, they included among the captives Russians, which was incomprehensible to all the other enslaved peoples. Through its intelligence service, the Central Intelligence Agency, America then even tried to involve the organized Ukrainian community in such an inane policy. However, America managed to enlist only very few people who agreed to become American agents and thus disseminate pro-Russian misinformation. The majority of the Ukrainian community was well aware of Moscow's historic aggression and understood that the USSR was just a continuation of the misanthropic Russian Empire.

A group that included the Russian Orthodox Church of the USA within the Russian American diaspora actively promoted this propaganda in the United States. However, even this duplicitous Russian community did not try very hard to conceal its anti-Ukrainian bias. For purposes of propaganda amongst Americans, an English-language monthly magazine was published by the Russian Publishing Company entitled "Russia." The editor was a Czarist remnant, Colonel Nikolai Ribakoff. The main topic, "Russia, the United States, and the Liberation Struggle," authored by Ribakoff, set the tone of a Russian liberation struggle but only to restore the Russian empire. One of the more telling articles was by Archpriest Peter G. Kohanik in 1952 entitled "The Greatest Lie of the Century 'Ukraine.'" Thus wrote the allegedly Christian Orthodox Archpriest:

> *...we all dislike the abhorrent Bolshevism and its sinful work in Russia and all over the world, but this does not mean that we should also hate Russia and her people. In trying to destroy Bolshevism, we have no right whatever to undermine the former Great Russian Empire by striving as the 'Ukrainian' Separatists do (assisted by good and honest, but misled Americans), to detach from her the 'Little Russia' (known at present as the 'Ukraine')...A study of Little Russian 'history' leads to the conviction that a 'Ukraine' as a nation, never existed...and, as such, they deserve no assistance in their separatist aims......those who support and recognize the various new republics, including the 'Ukrainian', which are now being planned and formed in or outside Russia are only doing a service to the enemies of Russia... At the present time, 'Ukrainianism' causes so much trouble to the Moscow Bolshevik rulers that they have been forced to purge many of its ranking officials...It seems that the Moscow Bolshevik rulers understand now more clearly the meaning of the 'Ukrainian' separatist movement. That*

is why they commence to resettle the 'Ukrainian'
population into other parts of the Soviet Union,
destroying (by intermixing the population) thereby the
invented 'Ukrainian' inhabitants.

Not even Putin has expressed more vitriol against Ukrainians. This is important not only for the sake of historical perspective but more so because it clearly shows that today's Russian Patriarch Kirill is not a new phenomenon. The Russian Church and the state have always been one. Recognizing Russian Orthodoxy as a religion means falling into the trap of Russian propaganda. Perhaps the most visible victims of this entrapment and propaganda have been representatives of the Vatican, in particular the current Pope. Unfortunately, there is little room for sympathy here, as they should know better. Even assuming a noble motive of ecumenical unity, there simply is no excuse, as Russia has, over the decades, exploited the Vatican in its hybrid war. Unfortunately, even Pope John Paul II was susceptible.

Another Russian, this time not of Orthodox Christian persuasion, but of the liberal poet-dissident cloth Joseph Brodsky, who came to the United States in 1977 and was given the opportunity to teach at such prestigious institutions as Yale, Colombia, Cambridge, Michigan, expressed his anti-Ukrainian feelings. In 1987, he had been awarded perhaps the most prestigious prize for literature, the Nobel. Apparently, the rest of the Free World was also duped. After the proclamation of Ukrainian independence in 1991, he wrote a vicious poem on Ukraine. This poem has never been published, but Brodsky did have the audacity to recite it personally boastfully and so it was picked up and translated into Ukrainian and English and perhaps other languages.

On Ukrainian Independence

"Dear Charles XII, the Poltava battle

Has been fortunately lost. To quote Lenin's burring rattle,

"Time will show you Kuzka's mother", ruins along the waste,

Bones of post-mortem bliss with a taste of Ukraine.

It's not the green flag, eaten by the isotope,

It's the yellow-and-blue flying over Konotop,

Made out of canvas – must be a gift from Canada–

Alas, it bears no cross, but the Khokhly don't want to.

Oh, rushnyks and roubles, sunflowers in summer season!

We Katsapy have no right to charge them with treason.

With icons and vodka, for seventy years we've bungled,

In our Ryazan, we've lived like Tarzan in the jungle.

We'll tell them, filling the pause with a loud "your mom":

Away with you, Khokhly, and may your journey be calm!

Wear your zhupans, or uniforms, which is even better,

Go to all four points of the compass and all four letters.

It's over now. Now hurry back to your huts

To be gang-banged by Krauts and Polacks right in your guts.

It's been fun hanging together from the same gallows loop,

But when you're alone, you can eat all that sweet beetroot soup.

Good riddance, Khokhly, it's over for better or worse,

I'll go spit in the Dnieper, perhaps it'll flow in reverse,

Like a proud bullet train looking at us askance,

Stuffed with leathery seats and ages-old grievance.

Don't speak ill of us. Your bread and wheat we don't need,

Nor your sky, may we all choke on sunflower seed.

No need for bad blood or gestures of fury ham-fisted,

Seems that our love is up if it at all existed.

Why should we plow our broken roots with our verbs?

You were born out of earth, its podzolic soils and its herbs.

Quit flexing your rights and laying all the blame on us,

It is your bloody soil that does not give, you watermelons, peace.

Oh, gardens and grasslands and steppes, varenyks [13] filled with honey!

We've had greater losses before, lost more people than money.

We'll get by somehow. And if you want teary eyes —

Wait 'til next time, guys, this provision no longer

applies.

God rest ye merry Cossacks, hetmans, and gulag guards!

But mark: when it's your turn to be dragged to graveyards,

You'll whisper and wheeze, your deathbed mattress a-pushing,

Not Taras' lies but poetry lines from Pushkin."

These thoughts exposed and left to posterity are probably worth reading in full because no one could make them up. Some terminology and reference require illumination for a non Russian or non Ukrainian, but even so, it is quite expressive of Brodsky's animosity, i.e.: Charles XII King of Sweden and Ukrainian Hetman Ivan Mazepa led the war against the then Moscovite Empire, but were defeated by Czar Peter at the battle of Poltava in 1709; "To show someone Kuzka's mother" is a rare Russian idiom meaning "to teach someone a lesson", infamously used by Nikita Khrushchev (1894 – 1971) in 1959 while addressing US Vice President Richard Nixon; Khokhly, singular Khokhol (literally "tuft of hair", referring to a typical Cossack hairstyle), is a Russian ethnic slur for Ukrainians; Embroidered towels are a hallmark of Ukrainian folk art; Katsapy, singular Katsap (probably from "yak tsap", "like a goat", alluding to beards customarily worn by Russians), is a Ukrainian ethnic slur for Russians; Taras Shevchenko (1814 – 1865) and Aleksandr Pushkin (1799 – 1837), Romantic poets traditionally seen as founders of, respectively, Ukrainian and Russian modern national literatures. Pushkin spent much time in Ukraine, exiled by the Czar for irreverence, and thereupon became a champion of the Russian Czar's anti-Ukrainian policies.

These were merely two examples of Russian chauvinist expressions towards Ukrainians, which at least in part explains why, on at least two occasions in the last one hundred years, the Russians have attempted actual genocides against Ukrainians. The recent abhorrent directive by the Moscow allegedly Christian Orthodox Church "to wipe Ukrainians off the face of the earth" has been used in the past. In 1932-33, the Kremlin murdered 7-10 million Ukrainians through an imposed famine referred to as the "Holodomor". A similar event, except with rockets and bullets, is taking place today. Fortunately, so far, the numbers are not as staggering, but then the Russians do not have control of Ukrainian territory as in 1932-33.

I recently attended the premiere of the Ukrainian film about the war in Ukraine dating back to 2014, "A Rising Fury," which was showcased at Lincoln Center at the famous Tribeca Film Festival in New York City. The director said it was difficult for the organizers to agree on the synopsis of the film because the proposal written by her was "too anti-Russian for them." American naivete extends from Government to the film industry.

But why should we be surprised by Americans? Mostly, they are naïve, accommodating, and willing to part with pieces of Ukraine in order to appease such as Henry Kissinger. I have Ukrainian acquaintances, including priests and simply pro-Ukraine Americans, ambassadors who are Russophiles (supporting the extensive use of the mother tongue), and working as lame American consultants through the CIA infiltrating even pro-Ukrainian Washington think tanks manifesting goodwill and managing to blur the focus from real issues.

Putin is not an outlier! He's simply a Muscovite! He is like the aforesaid Muscovite archpriest or the liberal dissident Russian poet Brodsky, who is not alone in his Ukrainophobia. There was the preeminent Russian dissident Oleksandr Solzhenitsyn, who wrote:

> "Not the whole of Ukraine in its current formal Soviet
> borders is indeed Ukraine. Some regions ... clearly

lean more towards Russia. As for Crimea, Khrushchev's decision to hand it over to Ukraine was totally arbitrary."

Solzhenitsyn's mother was Ukrainian. Does not Solzhenitsyn sound like Putin? There were, are, and will be others like him. There is, of course, the Russian mother whose soldier son rapes and kills innocent Ukrainian children upon her directive. Solzhenitsyn's antisemitism was prevalent as well. After all, he considered himself a Great Russian, and that meant chauvinism and the denigration of others because that is what Great Russians do.

Let's take a page from the Brodsky-denigrated Ukrainian poet Taras (Shevchenko):

"Fall in love with marigolds,

but not with the Muscovites,

Because Muscovites are strange people,

They do evil to you!"

This was written well before Putin and based on both history and Shevchenko's personal experience. He spent most of his adult life in Russia, mostly not by choice. However, he did have Russian friends who recognized his talent and encouraged him to write in Russian. He not only disappointed them, but became a Ukrainian force against which Soviet Russia was powerless. They allowed monuments to Shevchenko but attempted to alter his writings. Only God and Shevchenko proved to be insurmountable in Soviet Ukraine.

Bibliography

Conquest, Robert, "The Harvest of Sorrow", Oxford University Press, 1986

"Crisis Magazine," Joseph Pearce, "The Voice of a Prophet: Solzhenitsyn on the Ukraine Crisis," February 24, 2022

"Kobzar", Taras Shevchenko, "Kateryna", 1838

"Russia", Russian American Monthly Magazine, New York, December 1952

"Russian Universe," Sergey Armeyshov, "On Ukrainian Independence," Joseph Brodsky, translated by Artem Serebrennikov

"The New York Review of Books," Gary Saul Morson, "What Solzhenitsyn Understood," New York, May 12, 2022

"Witness", Whitaker Chambers, Regnery History, Washington DC, 2014

June 22, 2022

IN PURSUIT OF HISTORIOGRAPHY

My late father-in-law was a historian much respected by his peers, notably for his integrity. He was a Ukrainian American by birth and by choice. I once asked him whether, as a Ukrainian, he had difficulty pursuing the study of history since history is usually written by the victor, and Ukrainians have not often been victors. He stated, with no hesitancy, that his aim is always to learn the truth irrespective of existing historiography, and while that may be difficult under circumstances where his own nation has been less fortunate than others, it is important to look for sources first and then base your conclusions upon them. While he was paid modestly as all professors for his teaching, academic freedom was always paramount, and his research and publications were always meticulous.

As an attorney, I understood sources, perhaps mistakenly, to mean evidence, but my cynicism led me to understand that the sources he researched were not necessarily evidence that would be offered in a court of law. For historians, there is a broader understanding of sources. There are primary sources and secondary sources. True research is based on primary sources, which include items created at the time, such as artifacts used at the time, documents, memoirs, diaries, and even recordings. Such primary sources need to be authenticated as well, at times, even forensically and identified. The individual historian's interpretations of these primary sources can then be challenged by peer review (other historians). I respected that process, although, as an attorney, I was not satisfied.

My father-in-law was an especially honest and diligent scholar. However, as in any profession, there were and remain many charlatans and pretenders. Everyone, including historians and attorneys, possesses a certain amount of personal bias. That bias may be further exacerbated by monetary interests. It is important to understand that, as with attorneys, some historians are influenced by retainers and grants. For that reason, in a court of law, a historian purporting to be an expert, just as any other called to testify, is subject to impeachment based on bias, remuneration, and shoddiness.

Attorneys are recognized in that regard as they have a specific duty to represent only the interests of their clients. They are not permitted to lie but are expected to present only one side of the story. Still, in presenting only one side of the story, they need to adhere to the rules of professional ethics. However, many attorneys are rather flexible in both regards. This is widely known, and for this very reason, there exist disciplinary proceedings that sanction attorneys.

Academics face similar review committees if there are accusations of scientific misconduct, a charge which includes a range of unacceptable behavior such as misrepresentation of facts or plagiarism. And the punishment can range from censure, to sanction and to termination. However, because misrepresentation of facts may be presented as the historian's analysis and not a deliberate misrepresentation, official sanctions of academics, particularly if they have already been granted tenure at an academic institution, are rare. Thus, a stimulating teacher with a list of publications can find a position somewhere, irrespective of what nonsense he propounds. That only adds to my cynicism.

The current war in Ukraine has been ongoing since 2014, but its most recent manifestation as a full-scale invasion by the Russian aggressor has been much more recent. While the first day of full-scale war is generally recognized as February 24, 2022, Vladimir Putin revealed his version of Ukrainian-Russian history in the Summer of 2021. That speech was a proclamation of not only war but of genocide as he stated that Ukraine is not really a nation, whatever that means. He then proceeded to ascribe the history of Ukraine dating to Kyivan Rus to Russia despite the fact that, at that time, Moscow did not exist and would not for many centuries. Kyiv was established in the V century and Moscow in the XII.

Independent democratic Ukraine is fighting for its existence as a state and its right to its own history. A colonial Ukraine in the past, whether as a part of one empire or another, has produced historians on both sides of the Atlantic - including some agents of the colonizer and other self-loathing Ukrainian acolytes. Naivete and money for hire have afforded fora for expression to these agents and pseudo-scholars. Their so-called scholarly research provides ammunition for those who wish to destroy Ukraine, like Vladimir Putin, who, through his official spokesmen and even his religious abomination, in his exhortation to the Russian people, Russian mothers, no less, encourage the extermination of the Ukrainian nation.

Despite all their efforts, the enemies of Ukraine will not succeed. Ukrainian and foreign history has proven that. The Ukrainian people have persevered despite long periods of enslavement with only intermittent and relatively brief periods of statehood since Ukraine's Kyivan Rus era of statehood. Though Ukrainians have only begun to write their own history in words, it has long been engraved by the deeds of Ukrainian heroes. A Ukrainian victory in this war will be a celebration of the triumph of good over evil and a significant milestone in Ukrainian history. Yet another page will be written about the indomitable Ukrainian spirit.

This day of American independence seems like an appropriate day to urge all Americans to continue supporting Ukraine's independence because what happens in Ukraine will affect future world history and the world's freedom. That future freedom so much depends on American support. Thank you, President Biden and fellow Americans! You will be remembered by history.

July 4, 2022

"USEFUL IDIOTS"

During a recent debate between the Republican party candidate and pretenders for Congresswoman Liz Cheney's seat in the state of Wyoming, Ms. Cheney shone as a beacon of hope for the rehabilitation of her party. The pretenders could not have been more primitive. One said the war in Ukraine was provoked by Ukraine. Another said that President Biden's aid to Ukraine for the war effort was the Democrats' form of money laundering. Well, it was Wyoming, but I am not making this up.

Vladimir Putin has not been successful in the "military exercise," but apparently, he has been more than a little influential in disinformation and propaganda, at least among the above Republicans, witness the Wyoming congressional pretenders.

Yet, this is not strictly Republican. In 2019, first-term Congressman Ro Khanna from the Bay Area in California initiated an ill-informed action item among colleagues, which resulted in a missive signed by almost forty 40 members of Congress regarding "right-wing white supremacists" (I am not sure what that meant since black and white is not an issue in Ukraine) in the autonomous military battalions of Ukraine fighting in the Donbas region, specifically naming the preeminent Azov Battalion.

I would like to preface my opprobrium against Congressman Khanna by suggesting, at the very least, that the Congressman himself never conducted any serious research into this topic, never traveled to Ukraine to inquire, much less spoke with the leadership of Azov. In any event, the letter, I suspect, drafted by his office and signed on to by a bipartisan group of his colleagues, resulted in the Azov Battalion being singled out in the Ukraine appropriations bill precluding receiving military aid. Not surprisingly "The Nation" and the now late Stephen Cohen of Princeton, perhaps the quintessence of useful idiots at the very least, applauded Congressmen Khanna's effort.

How misinformed were Khanna-inspired members of Congress? Since the recent hostilities began on February 24, the Azov Battalion has been at the forefront of Ukraine's defense, particularly in the crucial most affected area, Mariopol, because it was the only Ukrainian access to the Sea of Azov and, ultimately, in the last bastion of Ukrainian resistance there Azovstal.

"The New Yorker," a highly respected and liberal like Mr. Khanna's publication, recently carried an article that included a section on both the Azov Battalion and the Right Wing sector, which are now integral parts of the Armed forces of Ukraine. The writer of the article, unlike Mr. Khanna, actually went into Ukraine and met the actors. As to the Azov Battalion and Ukrainian nationalism, the article reads:

> "The invocation of 'nationalist" as a derogatory term with fascistic connotations baffled many Ukrainians , who argued that their nation's history had been denied by the Russian denial of its right to exist...foremost concern (in Ukraine-ASL) was resisting an external and vastly more powerful aggressors...Much of the Azov Battalion...was currently defending Mariupol against a Russian onslaught that threatened to annihilate it...There is no question that leaders of the Azov Battalion and Right Sector championed a chauvinistic, illiberal ethos...Over all, such views were more marginal in Ukraine than in Russia-or, for that matter, in the US...In 2019, Right Sector and veterans of the Azov Battalion allied with other far-right groups to field parliamentary candidates and failed to win a single seat."

That spoke much about the Ukrainian electorate. Further, the writer pointed out that perhaps only 20% of the Azov and Right Sector people can be classified as extreme. The overwhelming bulk are simply patriots or nationalists in the unadulterated meaning of the term.

Let's consider the far-right and far-left contingents in the United States Congress and, perhaps, let's not forget the unqualified and criminal commander-in-chief in the prior White House elected nonetheless by the American people in 2016, at least electorally.

In any event, those fighting for the right of their nation to exist are sometimes considered extremists, particularly by the enemy. They also rely very much on internal discipline. Consider the Irgun fighting for Israel's right to exist, including later Prime Minister Menachem Begin. Consider Le Pen in France and many such extremists in democratic countries not faced with outside existential aggression. By comparison, Ukrainian society, including Azov and the Right Sector, is very benign.

In July of this year, Congressman Khanna met with Ukrainian Consul General in San Francisco to voice his support for military aid to Ukraine. This time indiscriminately.

In the words of that great cinematic philosopher, Forest Gump, "Stupid is as stupid does." I hope that is the only problem. There is a Fifth column, but that is another topic. The denigration of the Azov Battalion and the Right Sector in Ukraine is tantamount to Putin's Nazification of Ukraine. It aims at the naivete and susceptibility of the uninformed. Propaganda and disinformation by the enemy not only of Ukraine but the United States as well has to be recognized, at the very least, by our elected representatives. Otherwise, it feeds the Fifth Column.

Republican Governor Romney, as a presidential candidate in 2012, stressed that Russia is the greatest threat to global security. He was soundly ridiculed by Democratic candidate and President Barack Obama, who was not capable of recognizing the enemy. In fact, he made an off-the-record hushed overture to the enemy after initiating a "restart." In a recent interview, former NATO Commander General Breedlove insisted that Russia does not belong in any international institution, including the United Nations Security Council. That may be counterproductive for the moment and unmanageable in the future, but at the very least the General should be heeded on the great Russian threat.

We live, we learn. Hopefully, it's not too late. In any event, there needs to be independent research and analysis instead of acting upon disinformation and propaganda.

July 7, 2022

RUSSIAN CRIMES MUST BE STOPPED ON THE FIELD OF BATTLE

American Communist and later chief witness for the prosecution, Whitaker Chambers, explained his disillusionment with communism and remorse by comparing Russian communism with German fascism. The Molotov-Ribbentrop pact, the Soviet-Nazi alliance of 1939, was the breaking point. Hitler entered into the pact for a tactical reason: to undermine the alliance. Stalin entered because of clear ideological similarities, which he stated on more than one occasion. Lenin had often remarked that terror was necessary for the implementation of communism. In fact, Hitler borrowed much from the Russians, including concentration camps.

Russian warfare during World War 2 consisted largely of war crimes. In fact, when the Russians invaded Western Ukraine (then occupied by Poland) in 1939, they executed indiscriminately. As they were compelled to withdraw in 1941 as the Nazis invaded, the Russians murdered their prisoners of war, employing a scorched earth policy. Since they were the victors and allies of the United States and the United Kingdom, no indictments were filed, and no Russians were accused, tried, or executed for war crimes even though Russia perpetrated war crimes throughout the war.

War crimes, as recognized today, have been the mantra of the Russian soldiers dating back to at least the XVI century and the war ravaging of the notorious Czar of Moscow, Ivan the Terrible. In the XVIII century, when the Ukrainian Cossacks revolted against the rule of Moscow, Czar Peter, who later declared himself a Russian emperor, razed the Ukrainian capital, Baturyn, killing anyone he could. This, in fact, was Moscow's first attempted genocide against the Ukrainian people.

All of this had been ignored by the civilized world until now. Thanks to technological advances, everything is becoming transparent. More and more articles are appearing in the West about Russian crimes. They were glaring in Chechnya, outrageous in Syria, and now exposed to the world in Ukraine. Are the war crimes of Russian soldiers in Bucha and Irpin, executions of civilians with hands tied behind their backs, an aberration? Rockets fired on prisoners of war in Donetsk, mothers in Mariopil, and the kidnapping of children have been added to the list of crimes and proven that Bucha and Irpin were merely the beginning. Many have concluded that this is Russian warfare.

There is no justification for this Russian-acquired psychosis. Putin and Lavrov are clearly war criminals. So is the Russian soldier, and even his mother and the purported church of Moscow. The Russians are well aware that their style of warfare constitutes criminality and much more than simply the crime of aggression. Russian troops seem to believe that killing children or anyone else is the way that war should be.

Almost immediately with the formation of the International Criminal Court in the Hague, Russia withdrew its signature. Recently, it withdrew its membership in the Council of Europe and its signature from the European Court for Human Rights in Strasbourg. Russia has more judgments against it in the European Court than any other state. Ukraine remains a signatory to the ICC, and any aggression, crime against humanity, war crime, or genocide perpetrated on its territory remains within the Court's jurisdiction.

Early on, Ukraine, recognizing the fecklessness and ineffectiveness of international institutions such as the United Nations, the Council of Europe, and international criminal judicial tribunals, established its own separate unit at the General Procurators office charged with investigating, indicting, trying, and punishing Russian war crimes. To date, one such proceeding against a Russian sergeant for the blatant murder of a sixty-two-year-old man pushing a bicycle has been completed with an admission and a life sentence. However, this is one case among thousands.

Russian warfare of perpetrating crimes will not be stopped by an international institution or court. This Russian psychotic cancer has to be eliminated on the battlefield. Frankly, concern for Russian behavior has gone well beyond Ukraine. The world (not only other countries surrounding Ukraine) itself is threatened by this Russian psychosis, which has become almost innately a part of Russian culture, its egregious behavior, and arrogant scorn for the international community. Russia exemplifies the most heinous crimes: aggression, crimes against humanity, war crimes, and genocide. There is ample evidence of all four in the current war, but simply securing the evidence will not prevent the crimes.

August 10, 2022

WAR CRIMES SIX MONTHS LATER

Much has been written about the atrocities at Irpin and Bucha, two cities in the Kyiv region of Ukraine, and what was discovered there after the Russian defeat and withdrawal in March of this year. Photos from Bucha corpses of civilians shot execution style with their hands and feet bound appeared on global networks and screens. Back in March, Ukraine and more than forty other states appealed to the International Criminal Court in The Hague to investigate these events as war crimes. The ICC continues to conduct its investigation.

Obviously, the human remains have been interred, but very telling real evidence remains in the ruins. The cities have returned to some degree of normalcy, but with much less vibrancy, and lasting very vivid signs of war crimes remain. There are far fewer residents in Irpin, a city of over sixty thousand prior to the war. People are slowly rebuilding their places of residence, often places where they had been born.

In general, war crimes are defined as a deliberate gross violation of the laws and customs of war. This is a collective concept in international law that unites a group of serious violations of the rules of hostilities ("law of war") and the norms and principles of international humanitarian law committed deliberately or due to gross negligence.

In one of the many local residential complexes in Irpin, there remain ruins of residential buildings, as well as the bullet-ridden motor vehicles of former residents.

There is a white car with Donetsk license plates parked outside in a residential complex, probably belonging to refugees from Donetsk. The windows are shattered, and the basic structure is irreparably broken. However, what is most interesting is that on both sides, right and left, you can see at least several hundred holes through which bullets have passed. The car is an ordinary passenger car and fragile, without any armored equipment or plating, such as only the civilian population would use. Clearly, the enemy shot many times at the vehicle or the passengers therein.

The residential complex is called Irpinski Lipky. The buildings are almost totally destroyed by heavy artillery. Two inscriptions hang on the complex. One with a request in Ukrainian: The co-owners of this house really need help to rebuild. The second inscription gives the coordinates for transferring this aid.

The very fact of a war crime, abuse of the civilian population, is clearly established. Collateral damage? Definitely not! Missiles aimed destroyed people's home and private cars were shot at hundreds of times. The perpetrators themselves must be identified. This is probably not about one or two Moscow soldiers. It is more about their commanders, especially the commander-in-chief in Moscow.

Moscow's way of waging war includes gross violations, as is traditionally the case with a wild horde. The Geneva Conventions before the Second World War had no meaning for Stalin, the post-war Geneva Convention had no meaning for Brezhnev, and the Treaty of Rome in 1998, which formed the ICC, had no meaning for Putin. This was visible in Chechnya, Syria and today in Ukraine.

Perhaps the current war will serve to cross the "t's" and dot the "i's" on accountability, and there will be consequences, as the Russian Fedir Dostoevsky wrote in "Crime and Punishment." For the relevance of not only the ICC, and the structure and the very concept of the United Nations, the victory of Ukraine and the world is necessary. Ukraine and Ukrainians understand this. It is incumbent upon the civilized global community to recognize that the war in Ukraine is not only a Ukrainian war with Russia but a perhaps final test for civilization.

The Russian Federation, currently flexing its veto muscles at the UN Security Council, was never formally admitted to the UN, which was formed in 1945 when the Russian Federation did not exist. There is a certain process for a state to join the UN according to the UN Charter. There was a dissolution, the liquidation of the USSR in Bialowieza Puscha and Alma-Ata in December 1991, then a letter from Ambassador Vorontsov on behalf of President Boris Yeltsin, both then representatives of a state that was not a member of the UN. This letter did not talk about membership but addressed succession. Neither the issue of membership nor succession was discussed at any UN forum, and no decision was made. Russia argues that no one protested. But neither was a vote for membership taken.

The seat in the Security Council of the defunct USSR is vacant today. The Russian Federation can now submit a request to the UN for its acceptance as a member of the UN. On the basis that the RF is not a founder of the UN, and even more so given her behavior in the international arena over the past thirty years, the Security Council seat is not at issue. RF lacks any credentials to be considered a defender of world security in the UN Security Council.

This is in line with President Zelensky's recent speech at the UN General Assembly only in accordance with the UN Charter and legal requirements set forth therein.

A place for a demilitarized Russian Federation should be found in the UN eventually after hostilities so that the Russians can start the process of acting in accordance with the behavior of the civilized international community governed by the rule of law, justice, and the viability of civil society.

September 20, 2022

WHY THE RUSSIAN FEDERATION HAS NO VETO POWER AT THE UNITED NATIONS

The RF is not a member of the UN

China (Republic of China) was a charter member of the United Nations from 1945. It was not the People's Republic of China, which currently holds a permanent seat in the Security Council of the United Nations. In fact, the Korean War of the early 1950s pitted a coalition of the United Nations against Communist North Korea, Communist China, and the USSR.

In the struggle between Communist and Nationalist China, the Communists ultimately prevailed in the 1950s, but it was not until much later that the People's Republic of China became a UN member and succeeded to China's permanent seat at the UN Security Council. This required a formal application by the Peoples Republic pursuant to the UN Charter and a two-thirds vote of the UN General Assembly. This happened in 1971 largely as a result of President Nixon's and Henry Kissinger's efforts, two very dubious historical figures in terms of integrity. Many opposed argued that this was a bizarre reward for Chinese communist bad behavior.

The USSR was a charter member of the UN. On December 8, 1991, the leaders of the three most prominent Soviet Republics, Ukraine, Belarus, and Russia, in Biloveznka Puscha, Belarus, concluded an agreement dissolving the USSR. Two weeks later, in Alma Alta, Kazakhstan, eleven former Soviet Republics concluded a separate agreement dissolving the USSR. Thereupon, former Soviet Permanent Representative to the UN Vorontsev, acting on behalf of Russian president Boris Yeltsin, delivered a letter to the UN Secretary-General informing him of the dissolution and requesting accession of the Russian Federation to the USSR seat as a permanent member of the UN Security Council. Allegedly the UN Secretary General disseminated this letter among the UN member states with no further action taken.

Since then, the Russian Federation has acted as if its request had been approved and intimating both actual UN membership and a permanent seat at the U SC, participating both as a member of the UN at various fora and as a successor to the USSR at the UN SC. However, no formal application for UN membership by the RF was ever submitted. Nor has any vote been taken.

The UN has a process for UN membership. The State submits an application to the Secretary-General and a letter formally stating that it accepts the obligations under the Charter. The Security Council considers the application. Any recommendation for admission must receive the affirmative votes of 9 of the 15 members of the Council, provided that none of its permanent members have voted against the application. If the Council recommends admission, the recommendation is presented to the General Assembly for consideration. A two-thirds majority vote is necessary in the Assembly for admission of a new State.

In its Preamble, the Charter lays out its purposes of practicing tolerance and living together in peace, uniting strength to maintain international peace and security, ensuring that armed force will not be used except in the common interest.

Given Russia's offensive behavior in only thirty years culminating in the current aggression, which includes indisputable evidence of war crimes and probably more, such as crimes against humanity and attempted genocide, Russia's chances for immediate admission are negligible. The recent UN GA vote allowing President Zelensky to address the UN GA opening session virtually rather than in person of 101 in favor, only 7 opposed and 19 abstentions was symbolic of the international community's opprobrium.

Thus, upon motion by a UN SC permanent member, similarly to the Korean situation, the UN should send a coalition of its forces to Ukraine to assist the Ukrainians in the defense of their national sovereignty and territorial integrity.

In the long term, Russia should be admitted as a UN member (but certainly not a permanent member of the UN SC) for the sake of the UN's legitimacy as a venue for peaceful dialogue and conflict settlement, but only after Russia is demilitarized similarly to Nazi Germany in the late 1940s and accession to the Non-Proliferation Treaty as a non-nuclear state. This is a road map with viable variations certainly a possibility. It is a tall order and requires political will and integrity, certainly not a traditional characteristic of international approaches. This approach is one for the future viability of the UN as a peacekeeping mechanism on the international stage. It should also serve to settle the current conflict in Ukraine.

The Russians need to realize that their methods of conducting international relations have no place in today's world. Russia may renege on all opportunities and become a pariah, with continuing sanctions and designation as a state sponsoring terrorism. That, however, may be too much to expect from the traditionally servile and imperialistically predisposed Russian populace.

The process should begin immediately. Minister Lavrov, a war criminal himself, should never have been permitted to enter the United States during the recent UN events. Immediately, the United States, as a permanent UN SC member, should move to preclude Russia from all access to the UN due to the fact that it is not a member. In view of the bogus referendum in Ukraine's occupied regions, sanctions should be heightened; the Western countries should recall their diplomats, oust the Russian diplomats/spies from their territories, and declare the RF a state sponsor of terrorism. This is only the beginning. The end, as outlined above, is full Russian demilitarization and accession to NPT.

September 29, 2022

RUSSIAN WAR WITH UKRAINE AND UKRAINIANS AT THE UNITED NATIONS

On November 7, 2003, Valeriy Kuchinskyi, the Permanent Representative of Ukraine to the UN, sent a cover letter to the UN Secretary-General with a request to include in the documents of the 58th session of the UN General Assembly an attached Statement by the delegations of almost forty countries among them, to the surprise of most, that of the Russian Federation, Belarus, and Syria on the occasion of 70th anniversary of the Great Famine of 1932-33. In the text, the number of victims was stated to have been from 7-10 million, the word "Holodomor" was introduced (death by hunger), and the description "national tragedy of the Ukrainian people" was used. The Statement also referred to the memory of millions of Russians, Kazakhs, and other nationalities. The UN Secretary-General honored this request.

It is interesting to note in retrospect that at that time, the Permanent Representative of the Russian Federation to the UN was Sergey Lavrov, the current very aggressive and mendacious Foreign Minister of the RF. One explanation is that the RF and President Putin were overwhelmed by the war with Chechnya at that time.

Three days later, the Ukrainian World Congress, together with the World Federation of Ukrainian Women's Organizations, the only two Ukrainian non-governmental organizations that were and are members of the UN with consultative status, issued a "Statement of Support for Commemorating the Victims of the Great Famine of 1932-33 in Ukraine".

In May 2007, the UWC submitted a report of its activities during 2003-6 to the Committee of Non-Governmental Organizations at the UN for consideration and approval in accordance with UN regulations for non-governmental organizations. In January 2008, this Committee reviewed the report and adjourned pending further review. It posed two questions in the interim: what is the position of the UWC regarding the joint Statement on the Holodomor, which was made during the 58th session of the UN General Assembly, and what are the sources of the number of victims of the Great Famine in the UWC Statement.

The UWC replied that its position coincides with the assertions of almost forty states that signed the Statement, and the estimate of 7-10 million was made on the basis of the following sources: Robert Conquest's book "Harvest of Sorrow," the final report of the US Congressional Commission on the Ukraine Famine and the findings by the International Tribunal of eminent jurists which the UWC had convened; that the number of 7-10 million is composed of 7 million on the territory of the former Ukrainian SSR, and 3 million on other territories of the USSR, in particular, the Kuban, the North Caucasus, and Kazakhstan. Outside the Ukrainian SSR, the worst Famine was on territories densely populated by Ukrainians. The report of the International Tribunal includes statistics from two censuses of the USSR from 1926 and 1939.

At the session of the same NGO Committee in May 2008, none of the 19 states except the Russian Federation objected to the acceptance of the UWC report. Yet because of the Russian Federation, the report of the UWC remained in limbo.

On October 28, 2008, the Permanent Representative of the Russian Federation, Vitaliy Churkin, convened a press conference at the UN. The purpose of this conference was to boast to the UN press that the RF had managed to controvert Ukraine's efforts to include the commemoration of the Holodomor victims in the program of the 63rd session of the UN GA. A representative of the UWC present at the conference managed to ask Churkin a question, namely, whether this event of famine by forced collectivization and deprivation was not an attempt at the genocide of the Ukrainian people. Immediately, the UWC representative was surrounded by Churkin's security service, which caused the UN security to act as well. The UWC representative was accosted, threatened and asked to leave the press briefing room as other press representatives approached him for further comment.

Despite this, the commemoration of "Holodomor" victims continued in November-December of each year at the UN forum of various locations through the efforts of the Permanent Representation of Ukraine to the UN led by the Permanent Representative Yuriy Sergeyev.

This changed significantly when Viktor Yanukovych was elected or falsified as the President of Ukraine, and a like-minded Kostantyn Hryshchenko became the Minister of Foreign Affairs. Yuriy Sergeyev tried to do what he could. In 2014, under President Poroshenko, Volodymyr Yelchenko was designated as Permanent Representative. An annual commemoration of the "Holodomor" within the premises of the UN did not resume. It has not resumed under the current Permanent Representative of Ukraine, Serhiy Kyslytsya.

The aggression of the Russian Federation against Ukraine at the UN has intensified not only in relation to the observance of the "Holodomor" but in a more contemporary direction, often using the "Holodomor" as a weapon.

During the tenure of Russia's surrogate, Viktor Yanukovich, as President of Ukraine, the Kremlin addressed the issue of Ukrainians as a nation. In 2010-11, the Kremlin liquidated all federal Ukrainian structures within the RF. One of its major arguments for the liquidation was that the leadership of these structures had participated in events commemorating the "Holodomor." Yanukovich, on his part, within two months of taking office, publicly proclaimed internationally in Strasbourg that the "Holodomor" was not an attempted genocide against the Ukrainian nation.

As the policies of their puppet in Ukraine were thwarted and Yanukovich was forced to flee Ukraine for the RF, the Russians invaded Ukrainian territory, first Crimea and then the Donbas region, in February 2014. Simultaneously, they exploited the seat of the USSR at the UN Security Council to attempt justification of their aggression.

In tandem, they continued their own brand of cultural genocide against Ukrainians within the RF by liquidating regional Ukrainian structures. It should be noted that in each occupied territory of Ukraine, they destroyed Ukrainian texts and implemented a pro-Russian curriculum for schools.

In the Summer of 2021, RF President Vladimir Putin put out his own version of Ukrainian history, which did not mention the "Holodomor" and went so far as to question the existence of Ukrainians as a nation, suggesting absurdly that Ukraine was first created by Comrade Lenin when he forged the Ukrainian SSR.

As late as February 23, 2022, the Russian Permanent Representative at the UN, Vassiliy Nebenzia, insisted at the UN SC that the RF had no intention of invading Ukraine. The ultimate irony, but certainly not coincidentally, as per a rotational schedule, the RF chaired the UNSC in February 2022. On the 24th of that month, the Russians invaded Ukraine in a full attack from several sides.

Almost every village and town that was invaded became the scene of transformation from Ukrainian to Russian, beginning with schools. Russian texts replaced Ukrainian ones. Russian version of history overwrote Ukrainian history. In many places, the infrastructure was decimated, making the locations uninhabitable. Migration ensued while the Russians began a filtration system enabling the kidnapping of Ukrainian children and transporting them to Russia. Cultural genocide was brazen. In many areas, civilians were executed with their hands tied.

On April 7, 2022, the UN member states began to act, albeit symbolically, since the Russian usurpation of the UN SC seat made tangible action seemingly impossible. The RF was suspended from the UN Human Rights Council by vote of the UN GA. This meant very little in practice and only a little more in theory since 93 members voted to suspend, 24 voted against, and 57 abstained. It was a vote illustrating the UN member states concern with their own human rights record.

Immediately after the vote, Russia resigned from the UNHRC. The message here was to show that Russia did not care. It thumbed its nose at the UN caring very little for such matters as human rights. A month earlier, an action had been filed by Ukraine with the International Court at the Hague. The Court reprimanded Russia for its aggression. Russia ignored the reprimand.

Later, in March 2022, more than forty countries, including Ukraine, filed charges of war crimes at the UN International Criminal Court. Russia had withdrawn its signature from the Rome Treaty, creating the ICC, but the ICC maintained jurisdiction because the crimes were committed upon the territory of Ukraine, which is a signatory.

The most glaring problem with international law is the lack of ability to enforce its decisions. The UN ICC is somewhat deficient on grounds of jurisdiction and almost entirely on enforcement which precludes remedies, preliminary and long term. This court has taken on the task of investigating Russia's crimes in Ukraine. This is an ongoing process. In the interim, Russia continues its crimes. There is no mechanism for injunctive preliminary relief, and even were there, who would enforce it?

This is where international institutions should seek relevance. There is a genocide going on of an international order, and the law-abiding world community seemingly is powerless to stop it. But that is the point precisely. It's not powerless. It's unwilling. That is a major distinction. No one country should be in a position to impose its will upon the globe. The international community, acting through a majority, should be able to act for the sake of peace, security, and human rights.

Could a defense alliance such as NATO, composed of some thirty members, be a proper enforcement mechanism? NATO spokespeople continue to stammer on the Article 5 provision. There is, however, a preamble to the NATO charter which addresses security in the Northern Atlantic and sets forth NATO's apparent purpose to preserve it. Article 5 is a convenience for those unwilling to act.

Nations and states are inherently selfish. Assuming total lack of the moral element as a consideration, there remains personal concern or fear. There is ample reason to believe that the Russians, if successful at aggression in Ukraine, will move on to new pastures. Verbal sympathy and condemnation are simply not enough. Russia's suspension at the UNHRC does not prevent war crimes or genocide. Neither does it stop further aggression.

What is needed is an international effort, a coalition of willing nations and states who are prepared to go into Ukraine if only to stop the war crimes and genocide and prevent further aggression. The Ukrainian military will take care of the rest, as it has shown. Ukraine's efforts on the battlefield should buoy the international community. Ukraine leads an effort to harness the world's ostensibly second-largest military arsenal with much success.

This is not about Putin and waiting for an internal regime change in Russia. Russia created Putin, not the other way around. It was the dark soul of Russia that evolved this criminal. Putin, in his own way, is a fitting successor to Ivan the Terrible, Peter I, Catherine II, Vladimir Lenin, and Josef Stalin. Putin, Lavrov, Kirill are all cut from the same cloth. The Russian Orthodox Church is as much a criminal institution as the Kremlin, even if the current Pope Francis treats it as an equal for "ecumenical dialogue."

For the Russians, the dead are merely statistics. Their own soldiers are mere cannon fodder. Russian mothers are hardened by visions of glory - a Russian empire. Tens of thousands of Russian soldiers have been killed in this war. Are many Russian mothers in the streets of Moscow or St. Petersburg?

Good cannot prevail over evil if the good is manifested merely with sympathetic words or even a UNGA resolution or even defensive weapon support, but without more meaningful activity. Even the most naive among us has to take note that there is much wrong in this world. Like cancer, evil grows if unchecked. The future behaviour and the state of the world will depend on our integrity and action today.

This is where the member states of the UN need to step in with resolve. The UN can be a viable alternative to war and aggression as it was meant to be. The nonsense of veto power in security matters by the world's scariest aggressor forged in 1945 because of American sycophancy and Soviet infiltration can be rectified. The USSR was a charter member of the UN SC. But, the RF is not a member of the UN and the RF has no seat or veto power at the UN SC.

China (Republic of China) was a charter member of the United Nations from 1945. It was not the People's Republic of China, which currently holds a permanent seat in the Security Council of the United Nations. In fact, the Korean War of the early 1950s pitted a coalition of the United Nations against Communist North Korea, Communist China, and the USSR.

In the struggle between Communist and Nationalist China, the Communists ultimately prevailed, but well after the formation of the UN. It was not until much later that the People's Republic of China became a UN member and succeeded to China's permanent seat at the UN Security Council.

This required a formal application by the Peoples Republic pursuant to the UN Charter and a two-thirds vote of the UN GA upon motion of the UN SC. This happened in 1971 largely as a result of President Nixon's and Henry Kissinger's efforts, two very dubious historical figures in terms of integrity. Opponents argued that this was a bizarre reward for Chinese communist bad behavior.

The USSR was a charter member of the UN. On December 8, 1991, the leaders of the three most prominent Soviet Republics, Ukraine, Belarus, and Russia, in Biloveznka Puscha, Belarus, concluded an agreement dissolving the USSR. Two weeks later, in Alma Alta, Kazakhstan, eleven former Soviet Republics concluded a separate agreement dissolving the USSR. Thereupon, former Soviet Permanent Representative to the UN Vorontsev, acting on behalf of Russian president Boris Yeltsin, delivered a letter to the UN Secretary-General informing him of the dissolution and requesting accession of the Russian Federation to the USSR seat as a permanent member of the UN Security Council. Allegedly the UN Secretary General disseminated this letter among the UN member states with no further action taken.

Since then, the Russian Federation has acted as if its request had been approved and intimating both actual UN membership and a permanent seat at the UNSC, participating both as a member of the UN at various fora and as a successor to the USSR at the UN SC. However, no formal application for UN membership by the RF was ever submitted. Nor has any vote been taken.

The UN has a process for UN membership. The State submits an application to the Secretary-General and a letter formally stating that it accepts the obligations under the Charter. The Security Council considers the application. Any recommendation for admission must receive the affirmative votes of 9 of the 15 members of the Council, provided that none of its permanent members have voted against the application. If the Council recommends admission, the recommendation is presented to the General Assembly for consideration. A two-thirds majority vote is necessary in the Assembly for admission of a new State.

In its Preamble, the Charter lays out its purposes of practicing tolerance and living together in peace, uniting strength to maintain international peace and security, ensuring that armed force will not be used except in the common interest.

Given Russia's offensive behavior in only thirty years culminating in the current aggression, which includes indisputable evidence of war crimes and probably more, such as crimes against humanity and attempted genocide, Russia's chances for immediate admission are negligible. The recent UN GA vote allowing President Zelensky to address the UN GA opening session virtually rather than in person of 101 in favor, only 7 opposed and 19 abstentions was symbolic of the international community's opprobrium.

Thus, upon motion by a UN SC permanent member, similarly to the Korean situation, the UN should send a coalition of its forces to Ukraine to assist the Ukrainians in the defense of their national sovereignty and territorial integrity.

In 2019, Ukraine's Permanent Representative to the UN, Volodymyr Yelchenko, wrote an article on the effect of the RF's illegitimacy at the UN, using the aforesaid example of China and that of India and Pakistan from 1947 when the UN Sixth Committee reported that while India could continue its UN membership since it merely underwent a diminution of its territory, to wit: Pakistan. The latter had to undergo the entire process for UN membership under Article 4 since it was a new state similar to the Russian Federation in 1991. Unfortunately, while Mr. Yelchenko penned a cogent and persuasive argument, he took no steps at the UN to question the RF's legitimacy as a UN member and holder of a permanent member seat at the UN SC.

In the long term, Russia should be admitted as a UN member (but certainly not a permanent member of the UN SC) for the sake of the UN's legitimacy as a venue for peaceful dialogue and conflict settlement, but only after Russia is demilitarized similarly to Nazi

Germany in the late 1940s and accession to the Non-Proliferation Treaty as a non-nuclear state. This is a road map with viable variations certainly a possibility. It is a tall order and requires political will and integrity, certainly not a traditional characteristic of international approaches. This approach is one for the future viability of the UN as a peacekeeping mechanism on the international stage. It should also serve to settle the current conflict in Ukraine.

The Russians need to realize that their methods of conducting international relations have no place in today's world. Russia may renege on all opportunities and become a pariah, with continuing sanctions and designation as a state sponsoring terrorism. That, however, may be too much to expect from the traditionally servile and imperialistically predisposed Russian populace.

The process should begin immediately. Minister Lavrov, a war criminal himself, should never have been permitted to enter the United States during the recent UN events surrounding the opening of the UN GA in September. Immediately, the United States, as a permanent UN SC member, should move to preclude Russia from all access to the UN due to the fact that it is not a member. In view of the bogus referendum in Ukraine's occupied regions, sanctions should be heightened; the Western countries should recall their diplomats, and oust the Russian diplomats/spies from their territories, and declare the RF a state sponsor of terrorism. This is only the beginning. The end, as outlined above, is full Russian demilitarization and accession to the Non-Proliferation Treaty.

There is a solution to Russian aggression, war crimes, crimes against humanity, and attempted genocide. The UN may be the appropriate forum if only its member states followed the rules and did not simply acquiesce. Ukraine should take the lead on RF UN membership in tandem with its closest allies, the United States, the United Kingdom at the UN SC, and many other member states who have recently witnessed Russian medieval criminality in Ukraine.

That is the only off-ramp that the Russians would understand and not be able to abuse.

This year marks the 90th anniversary the single most heinous and largest in number Genocide perpetrated by the rulers in Moscow against the Ukrainian people – the "Holodomor", the Great Famine of 1932-33. It is fitting to honor the memory of the 7-10 million Ukrainian victims. Given Russian continued aggression against Ukrainians it is strategically important to include this genocide for observance commemoratively and as a lesson of history at the United Nations, the single largest and prospectively most effective international security structure representing the community of today's 192 member states.

November 7, 2022

RUSSIA'S OTHER PROBLEM

A federation is a group of states with a central government in which, in theory, those states may maintain independence in internal affairs. The Russian "Federation" is not that kind of "federation." It is an empire accumulated over half a millennia with direct central authority over all aspects of the affairs of constituent republics. Today, however, this central authority is threatened, largely because of Russia's war against Ukraine. Russia's conduct of its failing war suggests two resolutions of this invasion: Russia will not prevail in Ukraine, and as a result, the "Federation" is in peril.

One hundred fifty nations comprise the "Federation," among them are the Kazan or Volga Tatars. Their land, now Tatarstan, was forcibly invaded and occupied by the Muscovites, now known as Russians. This is the story of perhaps the largest national minority within the RF, numbering more than seven million.

In 1552, after many days of fighting during the siege of Kazan, the army of Ivan IV (known as the Terrible) stormed the city, plundered it, and then burned it. The male population of the city was completely slaughtered, and women and children were driven into slavery. Muscovites tied the naked corpses of the brutally murdered residents of Kazan to 50 logs and launched them down the Volga. Not a single village remained within a radius of 60 kilometers from Kazan itself. All of them were devastated and burned along with the inhabitants.

The modern Volga Tatars are the descendants of the well-known early and medieval states that have lived in the Volga region since ancient times. One of the last state formations of the modern Tatar people was the Kazan Khan-ate, which lost its independence in 1552. The capture of Kazan did not mean the fall of the entire state, although its army was destroyed, and the Khan was captured and sent to central Russia. The Tatars actively resisted for several more years.

The Russians pursued a policy of genocide and ethnic cleansing in the occupied lands. The Russians' calamitous policy forced the Tatars' migration from the Volga to the eastern parts of the Kazan Khanate. In this region of the former Kazan Khanate, the Russians did not rule until the beginning of the 18th century. Whereas the territories along the Volga and the city of Kazan were inhabited by Russians. The Tatar population was forbidden to settle along the Volga River for 200 years. In the 18th century, peasant uprisings began, which were supported by the Tatar population.

The first Russian revolution was actively welcomed by the Tatars. The Tatar population was among the most educated among the Muslim peoples of Russia. Therefore, the Tatars were represented in all political currents of that time. However, the czarist government, by amending the laws, created difficulties for Tatar voters. Thus, the majority of Muslims of Central Asia could not take part in the elections to the Third Duma, and according to the results of the elections to the Fourth Duma, the Kazan province became disenfranchised.

During the Soviet era, all activities of civil society were tightly controlled by the authorities. At the same time, the activities of organizations that did not recognize Soviet power and communist ideology were banned (legally or semi-legally, such organizations existed only in the early 1920s and reappeared in the late 1980s).

In the early 1990s, two ideological currents began to form in Tatarstan: the Tatar national movement and the Russian-inspired federalist pro-Russian movement. The peak of their political influence occurred in the early 1990s.

On August 24, 1990, a rally was held in Kazan demanding the adoption of the Declaration on the State Sovereignty of Tatarstan. Five days later, the Supreme Council of the TASSR began to consider this issue. A lively discussion ensued. On August 30, 1990, the Supreme Council of the Republic adopted the "Declaration on State

Sovereignty of the Tatar Soviet Socialist Republic." However, the Tatar national movement insisted on the adoption of the Declaration of Independence.

By the beginning of 1991, the situation in the USSR had become critical. The central authorities began to lose control over the union republics, and the Union entered a period of apparent disintegration.

In the autumn of 1991, the Tatar people gathered at their rallying site, demanding nothing less than independence. On October 15, 1991, an attempt was made to storm the Tatarstan parliament. On October 24, 1991, the Supreme Council of Tatarstan adopted a resolution on the act of state independence of the republic, preparing for a referendum that was supposed to reinforce the previously proclaimed state sovereignty.

The Chairman of the Supreme Soviet of the Russian "Federation," Ruslan Khasbulatov, in an interview with the Izvestiya Tatarstan newspaper, promised to deliver the leaders of the Tatarstan republic "in an iron cage."

The situation escalated. Russian authorities agitated people to ignore the referendum, to vote "No." The Republic of Tatarstan was flooded with leaflets calling for a boycott of the vote. This was the subject of a televised address by Russian President Yeltsin. On Saturday, the day before the referendum, the prosecutor of Tatarstan personally brought to the Chairman of the Supreme Council of the TSSR a notification that if the popular vote did take place, the head of the parliament would be held criminally liable on the basis of the decision of the Constitutional Court of the RF.

The Referendum on March 21, 1992, was an important step toward determining the status of the republic. The question was: "Would you like the Republic of Tatarstan to be a subject of international law, a sovereign state with the right to establish relations with the Russian Federation and other republics and states on the basis of equal treaties?" 81.7% of Tatarstan citizens took part in the referendum. 61.4% of them voted "yes."

On November 6, 1992, the Supreme Council of the Republic of Tatarstan, on the basis of the will of the people, adopted a Constitution of the Republic of Tatarstan. Tatarstan was the only one of all the republics within the Russian "Federation" that refused to sign a new federal treaty. They cited the Declaration of 1990, the results of the Referendum, and the new Constitution, thus demanding that it secure a special status in its relations with Moscow.

However, pressure on the leaders of the Tatar national movement and, in particular, the government increased. A disinformation campaign ensued. Statements of the Tatar leaders were distorted. Disinformation spread among the population that one of the leaders of the national movement spoke of the inferiority and "illegitimacy" of children from mixed marriages and the need to exterminate them.

The Tatarstan government began to gradually "surrender" sovereignty. First, sovereignty provisions were relaxed in the 1992 Constitution, then even more so in a 1994 Treaty with Russia.

In February 1994 the leadership of Tatarstan signed an agreement on the delimitation of powers between the authorities of Russia and Tatarstan. The agreement provided for special conditions for the Republic to join the Russian "Federation," which seemingly relieved tensions between Moscow and Kazan for years to come. For this compromise, Tatarstan was granted fairly broad rights of a sovereign subject, for example, the opportunity to conduct foreign economic relations and, to some extent, foreign policy activities.

With Putin coming to power in 2000, the complete rule of Moscow was restored. All regional specifics were brought "in compliance with the legislation of the Russian Federation." By 2017 the special relationship between Moscow and Kazan was terminated.

Also, in 2017, Putin prohibited the study and teaching of national languages in all the federated national republics. The decision resulted from the numerous complaints of Russians living in Tatarstan and other republics that they were being forced to learn a language other than their own. For Moscow, this was to be the final nail in the coffin of the Tatar language and culture – a cultural genocide.

However, it turns out that this was only Russia's effort to commit cultural genocide. The Kazan Tatars are very much alive, both culturally and politically. All this information was brought to my attention by Kazan Tatars who are intent on independence.

There appears to be a movement afoot.

November 6, 2022

YET ANOTHER PROBLEM FOR RUSSIA

The Kalmyks (Oirats) are a western Mongol people who settled in the Volga region in the early 17th century. They are mostly Buddhists by religion. According to the 2010 census in the Russian Federation they number almost two hundred thousand. Another four hundred thousand reside outside the RF, mainly in Mongolia and China. The republic of Kalmykia, located in the farthest part of Eastern Europe, is, in name, an autonomous republic within the RF. The last independent state of the Kalmyks was liquidated by decree of the Russian Catherine II on October 19, 1771.

On July 2–9, 1920, the First All-Kalmyk Congress of Soviets of the Working Kalmyk People took place, proclaiming the formation of statehood in the form of an autonomous region within the RSFSR. It was attended by delegates representing all the Kalmyk uluses of the Astrakhan and Stavropol provinces, Kalmyks living in the Don and Terek regions, in Kyrgyzstan, in the Ural region, and the Orenburg province.

The Kalmyk Autonomous Region was transformed on October 20, 1935, into the Kalmyk Autonomous Soviet Socialist Republic, but then abolished on December 27, 1943, and the Oirat-Kalmyk people were subjected to deportation. On January 9, 1957, the Kalmyk region was integrated into the Stavropol Territory, and on July 29, 1958, it was formed into the Kalmyk Autonomous Soviet Socialist Republic once again. On October 18, 1990, the Supreme Soviet of the Kalmyk ASSR adopted a Declaration "On the State Sovereignty of the Kalmyk Soviet Socialist Republic." The Declaration proclaimed the state sovereignty of the Kalmyk SSR and declared its determination to create a democratic constitutional state. This was motivated by the right of the Kalmyk people to self-determination and the desire of the people of Kalmykia for socio-

117

economic progress, cultural revival, and a radical increase in living standards.

However, under pressure from Moscow, the subsequent years proved to be a time of regression in sovereignty. In 1994, by a unilateral decision of President Ilyumzhinov and his supporters, the pseudo-Constitution of the Republic of Kalmykia, the so-called Steppe Code, was approved, in which the Republic of Kalmykia was recognized as a limited subject, not a state, as defined in the Constitution of the RF.

The authorities of Kalmykia were subservient executors of the will of Moscow and helpless in defending the national interests of the people and the Republic. Under Putin, Kalmykia, as all of the RF, experienced centralization and militarization, attacks on the cultures and languages of the non-Russian peoples.

Chauvinism, racism, xenophobia, ethnic discrimination, rampant great-power hysteria, even admiration for Stalin and other monsters of the past flourished in the RF. The territory that was illegally torn from the Republic of Kalmyia during the period of deportation of the Oirat-Kalmyk people was not restored. Illegal annexation of territories of the Republic of Kalmykia continued in favor of neighboring regions of the RF. Moscow pursued a colonial financial and economic policy that directly impeded the economic development of Kalmykia, as a result of which there was a massive decrease in the Oirat-Kalmyk population. During the years following the return of the people from deportation, Kalmykia occupied the last place in the USSR and is now within the RF in terms of providing the population with such basic necessities as drinking water. Activities of national organizations are suppressed, the terror of the federal authorities against civil and national activists continues.

Based on the foregoing, on October 26, 2022, a newly formed entity, the Congress of the Oirat-Kalmyk people, declared the need for the complete liberation of the Oirat-Kalmyk people from colonial dependence on Russia, its determination to seek secession of the Republic of Kalmykia from the Russian Federation and the proclamation and creation of a sovereign independent state.

The Congress of the Oirat-Kalmyk People has appealed to all states of the world, governments, and parliaments to recognize the need to liberate the Oirat-Kalmyk people from the colonial oppression of the Russian Empire and recognize their legitimate right to self-determination and the creation of an independent state.

This is only the beginning. In Europe, a new structure of joint efforts by enslaved peoples within the framework of the RF was formed called the League of Free Nations. This structure includes the following nations: Bashkir, Buryat, Cossack, Kalmyk, Moksha, Tatar, Chechen, Erzya, and Yakut. On November 26, 2022, a similar and expanded structure called Americans Against Russian Imperialism took shape in the United States. Currently, it includes Tatars, Kalmyks, Kazakhs, Armenians, and Ukrainians. Many other nations have expressed interest in the dismemberment of the Russian Federation.

December 5, 2022

FURTHER COMPLICATIONS FOR RUSSIA AND OPPORTUNITIES FOR GLOBAL SECURITY

The Buryats are a Mongolian-speaking people living on both sides of Lake Baikal, as well as in Mongolia and China. The total population is estimated from 550 thousand to 690 thousand. The Buryat language belongs to the Mongolian branch of the Altaic language family and is one of the state languages of the Republic of Buryatia, along with Russian. The traditional religions of the Buryats are Buddhism and Shamanism. At the beginning of the 17th century, the Muscovite state began the conquest of the Buryat land. The conquest of ethnic Buryatia lasted for about a hundred years and finally ended sometime after the signing of the Burin Treaty between Russia and China in 1727.

The Buryat national movement originated at the turn of the 19th-20th centuries as a response to the tightening of Russia's repressive policy towards the Buryats. The emergence of a stratum of bourgeois nationalists in the Buryat milieu was a unique phenomenon in the history of national movements in Central Asia. Due to an imperialistic allegedly administrative land reform undertaken by the tsarist government at the beginning of the 20th century, the Buryat population rose in active opposition to protect its land.

After the February Revolution in the Russian empire, by a decision of the National Congress of Buryats of the Trans-Baikal region and the Irkutsk province in April 1917, a national state of the Buryats was formed - Buryat-Mongol Ulas. In 1923, the Buryat-Mongolian Autonomous Soviet Socialist Republic was formed as part of the RSFSR. During the Stalinist repressions in 1937, the Buryat leadership was arrested, either shot, or sent to concentration camps. A wave of arrests hit thousands of citizens of the Republic.

On September 26, 1937, almost a third of the territory was torn off from the Republic.

Demands for the reunification of the Buryat people within the boundaries of a single republic sounded with renewed vigor at the end of the 1980s and the early 1990s. Regional political associations were created. The core of the platform of these organizations was the revival of the Buryat-Mongolian people through territorial reunification and the re-establishment of a single Buryat-Mongolian Republic.

In 2020, the Buryat Democratic Movement (in exile) officially appealed to the President of the Russian Federation with a demand, based on the existing law of the Russian Federation and the obligations assumed by the Russian Federation to comply with international legal norms, as well as archival historical documents, to restore the Republic of Buryatia within its 1937 borders and to carry out the necessary actions for the rehabilitation of the Buryat nation and the Republic of Buryatia. This appeal was ignored.

In 2014, in connection with the Russian invasion of Ukraine, activists and supporters of the Buryat national movement repeatedly condemned the illegality of Russia's actions. They strenuously objected to sending soldiers from the territory of Buryatia and Siberia to participate in illegal action. Many Buryats had been conscripted. By 2016, many Buryat activists had emigrated and formed the Buryat Democratic Movement outside the RF. With the start of Russia's full-scale war against Ukraine in 2022, the Buryat Democratic Movement (in exile) was one of the first (among the people held captive by Moscow) to issue an official statement in support of Ukraine and condemn the illegality of Russian military aggression.

The Buryat emigration formed a consolidated movement, "Buryats Against the War," from which the "Free Buryatia Foundation" emerged, which includes activists in the EU countries, the USA, and Mongolia, as well as groups that remain in Buryatia in the underground. Together with other national minorities oppressed within the RF, the Buryats have joined the League of Free Nations based in Europe.

The Buryats are one of many nations oppressed within the RF who have not only voiced their condemnation of Russia's war, manifested support for Ukraine, and reawakened their own national aspirations. It is important to note that the Russian Federation is not a federation but a prison of more than 100 non-Russian nations oppressed for centuries by the Russians. That prison is a time bomb ready to go off at any moment. Russia's brutal yet losing war in Ukraine has certainly been motivation as a combination of conscriptions, repressions, and economic sanctions is proving to be too much for the non-Russians and serving as motivation and opportunity for revolt and self-determination.

The lessons of history regarding empires are that an empire almost always takes on more than it can manage, which decays with time. Repression serves the empire well, but oftentimes, the patience of the repressed can break, which results in more courage and risk-taking, especially when the weaknesses of the oppressor are exposed. The result may be revolt. This is what should happen in the Russian Federation. The first signs are apparent.

The democratic world has not only a moral obligation, but also a political opportunity to support legitimate aspirations, in particular when they serve the interest of world stability and peace in the long term. The antidote to empire is democracy. Even people who do not have a tradition of democratic rule and respect for human rights, under the influence of an open global society where everything is transparent, begin to value the rights and opportunities of a free society. However, it is necessary not only to talk about supporting the good to overcome evil and taking advantage of new opportunities but also to act accordingly and decisively.

December 10, 2022

THE DISMANTLING OF THE
RUSSIAN FEDERATION

The Erzya National Congress convened in exile in the Estonian city of Otepaa on September 30, 2022, to consider the intensifying repressions in the Russian Federation. The delegates, after discussions, adopted significant resolutions on new goals and objectives of the national movement, including the struggle for independence of the Erzya and the secession of the Erzya territories from the Russian Federation.

Erzya is one of the most numerous Finno-Ugric peoples of the RF, which live in the Volga region. The total number is about 500 thousand people. The Erzya language is a Finno-Ugric language of the Finno-Volga group, one of the three official languages of the Republic of Mordovia, along with Moksha and Russian. The Erzya profess Christianity (Orthodoxy and Lutheranism), as well as the traditional national religion, Ineshkipaziya. They are one of the few peoples enslaved by Moscow that have their own system of national representative bodies. It consists of a congress of delegates from the Erzya political parties and public associations, a council of elders, and a national court.

The Erzya National Movement has officially condemned the unleashing of a war against Ukraine by the Russian authorities three times: once in 2014 and twice in 2022. Arson of the military enlistment office in Ruzaevka (Republic of Mordovia), as well as the distribution of anti-war leaflets in Saransk in July 2022, are associated with the Erzya underground. There are Erzya volunteers fighting in Ukraine against the RF Armed Forces, and there is confirmed data on losses among Erzya fighters.

The Russian authorities have tried to take control of the key organs of Erzya through intimidation and persecution of activists, and having failed; they formed parallel representative bodies headed by public sector workers, people dependent on the authorities.

"It was the intensification of repressions in our native lands, the creation by Moscow of fake structures for the self-organization of our people, as well as new military-political challenges in the Russian Federation that prompted us to immediately convene the Congress on emigration. We`ve prepared it in record time — less than three months. There were no discussions about the venue of the Congress. Estonia is the rising dawn of the Finno-Ugric world, our intercessor and our hope. The Estonian people are our kindred people, we came from the same historical and cultural cradle. Therefore, just as Turkey is not a foreign state for Azerbaijanis, so Estonia is not a distant land for us," explained the Chairman of the Organizing Committee for the convocation of the congress.

On the morning of September 30, the leadership of the parish, Estonian politicians and cultural figures, journalists, and scientists arrived in Otepää. The whole city was covered with Estonian and Erzya flags. The national flag in Otepaa is felt very palpably – the first Estonian flag was consecrated in the local church in 1884. The opening of the Congress was marked by a ceremony of raising the flag of Estonia and the Erzya national flag. This year, the Russian FSB and the police began to persecute the Erzyans in their homeland — in the Republic of Mordovia for Erzya flag raising.

The Congress began with a minute of silence, honoring the memory of an Erzya warrior — a soldier of the Armed Forces of Ukraine, Oleksiy Veshchevailov, who planned to go to the Congress as a delegate but died on September 26 in a battle with the Russians in the Bakhmut direction in the Donetsk region of Ukraine. Other Erzya warriors fighting on the side of Ukraine were supposed to go to represent the Erzya military brotherhood. One of them did manage to get a 4-day layoff and get to Estonia. When the young Erzya, in the uniform of a soldier of the Armed Forces of Ukraine, entered the conference hall, he instantly drew the attention of the press and the Estonian public.

"The importance of this event for our nation is difficult to overestimate. In fact, our people found themselves behind the Iron Curtain. More than a third of the delegates could not get to the Congress. The Russian authorities put pressure even on those Erzya who remained in the Russian Federation and were involved in the preparation and holding of the Congress remotely. There were people who could not cross all the borders and did not get to Estonia. However, despite all the obstacles, we were able to convene the Congress and involve not only elders but also young people in it," said Olexander Butyaykin, a fighter of the Armed Forces of Ukraine, a young veteran from Erzya.

Very acute political issues were brought to the attention of the delegates. A consensus was found on the most difficult topic – state building. The survival of the Erzya as a people within the RF was deemed impossible. The delegates chose the formation of the federal state of Erzyan Mastor.

The Congress identified the Republic of Mordovia, Penza, Ulyanovsk, Nizhny Novgorod, Ryazan, and Samara regions as illegitimate territorial-administrative formations and the "authorities" of these formations to be bodies without representative capability.

After heated discussions, the delegates stated that the continued presence in the RF of territories where the Erzya people densely reside means the final disappearance of the Erzya as a people: "Not a single aspect of the policy of the Russian Federation or the Republic of Mordovia is aimed at preserving the Erzya people, their national identity, culture, language, religion. Moreover, the policy pursued by the Kremlin towards the Erzya, as well as other Finno-Ugric peoples, is aimed at our speedy dissolution in the Russian ethnos. The Russian Federation is pursuing a policy of covert ethnocide against the Erzya."

Erzya not only accused the Russian authorities of ethnocide but also directly declared their desire to create a separate state, outlining in detail its borders, political form, and state structure: The realization by the citizens of Erzyan Mastor of the right to preserve and develop their national identities, languages, and cultures will be enshrined in the Constitution. The territory of the state will include the lands of the Republic of Mordovia, Penza, Ulyanovsk, and parts of the Nizhny Novgorod, Ryazan, and Samara regions. The state will have the following administrative structure: 8 cantons (of which two are Tatar national) and the autonomous Moksha Republic. The capital of the federation would be Saran Osh. The national emblem and the anthem were approved.

The Congress also decided that until the independence of Erzyan Mastor, the struggle of the Erzya people for self-determination would be headed by the national representative bodies and the chief elder. Only Erzyans can take part in the formation of representative bodies. The Congress recognized people as Erzyans who openly and publicly declare their belonging to the Erzya nation and are able to prove their kinship with a person of Erzya origin — without regard to the level of family ties. Also, an Erzya is a person who has mastered the Erzya language at a level sufficient for free communication and recognizes himself as part of the Erzya nation – without even having a drop of Erzya blood.

The Congress condemned the invasion of the Russian Armed Forces into Ukraine, and mobilization on the lands of indigenous peoples. They expressed solidarity with the protesters in Dagestan, Yakutia, and other colonial republics, supported the declaration on the decolonization of Russia adopted in Prague on July 23, 2022, at the Forum of the Free Peoples of Russia, and called on all enslaved peoples of the Russian Federation to fight for the collapse of the empire and the creation of independent states on the occupied lands of these peoples.

Komi, Karelians, Izhors and Mari took part in the work of the Congress as guests. On the sidelines, Estonian politicians and even the military were seen, who came to Otepaa to hold a series of closed meetings.

A member of the Presidium of the Congress, a political emigrant of the new wave, shared his impressions.

"Estonians' interest in us, as a kindred people, has increased markedly. The main thing is that the Congress abruptly brought the Erzya theme out of the folklore plane into the political one. Energy is felt in the air: both Erzya and Estonians understand that Russia has entered the final stage of its existence, and in 2024, the borders of new states will be determined."

One may say "wishful thinking". But then there are some one hundred nations in the RF repressed by the Russians, many of whom have voiced not only discontent but a desire for freedom and statehood. The Erzya people have at least two brotherly NATO members who are both allies- Estonia and Finland. And, frankly, this is only the beginning. Ukraine will support the Erzya. Russian Christmas, a time for great Russian orthodox Christian hypocrisy with a mantra of kill your neighbor, is still two weeks away, but given Russian losses on the battlefield, President Zelensky's recent historic and moving address to the Congress of the United States and the clearly manifest aspirations of the non-Russians within the RF, the New Year has to be a matter of great concern for Russian imperialists and Christmas should be less than merry for Vladimir Putin, Sergei Lavrov, pseudo-Patriarch Kiril and people of their ilk.

December 23, 2022

THE BASHKIRS

The Bashkirs are an ancient people of Eurasia, formed in the Southern Urals as an independent ethnos in the first half of the I millennium AD. The first written mention of individual tribes that became part of the Bashkir people is found in the writings of Herodotus (V century BC). The territory of the historical lands of the Bashkir people, the so-called "Historical Bashkortostan," includes the lands of today's Chelyabinsk, Orenburg region, parts of Sverdlovsk, Kurgan, Perm regions, and the Republic of Tatarstan.

The number of Bashkirs in the world is 1 million 700 thousand people. 1 million 172 thousand Bashkirs live in the Republic of Bashkortostan. The religion is Sunni Islam (Hanafi Maskhab).

Some of the Bashkir tribes in the middle of the XVI century concluded an agreement with the Moscow state and became part of it with their lands. Most of the remaining tribes were eventually conquered and forcibly annexed. According to the Agreement, the Bashkirs had to pay a small yasak, protect the southern territories, and participate in all the wars of the Moscow state. In response, Bashkirs were assigned their lands, where they were sovereign owners (patrimonial rights) and were granted full internal self-government.

However, after only a short time, Moscow violated the Treaty, seizing Bashkir lands and conducting attempts at forced Christianization. The Bashkirs responded with uprisings. Bashkir uprisings shook Russia for more than two hundred years, many of which ended with the victory of the Bashkirs. Bashkirs took an active part in the peasant war of 1773-1775 and fought against the tsarist government.

After the February Revolution of 1917, when national consciousness began to awaken among all peoples, the Bashkirs chose their own government, formed their own national army, and founded the First Bashkir Republic – Bashkurdistan. For the recognition of the republic, they had to fight both with the reds and with the whites. After the signing of the Agreement between the Bashkir and Soviet governments on the recognition of the Bashkir Republic on March 20, 1919, a year later, Lenin violated this Agreement and annulled many of its clauses that were under the jurisdiction of the Bashkir government.

The 90s of the XX century saw a new chapter of a Bashkir national movement for the sovereignty of the republic. The Bashkir intelligentsia and the Bashkir public created the Bashkir People's Center "Ural," the Bashkir youth organization "Union of Bashkir Youth," which became the driving force in the struggle for the sovereign Bashkortostan. In 1993, a Constitution of the Republic was adopted, which reflected many aspirations of the Bashkir people. In 1994, a Federation Agreement was signed between the Republic of Bashkortostan and the Russian Federation on the delimitation of powers and jurisdiction, according to which Bashkortostan was endowed with many rights as a republic within the RF.

However, with the arrival of Vladimir Putin, many of the republic's rights were taken away by the Kremlin, and the Constitution of Bashkortostan was rewritten under pressure from Moscow, with many articles and paragraphs stricken.

In response, the Bashkirs formed national organizations "Cook Bure" and "Bashkort," which have raised issues of protecting the rights and interests of the Bashkir people, the return of the sovereignty of the Republic, and the Constitution of Bashkortostan from 1993. The Russian authorities began repressions against the Bashkir national activists, criminal cases were opened against the leaders of the "Cook Bure" and "Bashkort," and activists were imprisoned. In 2020, the "Bashkort" was banned. One of the founders, Ruslan Gabbasov, fled from Russia and found political asylum in Lithuania. He then formed the Bashkir National Political Center which coordinates political activities aimed at gaining independence of the Republic of Bashkortostan. The Bashkir National Political Center has joined the League of Free Nations, where representatives of national and regional movements within the

RF are striving for their nations' independence from Russia.

In Bashkortostan there is a massive reduction in the use of the Bashkir language among the population itself as a language of communication. Communication in Bashkir is not accepted in any institution; almost all websites of state, municipal, and educational institutions do not allow registration in the Bashkir language. Language has been weaponized, and Russification is rampant. In the 2021-2022 academic year, 99.4% of students (504,977 people) studied their native languages, of which 345,509 (68.02%) chose Russian as their native language; Bashkir — 105,035 (20.63%); Tatar — 46,541 (9.2%). Native languages of the national republics of the RF, except Russian, ceased to be part of the compulsory school curriculum. In January 2019, the Advisory Committee of the Framework Convention for the Protection of National Minorities of the Council of Europe criticized Russia for its national policy. Experts expressed concern about the "growing dominance of the Russian language" while at the same time "the lack of effective support for the languages of national minorities."

As part of Russia's "divide and impera" pattern, in Bashkortostan, nominal volunteer battalions were formed in the summer by the authorities, demonstrating, in their view, the active complicity of the region in the war between Russia and Ukraine. "Volunteers" were promised large "combat" payments, equipped and escorted to the front. The real losses among the personnel were hidden or underestimated, and cases of refusal of volunteers to participate in battles were hushed up. The combat capability of the battalions were and continue to be very low. The head of the Bashkir National Political Center, Ruslan Gabbasov, and his associates addressed an open letter to Vladimir Zelensky, in which the Center called on the President of Ukraine to initiate consideration by the Verkhovna Rada of Ukraine of the draft resolution "On recognition of the Republic of Bashkortostan as an occupied territory."

"With this step, Ukraine will not only morally support the Bashkir national movement, whose main goal is to gain independence for our Motherland, but will also give us strong trump cards in the fight against the Kremlin and its puppets in Bashkortostan," Gabbasov explains. "It is important that Ukraine begins to establish contacts with the national liberation movements, which already today demonstrate their desire for liberation and the creation of independent states," the letter concludes.

It seems to be a morally correct and strategically prudent proposal. The dismantling of the Russian Federation is a political necessity for global peace and security.

December 15, 2022

THE SAKHA (YAKUT) PEOPLE

The Republic of Sakha (Yakutia) is located in the Russian Far East, along the Arctic Ocean, with a population of roughly 1 million. Yakutsk is its capital and largest city. The republic has a reputation for an extreme and severe climate, with the lowest temperatures being recorded. Regular winter averages commonly dipped below −35°C (−31°F) in Yakutsk. The hypercontinental tendencies also result in warm summers for much of the republic.

The Sakha, or Yakut, people are the descendants of Turkic nomads and originated in the region around Lake Baikal. But in the thirteenth and fourteenth centuries Mongols arrived from the south, along with other peoples, and the Sakha moved north and east, settling eventually in the basin of the river Lena, later called Yakutia. Yakutsk was founded in 1632. In 1638, the Yakutsk province was established.

Moscow colonized and incorporated the area into the Czardom in the early-mid 17th century, obliging the indigenous peoples of the area to pay fur tribute. The initial period following the Russian conquest saw the Sakha population drop by 70% as the Russian population there increased.

Yakutia saw some of the last battles of the Russian Civil War, and the Bolshevik authorities reorganized Yakutsk province into an autonomous republic, the Yakut Autonomous Soviet Socialist Republic, in 1922. The Soviet era also saw the migration of many Slavs, specifically Ukrainians, into the area.

With the demise of the USSR, the Russian Federation was established and, within it, the Republic of Sakha Yakuta. The 1990s were economically brutal for much of the RF but politically empowering for RSY. Glasnost'-era ethnic-consciousness movements retained their momentum and led to a Sakha cultural revitalization. The RSY enjoyed greater financial autonomy over the profits of its natural resources, thanks to an agreement signed between RSY's leaders and Boris Yeltsin. Although Russians still continued to overall outnumber them, the Sakha regained some of their demographic strength as tens of thousands of ethnic Russians returned to Russia proper. This trend began to reverse when Vladimir Putin took office. Under his regime, Moscow has re-centralized power over its peripheral areas. The state has commandeered controlling interest in RSY's diamond industry by becoming the majority shareholder of its monopoly company. In 2016, the RF initiated a homesteading act to repopulate Russia's peripheral areas by granting free land to citizens willing to resettle there. A Sakha representative living in the United States observed recently:

> "My people got acquainted with the Russian world 400 years ago, the "pioneers" in search of the ends of the earth came to our lands with fire and sword. They killed men, raped women and children. My ancestors resisted, but the technological advantage allowed the Russians to quickly conquer all of Yakutia. These were dark pages in the history of my people, full of pain and suffering, and only the vast size of my land and the dispersed living of my people made it possible to survive in such difficult conditions. Years passed, the country changed, the kings, emperors and secretaries changed, the attitude built on the principle: metropolis-colony did not change. Moscow continues to pump out resources: gas, oil, gold, diamonds, etc. In response, we get polluted rivers, toxic waste and industrial waste. I, being a full-fledged citizen of the country, am a second-class person, I have fewer rights in my country than whites, chauvinism and nationalism are the state policy of the country. We were silent for a long time because we are afraid, we are shut up, we are kidnapped, we are killed and this is happening today. Even I, being safe here, by saying these very words

endanger my relatives who now live there. But I have no right to remain silent, I want the whole world to recognize the Sakha people: modest, hardworking, kind, talented and eco-friendly people."

On September 21, 2022, by decree, the President of the Russian Federation, V.V. Putin, announced an additional mobilization of the military in the RF. There was an official statement in the media from the Ministry of Defense that 300,000 reservists would be called up. While the official Russian authorities concealed the real statistics, an analysis of the first days of mobilization from September 22 to September 25, 2022, conducted by anti-war activists in the RSY, the Republic of Buryatia, the Republic of Tyva, and the Republic of Kalmykia, as well as independent Russian media showed ethnic selectivity and a blatantly disproportionate number mobilized from ethnic regions compared to the central regions and cities of the RF. Thus, from the small settlements of the Far North, almost the entire able-bodied young male population has been mobilized.

This recent disproportionate mobilization has further annoyed the Sakha people. Sakha representatives joined the U.S. based Americans against Russian Imperialism. One stated that the national minorities within the RF are being used as cannon fodder in an unjust war.

January 11, 2023

PUTIN IS NEITHER MENTALLY NOR PHYSICALLY ILL

He is pure evil. He is a killer. That is all. Contorted or gratuitous explanations are not necessary to explain his behavior. Many in the West have twisted themselves into knots attempting to explain Putin or perhaps offer hope that somehow the war will end with Putin's demise.

The latest distortion was in connection with Putin's New Year's address. Some even reported that Putin must be physically ill since he was coughing throughout. Resorting to Russian-style disinformation is not necessary. Putin simply cleared his throat several times. The total video, lasting some ten minutes, was clear evidence of misinformation or attempted sensationalism, only to be contradicted by the video itself. Putin was in complete control. He obviously helped stage it. Some of his main actors were participants.

Putin's speech was a montage of lies. But his mendacity was clear-sighted and intentional. He went out of his way to appear on screen not as a severe dictator but as a conciliator towards not only the Russian people but all the peoples of Russia. This indicated that he was cognizant of his own political vulnerability within Russia, not only among the Russians but the captive nationalities within. This continued reference to the people of Russia rather than the Russian people was striking and most intentional. Putin is not delusional. He is aware of internal turmoil within an empire which he maintains by force and repression.

Depicting Putin as either mentally or physically ill is not conducive to Putin's demise or bringing about peace. Russia and Russians are built upon and fed by lies. Perhaps the best example of that is the alleged Russian Orthodox church. Some Western experts have represented the idea that a messianic vision of Russian Orthodox somehow serves as an impetus for Russian behavior. Religion often serves as an opiate, often for both good and bad. But

Russian Orthodoxy today is neither a church nor a religion. Analyzing Russian Orthodoxy through the centuries may require a separate analysis, but what is indisputable is that the Russian symbol, the two-headed eagle, was stolen from Constantinople Christianity, and even the Moscow Patriarchy was achieved at the point of a gun.

One publication recently even suggested that Putin takes his cue from the alleged Russian Orthodox Patriarch Kirill. Nothing can be further from the truth. Putin is the general. Kirill, at best, may be a colonel. The Russian Orthodox Church is a state institution; in fact, its latest version is a creation of Stalin from the 1940s. The West certainly lends too much-undeserved recognition and credit to that appendage of Russian special forces.

These distortions are not helpful in the struggle against Russia. I am not ascribing motives to those who distort. Let's call it naivete as we do when explaining the actions of Pope Francis, lest we offend him and the Catholic Church. Disinformation, particularly by respected sources, even without malice or intent to misinform, is very dangerous because it impacts public opinion. The struggle against Russian imperialism must be a global effort. While fringe reactions and behavior are to be expected, the fringe should be neutralized by rational consensus and global effort.

There are weaknesses within Russia, but a debilitated Putin is not one of them, especially when one recognizes that Moscow has been producing Putins for centuries. The greatest weaknesses within Russia are that it is a prison of some 100 captive nations, that its economy is not productive, and that as a result of the lack of financial wherewithal, its military might is grossly exaggerated. Whatever it might possess was stolen, including its nuclear capability. Winning the war requires dismantling the Russian empire, not victimizing its principal criminal or inducing complacency, suggesting that the main evil is almost at an end. Vladimir Putin remains the main perpetrator, but the accomplices are the Russian people, Russian culture, and history.

January 3, 2022

WHAT DOES "END OF THE WAR IN UKRAINE" MEAN?

There is a joke going around Ukraine that the Russian-speaking population went to bed on Wednesday, February 23, 2022, saying "good night" in Russian, and on Thursday, the 24th, they woke up saying "good morning" in Ukrainian.

By noon on the 24th, I was taking part in a protest march around the city of New York, traversing the Russian Mission to the United Nations, the UN itself, and then the Russian Consulate shouting, "Stop the war, save Ukraine, save the world!"

Today, I say only "To victory!" like all the people in Ukraine, especially its soldiers. How times have changed! Russia thought this was an exercise to last a week.

The end of the war on the basis of an agreement as proposed once by the West and more recently by Moscow is not a solution to the problem of Russian imperialism and the need to protect the people and territory of Ukraine. Today, we end the war; tomorrow will be the beginning of a new one. If someone thinks that this is not so, let him read the history of Russia.

The first anniversary of this merciless and completely unjustified war— a war that is marked by military aggression, as well as horrific war crimes, crimes against humanity, and a clear intent of genocide, is approaching. These crimes are being investigated by the International Criminal Court, although you would have to be blind not to be able to reach that conclusion yourself based on currently available evidence. At this time, twenty percent of the territory of Ukraine is under occupation. The country has suffered significant human casualties, and its territory and infrastructure have been severely damaged.

Meanwhile, the armed forces of Ukraine have not only repelled the strongest attacks of the enemy but also, in some instances, launched successful counterattacks. The West has not just promised but delivered high-quality weapons to Ukraine, albeit mainly defensive ones, and given assurances and then delivered more sophisticated ones.

We need total victory. Russia's unconditional surrender, that is, the release of the entire territory from the occupier and a return to the borders of 2013, is imperative. But that is not enough. The end of the war by returning to the state of 2013 means that Russia could mount a similar war after only a few months, having had sufficient time to regroup. Moscow's signature on a document is not worth the paper on which it is written. Putin and Kirill's "Orthodox Christian" appeal for a Christmas ceasefire proved this most recently.

Unconditional surrender is, without the slightest doubt, merely the first step. The second step is the reconstruction, through funding by the RF, of destroyed Ukrainian territory and infrastructure. The third is the expulsion of the RF from the United Nations and, of course, its Security Council. The RF is not a member of the UN; the USSR was. These are two very different entities, as one was dissolved before the other was formed. The fourth is the dismemberment of the RF into the constituent nations located therein, according to the free will of these peoples. Call it referenda. The fifth is the full demilitarization of Russia of both its nuclear and conventional weapons and the removal of the nuclear arsenal, under the supervision of the UN, to Europe's nuclear states, the United Kingdom and France.

The sequence of these steps can be changed, but not the first one, a step that is a sine qua non and can be realized either by Ukraine's complete victory on the battlefield or the voluntary withdrawal of all Russian armed forces to the territory of the RF. The longer this takes, the more compensation will be due from Russia.

These assumptions are not delusionary but a common-sense conclusion based on today's realities. The RF is a pariah state, considered an outcast in the international community. It is under heavy sanctions, and it is losing on the battlefield. Even China, which has different trade interests, has no desire to subscribe to Russian aggression. Only North Korea, Iran, and Assad's Syria remain allies, and they themselves are pariah states. Former Soviet states are irrelevant because many operate in fear.

These points, with the exception of the dismemberment and demilitarization of the Russian Federation, are congruent with the points laid out by President Volodymyr Zelensky of Ukraine. Whatever is missing from President Zelensky's peace plan is simply not within his purview. Yet he believes in a common-sense world community and understands the opportunity for those who are currently enslaved by the RF to gain their freedom and for the international community to rid itself of the anachronism of empire in the 21st century whereby one nation enslaves and oppresses another before the eyes of the whole world.

It is time to stop Russia's comical and harmful discourse on ending the war because it only benefits the Kremlin. It is time for serious proposals to foster victory for Ukraine by strengthening its defensive combat capabilities, providing help to rebuild the country, establishing an environment of freedom from fear of its neighbor, and accommodating the captive nations of the RF. These nations have to rise up by themselves and express their will—but with our help. All peoples have the right to self-determination, and every individual on the planet is entitled to all human rights. This is what the end of the war has to mean. Anything less is unacceptable.

January 9, 2023

EPIPHANY

I am back in Lviv four days before the observance of the Baptism of Jesus according to the Old Julian Calendar and nine days after the Latin Rite observance of the Epiphany. Ballistic missiles had been launched by the Russians yesterday throughout Ukraine. Particularly hard hit was the Southeastern city of Dnipro, where a residential structure was targeted with significant civilian casualties. Kyiv, our point of departure, was also hit, but the train left only one-half hour behind schedule. Life goes on.

In fact, there is much cause for optimism despite the recent bombings throughout Ukraine, including the Western cities of Lviv and Ivano Frankivsk. Children were singing Ukrainian songs in the Kyiv Metrograd yesterday. Western tanks and Patriot anti-missile systems are on the horizon.

Ukrainians, indeed, are an indomitable people. Sure, they complain as much as anyone, but they invariably manage to grasp the positive. One of their favorite phrases is that heroes never die despite the fact that Ukraine's heroes are dying every day. My wife spoke with a friend in Kyiv who told her that her brother had just been killed at the front. They decided not to tell her mother but they did tell her father. The heartbroken father died the following day. The mother remains alive, hoping to see her child again.

This whole year has been an Epiphany for many. The previous day, I met with first-year students at the Kyiv National University. We devised a strategy for victory and the dismemberment of the world's last empire. They were very excited to contribute. We spoke about America as well. They were grateful but circumspect. They felt that America owed them something because it was at America's insistence that Ukraine surrendered the world's third-largest nuclear arsenal. I assured them that America and Americans were with them. We also spoke about their own future. They were proud to be part of the Ukrainian nation, not only because of its manifest courage but also because it so strongly believes in genuine freedom and democracy.

Ukrainians believe that they are saving the world, and they have accepted this mission. They are grateful for the support they receive from the very people they believe they are saving and whose battles, as well as their own, they fight. Still, some would-be allies are puzzling. Perhaps not so much Hungary with its fascist leader, but still a member of both NATO and the EU and with a diaspora of both nations respectively located. Still, certainly, Belgium seems an aberration, selling out for diamonds despite being the seat of both the EU and NATO and benefiting therefrom financially as well as politically. Germany and France have been less than fully supportive, still perhaps more than in the past. Israel has been a quandary since Iran. Israel's worst nightmare is a staunch ally of the Russian aggressor. Unfortunately, Israel is notorious for its self-interest, but here it appears to be blind as well.

The Ukrainian European diaspora has been less than vocal. A recent conference of European Ukrainians held in Serbia, of all places, failed to address the less than meaningful support for Ukraine by some European countries. Serbia, of course, is a known quality, often referred to as the Russia of the Balkans and notorious for war crimes. Still, the Ukrainian European diaspora has seemed not only powerless but downright inactive. The Ukrainian World Congress ostensibly maintains a Mission in Brussels with little efficacy.

On Sunday I went to St. Andrew's Ukrainian Catholic Church in Lviv and prayed four times for the Pope as is prescribed by the Ukrainian liturgy, asking for God's mercy. In the past, I had been dismayed by these incantations because of the Pope's lack of tangible concern for the people of Ukraine, but I have had an Epiphany regarding the Pope. Perhaps Pope Francis will have one too.

As the liturgical Christmas season draws to an end, as well as my time with my Ukrainian brethren in Ukraine, I am optimistic but concerned. The New Year offers much hope and many challenges. The feast of the Epiphany, the coming of the Magi, and the Baptism of Christ provide much focus. 2023 could be the year of a lasting global Epiphany free of war crimes, aggression, tyrants, and empires.

January 16, 2023

RUSSIAN THEATRE

Russia's Aggression in Ukraine will bring about new theatre in the Russian Empire.

Two events of recent production, United States President Biden's unannounced visit to Ukraine and Vladimir Putin's Russian version of the "State of the Union" address, evoked different comparisons, yet strangely with similar apparent conclusions. A long-time friend of mine from Russia (He is not Russian. There are more than 100 different nationalities in the Russian empire.) commented on the two productions:

"And where do they give sausages?"

Foreign Minister Sergei Lavrov called US President Joe Biden's visit to Kyiv theatre.

".. there is a performance. So it continues. Everything works in this way, from the point of view of our former Western colleagues and from the point of view of saving the Nazi regime."

Let's try to contribute our 5 kopecks.

We can agree to a certain extent about the performance with Lavrov.

As one of the world's most famous playwrights, William Shakespeare, said, 'All the world's a stage.' Long before Shakespeare and after him, analogies were drawn between the world and the stage, people and actors. Everything is understood by comparison.

Biden's visit was theatre, with a good direction and a wonderful performance by the actors.

In contrast to the performance on February 21 in Moscow, where the absurdity was visible to the naked eye.

Joe Biden, who hardly ever flaunts his muscles to the public, did not fly with cranes, did not find ancient shards at the bottom of the sea; he came to a warring country and assured to the sound of sirens: 'I am with you.'

An anti-aircraft complex was installed near Luzhniki in Moscow. However, it did not reach the sirens. And then there is the impression that there is no war, and if there is, it has somehow turned into a patriotic accompaniment to the narratives of the 'Russian world.' In Luzhniki, there was an atmosphere of free porridge and sausages: "Where do they give sausages?" That's what everyone asked.

"Anti-aircraft fire and the actors' rhetoric reminded us of the war."

All is not well in Russia. Each day, centrifugal forces are at play. Nations captive in Russia with governments in exile are joining forces, some even proclaiming independence. Letters were sent last week to United States Senators by a new structure calling itself Americans against Russian Imperialism. The thrust of the letters was as follows:

> "We are Americans representing ten nations that are either colonies within the current Russian empire, the Russian Federation, or nations with independent states that border on the RF and continue to suffer from Russian aggression. We are ethnically Armenians, Bashkirs, Buryats, Cossacks, Erzya, Kalmyks, Kazakhs Sakha, Tatars and Ukrainians. We reside from New York to Hawaii.

> The recent Russian aggression in Ukraine has opened the eyes of the world to the danger that Russian imperialism represents to the entire democratic global community. We have formed an alliance to strive for the legitimate independence of all nations affected today by Russian imperialism. We seek long-standing peace and security, which can be achieved only through the disintegration of the Russian empire and the formation of independent states as desired by the nations within the RF today.

> In order for peace to prevail, the world must recognize

that Russia is an empire and that the people and nations within and on its borders have a right to be free. Our goal is in the interests of the whole world, as peace and security can only be achieved by allowing for the self-determination of all peoples and preventing aggression by its neighbors. A simple end to Russia's hostilities against its neighbor Ukraine is inadequate, as Russia has proven over centuries that it will cease aggression, only to fortify and begin anew."

The disintegration of the Russian empire would be much more than theatre for Minister Lavrov and his boss. Yet that eventuality is very much within the realm of possibility. Russia's next annual "State of the Union" will be much different most assuredly. Yes, it may highlight even an entirely different cast of actors and a new message. Even the sausages may taste different, or there may not be any sausages.

February 28, 2023

THE MISSION OF AMERICANS AGAINST RUSSIAN IMPERIALISM

Russia's full-scale aggression against Ukraine has resulted in several perhaps unforeseen results which have become significant phenomena that should lead to the demise of the world's largest empire.

Firstly, Ukrainian resistance has been magnificent and overwhelming, so Russia today controls little more of Ukrainian territory than it did on the eve of the full-scale invasion on February 24, 2022. In fact, Ukraine has produced counteroffensive measures that have addressed territory taken by Russia at the time of its initial aggression in 2014.

Secondly, Russian military losses have been extreme, so it has become apparent to the world not only that Ukraine possesses, with the support of its allies, military capability second to no country in Europe and that even aside from the morale factor, Russian military might is very much outdated and exaggerated.

A third phenomenon has been the situation within the Russian Federation, certainly, more appropriately labeled the Russian Empire. The RF is not a monolith, certainly not homogeneous, and is a product of the repression and oppression of non-Russian peoples who have lived on their land and had their own states for centuries. Indeed, the territory of the RF is a result of conquest and actually belongs to many nations.

> *"In order to realize the right of self-determination by our peoples and territories of the Russian Federation, we created the Free Nations' League - a horizontal network structure that brings together organizations, movements, and individual activists who share our goals and views.*
>
> *We set ourselves the following tasks:*

Consolidation of anti-imperial forces; training of personnel for state building; search for allies in the international arena; the acquisition of real sovereignty by the subjects of the Russian Federation; realisation of the right to self-determination."

This is the Mission Statement of the Free Nations League. What nations comprise the Free Nations League? Bashkirs, Buryats, Erzya, Ingrians, Kalmyks and Tatars.

The League also includes activists of the Ingush and Yakut national movements, as well as the smaller peoples of the North as observers.

A similar network named Americans Against Russian Imperialism has been formed in the United States of Americans belonging to the following ethnic groups: Armenians, Baskirs, Belarusians, Buryats, Cossacks, Erzya, Kalmyks, Kazakhs Yakuts, Tatars, and Ukrainians residing from New York to Hawaii. The mission of this group is very similar:

"We are Americans, representatives of nations long-suffering under Russian oppression. Some have managed to form their own independent states following the demise of the Soviet Union but continue to be unduly pressured by the so-called Russian Federation, which, in essence, is a ruthless Russian empire. Others continue to languish within the empire itself. Our purpose in forging this structure is to familiarise our fellow Americans with the plight of our ancestral nation and seek joint cooperation and assistance in bettering the current conditions aimed ultimately at establishing independent and democratic states free to navigate their own course, history, and culture. We sincerely pray that our fellow Americans will be sympathetic to our cause and helpful in accomplishing our purpose."

March 19, 2023

EASTER IS A SPECIAL HOLIDAY FOR UKRAINIANS

Resurrection and salvation are special phenomena for Christians of any denomination. All the more, they are significant for Ukrainian Christians. Christianity is not just a religion. Such an understanding is very narrow and, frankly, primitive. Christianity is a way of life. It is the victory of good over evil. This is the essence of morality. Jesus Christ taught us, in the two commandments that he left us, to love God and our neighbor as ourselves. That is the essence of Christianity. All other prescriptions or commandments, including the "law of Moses" or "Church dogma," are secondary. They may be conducive, but they are relevant for us today only as they evolve from the subsequent or prior commandments of Jesus Christ.

Today's war in Ukraine is a struggle for the life of our people. It is also an extreme competition for the victory of good over evil. It is like Jesus' Way of the Cross for our people, which must end with the Resurrection. Jesus came to earth to save the world from original sin and to introduce spiritual morality and goodness into the world. In the process of his messianic work among the people, he encountered various manifestations of evil, diabolical actions such as killings and the not-so-laughable Pharisees, which would seem to be not so harmful or heinous, but, in fact, no less damning and widespread as the grievous sinners. Jesus did not overcome these phenomena in the long term because man is free to make mistakes, but he did manifest that one must believe in good, in God, and in the constant struggle against evil. He emphasized that indifference and, more so, impudence are also sins.

We see today how these manifestations of evil pervade the whole world. Moscow, and not only its government but also the people, is the personification of evil through a culture of imperialism. Ukraine's bard Taras Shevchenko described the Muscovites

(Russians) as "evil people." Yet this does not mean that a Muscovite child is evil at birth. However, as a result of Moscow's imperial culture, in many cases it grows into an evil Muscovite. This is how he is brought up by his evil Muscovite mother, who grew up in the bosom of the empire and is willing today to give birth to sons so that they fight for the empire.

Supplementing this evil is considered a lesser evil but still, an evil - a kind of arrogance or indifference to blatant evil, considering oneself defiantly special or exceptional.

We Ukrainians are called by Jesus today to fight against these manifestations of marginal evil as well, diplomatically and through the example of our heroism. We continue to fight against the main egregious evil of Russian imperialism, but we also struggle against modern manifestations of indifference and a sense of exceptionalism, which is noisily preached in particular in America. There is an almost bizarre example of this, today's assumption that is for the month of April, by Russia, the world's worst aggressor of the chair of the UN Security Council. Argumentation would be unnecessary. There is no need to talk about global morality or irony here. There has never been a better case made for the need for UN reform.

The resurrection and victory of Jesus over death, as well as good over evil, manifested itself in the last year in the world: Ukraine passed the test of its defense, and military capability proved itself more than capable despite global predictions. Seeing this, the freedom-loving democratic states of the whole world came to the defense of Ukraine not only in word but also in deed by delivering not only humanitarian aid but also lethal weapons. Some came because they felt they could be next. But most came because it was the right thing to do. Recently, the International Criminal Court issued an arrest warrant for Vladimir Putin for war crimes. This has caused concern even in countries forcibly indoctrinated to be friendly to Putin.

At this time, the triumph of the Resurrection of Jesus Christ manifests itself not only in a historical or spiritual context but in today's not only political but also humanitarian and politically strategic order. Ukraine and its people are victims of this Cross, but it and its people are primarily the executors of the Resurrection and the victory of good over evil. Apparently, in this case, the Lord chose us and gave us a daunting task. We are fulfilling this assignment.

Therefore, let us carry out our beautiful Easter traditions, paint our eggs, and bless our baskets with deep faith and hope. I'm not a preacher. I am just a Ukrainian Christian who believes that the Lord chose us to be His instrument in the victory of good over evil.

Christ Has Risen!

Indeed, He Has!

April 8, 2023

TWO VERY DIFFERENT SOULS

The Russian culture of empire, taking what is not yours, versus the Ukrainian culture of simply defending its own.

This is a personal perspective by a Ukrainian-American born in the United States of immigrant Ukrainian parents, educated in the American system and grounded in American culture of splendid democratic values, an appetite for capitalist gains, aka the American dream, and an erroneous belief in American exceptionalism. To address the last, neither America nor Americans are exceptional. The founding fathers were not. There were both good and bad.

America is responsible for much good. It is equally responsible for much bad. Today's culture of coming to terms with evil is the appropriate approach. Blindness in this regard can only result in more evil. Nevertheless this is not about American culture or its soul but about two neighboring nations which are today very much on the American mind as well as that of the global community.

The aforesaid comment on America is intended to raise consciousness in every society that introspection of one's culture and soul is a necessary albeit complex process for all peoples. Ukrainian and Russian cultures, despite geographical proximity and a mutual albeit unfortunate history, are striking examples of how two cultures and, resultingly, two souls can be very different.

Russian Czar Peter I was dissatisfied with the history of the Moscow state, so he changed the name of Moscow to Russia since Kyiv had been known as the capital of Rus'. Later, Czarina Catherine II decided that changing a name was inadequate. She commissioned Russian historians to compile or compose historiography. One of them, Russian writer and historian Nikolai Karamzin, wrote critically about Russian historiography, stressing that it is based on lies. Precisely, this is the basis for the Russian soul.

It has been said that a Russian mother who feels intensely for her Russian son, the soldier, feels more intensely for the Russian empire. The son is brought up to be willing to die for that empire, right or wrong. That culture, as well as severe penalties for public assembly in Russia against the war, are the reasons why Russian mothers today, who have suffered tremendous losses, fail to manifest their sorrow through civil disobedience.

Russian historiography, which feeds the Russian culture, is predicated on the idea of Russia as a great power, an empire, and a third Rome. That mandates much theft in terms of history and aggression in politics. Let's consider only two examples according to the Russians: Kyiv is the mother of Russian cities, and the symbol of Russia is the two-headed eagle since Russia is the third Rome. Presenting a false narrative of history requires victories on the field of battle as the victors become the next historians. For that reason, victory on the battlefield, irrespective of human cost, is mandated for the empire to persevere.

The real facts are very different. Kyiv was founded in the V century. Moscow as an entity was founded in the XII by a Kyivan who was deprived of the Kyiv throne essentially by the rules of a primogenitor. Russia's representation of itself as the bulwark of Christian Orthodoxy is also entirely false. The Holy Roman Empire in Constantinople fell to the Ottomans. In this vacuum, Moscow assumed the mantle and, at gunpoint, forced the Patriarchy in Constantinople to recognize a Moscow Patriarchate.

Ukraine and its soul are essentially different. Ukrainian history is some half a millennium older. More importantly, excepting the Middle Ages when might be considered right and conquerors were glorified, Ukraine has a tragic history, and even at times of glory, Ukraine has always manifested a satisfaction with its own and a reluctance to conquer that which belongs to others. Examples abound but a most striking one is that of the Cossack uprising against Poland in 1648. The Cossacks, under the leader Hetman

Bohdan Khmelnytsky, arrived at the gates of Warsaw but then withdrew, deciding that they were free men, protectors of their own and not conquerors of others.

Both Ukrainians and Russians are born children of God if you are a believer and simply children of their parents by science. What distinguishes them is the culture wherein they are raised. Russians are reared to believe in an undying empire. Ukrainians are brought up to protect their own. These are two very different cultural underpinnings.

I began this piece with a brief overview of American exceptionalism. Russians believe in their own exceptionalism. The difference is that in America, reason prevails, or at least the ability to express one's views and to assemble publicly in order to share that view. In Russia the rule is to remain silent with the hope of triumph so that the empire may go forth and prosper. The choice for the global community is very clear. Ultimately, perhaps good will never absolutely triumph over evil, but at least effort may lessen the suffering of those exposed to evil. Ukraine is commencing a counteroffensive. All hands on board.

May 6, 2023

POLITICS

Dealing with Rogue Allies and Making Friends

The word politics comes from the Greek word "polis," which refers to "city." Politics would refer to the affairs of the city in its widest scope. Inasmuch as the Greeks ruled city-states, the term applies, in fact, to countries or states. A person in today's structured society is an integral part of some city or state. Almost everything in one's life can be deemed political.

U.S. Speaker of the House of Representatives in the 1980's Tip O'Neill, coined the phrase, "All politics is local." Ukrainians have a similar sentiment that the shirt is closer than the coat. In any event, politics means anything and everything that affects a person, his family, his home, and his community. So, in sports, a fan is a political animal. An often misused statement that there should be no politics in sports is one of the more nonsensical yet ubiquitous statements. The Olympics are an obvious example. I root for the United States or Ukraine today. Irrespective, I always root against Russia or Russian athletes. In American sports, I root for the Mets, Jets, Knicks, and Rangers because I was born and raised in New York. Enough!

Why is this topic relevant today? Because Indian Prime Minister Modi was recently scheduled in Washington for a state visit in June. A state visit is a big deal. It is not accorded to everyone. If politics had a strong moral component, Modi would have been shunned or even assailed. Sure, he is popular in India. There are 1.3 billion people in India. There are many immigrants from India in the United States. That is one solid justification for a state visit - to make a billion people our allies. Still, Modi is an autocrat, chauvinist, and a killer. In the name of his version of God, he murders people, particularly those within India of the Islamic faith. India and China are the world's largest importers of Russian gas.

Several years ago, I traveled to Bulgaria to visit the Ukrainian community there. One of the highlights of my visit was a conversation I had with a nondescript. Bulgarian, an every-man. When he learned that I was from America, he offered a bit of philosophical humor. He stated that Bulgaria, having joined NATO, is now an ally of the United States. However, in the past, he pointed out, Bulgarians were aligned with the Roman Empire, the Ottoman Empire, the Reich of Nazi Germany, and lastly, the Soviet Empire. These empires no longer exist, he pointed out, so we Americans better be careful. We both laughed. In all fairness, Bulgaria finally stepped up to help Ukraine in the war as late as December 2022.

Bulgaria is not an aberration. The words "politics makes strange bedfellows" come to mind. Perhaps more disturbing is Hungary under Prime Minister Victor Orban. In modern history, Hungary has always been on the wrong side: in World War I with the central powers and in World War 2 with the Axis powers. Hungary is a member of NATO. Yet Victor Orban appears closer to Vladimir Putin than he is to the United States. More importantly, because of the rules of international organizational governance like NATO, Hungary, a negligible country by population, might, and general wherewithal, run by a madman, carries a decisive voice on Ukraine's future.

Several years back, I had an opportunity to travel with a Hungarian delegation from the city of Lviv to Ivano Frankivsk, where a monument had been erected to a preeminent Hungarian poet. The delegation included the Ambassador of Hungary to Ukraine, some lesser diplomats, but also the vice speaker of the Hungarian Parliament. These were all Orban's people. The vice speaker was particularly loquacious. They behaved as if they were doing Ukraine a favor by participating in the event. Naturally, that did not sit well with me, but that is another story. We did some wining and dining and there were some words exchanged. By the way, the vice speaker, like his boss, was a big Trump supporter. I often wonder where these people come from. God should have simply broken the mold. Hungary is not a total NATO rogue state as it has accepted almost 200,000 Ukrainian migrants.

The Polish parliament recently voted to support Ukraine's imminent NATO accession. Poland has been at the forefront throughout the war and has been a paragon NATO member in supporting Ukraine, and this despite a troubled Ukraine Poland history. Questions may be posed such as what are two Western, in essence, belligerents such as Bulgaria and Hungary doing in NATO. They certainly have not helped much in the war effort.

On second thought, ultimately, it is better that they are within the civilized European community and exposed to Western values and culture, most importantly, a democratic form of government, respect for human rights, and the like. Orban has been prime minister far too long. The same applies to Prime Minister Modi. It seems that there are significant issues of xenophobia and chauvinism. Working with these questionable persons and/or countries may bring them closer to us. But there must be some accountability. Politics, while not affording principles or moral integrity, does fashion a quid pro quo.

May 10, 2023

THE ONLY SOLUTION

The End of Empires

Many proposals have been made regarding ending Russian aggression in Ukraine. Many have offered off-ramps, surrendering to Russia's and Putin's supposed need "to save face," thereby forging a frozen conflict. Ukraine has insisted that the only end of war reality is a return to the January 2014 borders. Neither proposal is a solution in the long term.

As long as Russia remains an empire, global security, and Ukrainian sovereignty remain at issue. Accepting the Ukrainian proposal means simply that the next Russian aggression is temporarily postponed. People cannot live in constant fear.

Since the second phase of the war on February 24, 2022, at least three movements have evolved. The first was the Free Nations League, a coordinating body in Europe comprised of nations currently held captive within the Russian empire known as the Russian Federation. The second was an American association of nations within the Russian empire as well as several outside of it but within the sphere of continuous Russian pressure. And now these nations have agreed to join efforts with nations held captive or repressed by another evil empire, the Chinese People's Republic.

"The end of evil empires" is the mantra of this joint effort. Looking back to a time during the Cold War when the United States, in its wisdom with significant prodding by East European nations, passed legislation designating the third week of each July as a time to remember those nations that were a part of the Soviet Union or its satellites known as "Captive Nations." Ultimately, but not fully, this action prevailed.

In July 2023, there will be a march in Washington from the Capitol to the White House displaying the flags of some twenty nations currently suffering under Russian and Chinese oppression.

The significance of this event lies predominantly in its creation. These are very different nations, entirely different cultures with little in common except for the desire to be free.

Why should the United States pay any attention to this movement? The first reason is an obvious moral one. In this regard, America has a role to play in view of its own history.

However, even a cynic can find justification to support this cause.

Since World War II, a conscious effort has been made by the global democratic community to ensure global security. As the League of Nations faltered, the United Nations has ensued and persevered, albeit not successfully, on all fronts. Its purpose was multi-fold but its foremost goal was directed at global security. A monster, however, was forged: the UN Security Council. People throughout the world disparage the work of the UN and scoff at the waste of the UNSC. This is a lesson learned.

However, the ridicule is misplaced or misapplied. I recently spoke with a representative of the Uyghur people who are being mercilessly and intentionally slaughtered by the Chinese in East Turkestan, known in China as Xinjiang province. He laughed at the lack of efficacy by the UN. Rather, he suggested, the repressed nations should seek a dialogue with the United States, Congress and the White House.

He is right and wrong. Freedom and global security need a champion, but the United States cannot do it alone. God knows we have our own problems. However, the United States must continue to lead the global community. It is easy to disparage international structures because, so far in history, they have proven to be feckless. However, international organizations and associations are the future. The Internet, the global economy, global environmental issues, and poverty have proven that.

I refrain from domestic criticism because that merely evolves into bickering. I certainly wish that Ukrainians in America, Democrats or Republicans, would wake up on a single issue. That issue is Ukraine, and that issue ultimately mandates the end of the Russian empire. Let us widen our horizons and work towards the end of all evil empires. I certainly feel for the Uyghurs in China and pray that they feel for the plight of Ukrainians suffering from Russian aggression. I try to stay away from John Lennon, but in this instance, the phrase "The world will be one" resonates. But, John, there must be nations and religions because people need both. Imagine if there were no empires. The world will be free and secure, and only then will it be one.

May 15, 2023

BEWARE OF RUSSIANS

No More Appeasement

The recent "almost civil war" and "imminent coup d'etat" in the Russian Federation has caused some turmoil and, at its conclusion, recognition that it was "much ado about nothing." Putin and his former chef Yevgeny Prigozhin, notwithstanding, Russians remain in control. The only positive result may be that the brutal Wagner forces may be out of the war in Ukraine, only to be replaced by equally brutal but less capable Russians. Those most hopeful, or at least with the most vivid imagination, perhaps forget that Putin and Prigozhin are peas in a pod or equally war criminals, with the only difference being that one has been issued a warrant for arrest by the International Criminal Court.

A Ukrainian from the RF, Marika Semenenko, recently pointed out in "The Moscow Times" that opposition leader Navalny's closest adviser, Leonid Volkov, described activists who demand Russia's decolonization as "freaks." Navalny's supporters continue to repeat that the war in Ukraine is "Putin's war" and that the Russian people are its victims. The chairwoman of Navalny's Anti-Corruption Foundation, Maria Pevchikh, has described the regime's authoritarianism as domestic abuse. In any event, one thing is abundantly clear: Russian liberals who oppose Putin continue to support Russian hegemony over ethnic non-Russians from the national republics. Many extend that hegemony to include Ukraine and Belarus.

It is important to note that the so-called Russian liberals have not issued any statements of condemnation, oral or written, about the atrocities and war crimes perpetrated by the Russians in Ukraine, whether they be of the Wagner or Russian standard defense variety. Recently, "The New York Times" reported about a newly liberated village in Ukraine's Donbas, which revealed graffiti that can be attributed only to Russian soldiers, rank and file, expressing not only vitriolic hatred towards Ukrainian civilians but total disregard for their mutilation and in fact, satisfaction.

Political pundits, experts, and fortunetellers are equally accurate. No one can tell how the Russian invasion of Ukraine will end. The West continues to foster diplomatic talks and continues to arm Ukraine in order allegedly to enhance Ukraine's bargaining position. There is nothing wrong with that position.

There is a long history of the civilized world dealing with Russia almost as if Russia was a normal partner or adversary. Marika Semenenko makes a very salient point in comparing Russia to other empires. Her distinction refers to empires of the second and now the third millennia but does not include China as a similar empire. The Russian Empire is not separated by oceans. It is essentially contiguous. There is a long sharing of history. While the British and other empires were cruel, they never sought complete assimilation and always recognized their colonies as such. Russia purports to incorporate its empire under one umbrella, at least in the case of Belarus and Ukraine.

The history of Ukraine clearly predates that of Russia and thus becomes a sine qua not for Russia's right to Ukrainian lands and history. What kind of a respectable empire would Russia be if its origin began only in the XII century and, even then, was founded by a Kyivan exile prince only to serve for three centuries as a vassal state to Turks and Tatars?

The West has a very difficult time understanding Russian culture and psyche. Putin, Prigozhin, and Navalny are all Russian imperialists. Putin and Prigozhin are killers and war criminals as well. Navalny has simply not had a chance.

Suggesting and urging an end to the war in Ukraine with a diplomacy option is essentially negotiating with war criminals. If Putin would come to the negotiating table, would the warrant for his arrest as a war criminal be withdrawn and then expunged by the International Criminal Court? And what could happen within twenty-four hours following the ceasefire?

Ukrainians certainly do not want to find out. They do not want to put Putin out of his misery. They need to put Russia out of everyone's misery.

For that to happen, the national minorities in Russia have to be heard. Ukrainians would breathe a sigh of relief if Armenia, Belarus, Kazakhstan, and other so-called independent "stans" were free of Russian pressure and the Bashkirs, Buryats, Chechens, Circassians, Erzya, Kalmyks, Kazan Tatars, Sakha, and other nations heinously persecuted by Russia could raise their national flags and join the community of free nations via the United Nations. That would be a just and lasting settlement. Anything less would be yet another form of appeasement. We know how well appeasing Russia works.

June 28, 2023

THE VILNIUS NATO SUMMIT

It happened fifteen years ago in Bucharest. NATO's most significant and powerful member, the United States of America, was prepared to offer Ukraine and Georgia a NATO Membership Action Plan, only to be stymied in its efforts by two militarily insignificant and historically Russia-appeasing members, France and Germany. Instead, Ukraine and Georgia were accorded a meaningless NATO assurance that the two countries would one day become NATO members.

The dishonest broker in this was the Chancellor of Germany Angela Merkle, with ties to East Germany, and KGB agent Putin from Dresden, who proceeded to pursue this disingenuous role for more than the ensuing decade. Merkle served as German chancellor for 16 years. Her biography as a member of the Communist Free German Youth, her choice to study Russian so that she could move up in East German society, her meeting and wedding her first husband in the USSR, her reluctance to join the East German dissident movement, certainly merits some attention in explaining her longtime affinity for Russian global criminal Vladimir Putin and her obstruction of Ukraine's accession to NATO membership.

Russia was emboldened. One month later, Russia attacked Georgia and invaded its territory, which resulted in a frozen conflict in Abkhazia and Southern Ossetia, which remains to date. Russian President Medvedev, by decree, declared the two regions independent states. Simultaneously, Russia targeted its efforts on Ukraine through energy and other mechanisms, fomenting discord among Ukraine's political leaders, which resulted in a fraudulent election and a victory for Russia's surrogate, Victor Yanukovich. The West appeased once again with an endorsement of the Russian puppet by "The Financial Times" and a recognition that the election was free and fair by Western governmental election monitors.

Yanukovich proceeded to extend Russian control of the Crimean port of Sevastopil for an additional 25 years and depleted the Ukrainian military to less than 10 thousand able bodies. By the time the people of Ukraine were able to oust the Russian surrogate in February 2014, Ukraine was ripe for a Russian invasion. And so Russia took Crimea, annexed it by a Russia-style fake referendum, and then invaded the Ukrainian Donbas region.

Ukraine began to rebuild its military, but NATO insisted on simply reiterating its tired old refrain about Ukraine's future NATO membership. Russia was emboldened further, and so on February 24, 2022, Russia invaded Ukraine with full force, targeting not specific eastern regions but the capital, Kyiv itself.

Ukraine's President Volodymyr Zelensky has often opined that the ongoing war in Ukraine today is the fault of the West. In fact, it is the result of the dis-ingenuity and maybe more of leaders like Chancellor Merkle, the fecklessness of Presidents Obama and Macron, the political ignorance at best, and perhaps, the sedition of President Donald Trump and his MAGA and GOP cohort.

Another NATO Summit is on the horizon. There are two ways of ending the war in Ukraine. One way is through a total Ukrainian victory, which requires not only a return to January 2014 borders but the dissolution of the neighboring evil empire through decolonization to preclude imminent and future aggression. This option would take a lot of time and cost many lives. The second and more viable solution is for the Vilnius Summit to accept Ukraine as a NATO member expeditiously not unlike Finland.

Some have argued that Ukraine may not be accepted while the war is in progress. There is no such prohibition in the NATO Charter. Others have pointed to Hungarian strongman Viktor Orban who has announced his opposition to Ukraine's NATO accession. Orban should be reprimanded privately that while the NATO Charter does not include an expulsion provision, a case can be made for expulsion if a member fails to carry out their duties. There is no prohibition of expulsion. Orban has previously announced that Hungary will not arm Ukraine and, egregiously, that it will not permit the transit of lethal arms to Ukraine over its territory. Ukraine is by far and perhaps, excepting Turkey, the strongest potential NATO member in Europe. Hungary is one of NATO's meaningless accouterments. Even an unhinged Orban has to understand this reality.

Now is the time for NATO to stand up to Russian aggression meaningfully with determination, not appeasement. The result will be a further weakening of the Russian rat currently cowering in a very tight corner of the Kremlin.

July 5, 2023

A FORGETTABLE NATO SUMMIT

As an American and even more so as a Ukrainian American, I cringed watching at least two performances in Vilnius, one by the President of the United States and the other by the NATO Secretary General. The first was a sit-down press briefing by President Joe Biden and Turkish President Recep Erdogan. President Biden could not level more praise upon his counterpart. This sycophantic performance was reminiscent of President Biden's recent adulation of Indian Prime Minister Narendra Modi in Washington. Politics does indeed make strange bedfellows, but there should be a limit to duplicity. Prime Minister Modi in Washington did not become any less of a genocidal murderer. President Erdogan, by allowing Sweden into NATO, did not become any less an autocrat.

And then there was poor Secretary General Jens Stoltenberg. Frankly, he was carrying out a mission as instructed, in particular, by the United States. At a press conference he kept repeating the same line to all questions, reiterating ad nauseam the package that Ukraine was receiving. But all questions were not the same. A Ukrainian press representative asked Stoltenberg what conditions had to be met by Ukraine to receive a NATO invitation. Stoltenberg ignored that question entirely. At one point, an exasperated Secretary General replied that Ukraine's membership in NATO would not be an issue at all if Ukraine lost the war.

The Ukrainian package consisted of multiyear aid, the formation of a NATO-Ukraine council rather than a committee, and a one-step process elimination of the MAP requirement. The promise of multiyear aid is not enforceable and may be withdrawn at any time. Russia had a NATO council arrangement with no efficacy. There is no such structure in the NATO Charter except for NATO members forming a council. Finally, the two-step process has become anachronistic since both Finland and now Sweden did not have to encounter MAP. The NATO Charter is silent on MAP in any event and speaks strictly of invitation. So, in essence, Ukraine received nothing of substance.

Naturally, Ukraine's President was deeply disappointed and said so. He recognizes that global security continues to depend entirely on the lives of Ukrainians alone. Russia had been in a no-win situation. It certainly could not conquer all of Ukraine. At best, it could retain its 2014 ill-gotten gains of Ukrainian territory and not much more. Russian President Putin had become a global pariah and was under an arrest warrant from the International Criminal Court. The Vilnius Summit gave Russia and Putin a new life with the possibility of rehabilitation. A good day for Russia and a bad day for Ukraine makes the world less safe.

Where does Ukraine go from here? The war itself has proven that mostly Ukraine has been right and the U.S. has been wrong. Ukraine asks for weapons. America replies you do not need them. Time passes, Russian brutality increases, and America relents belatedly to Ukrainian requests. The most recent examples are the F16s and cluster munitions.

Patriotic Americans naively came away with a message for Russia that NATO is very much alive. Russia received an entirely different message – that appeasement continues to be America's policy and that no matter how brutal Russia is, America will forgive and look for a diplomatic off-ramp. This is an inveterate weakness of American foreign policy going back one hundred years.

There is no easy solution. America and President Biden have to learn the hard way. Unfortunately, the hard way is very costly in terms of life and infrastructure for Ukraine. NATO membership in Ukraine would have sent a loud and overwhelming message to Russia that there are only two options: withdraw entirely or face the dissolution of the Russian empire.

Perhaps in the long term, because of the protracted time, American and President Biden's fecklessness will serve to rid the world of the evil empire. A prolonged war will enable civil unrest and national uprisings within the Russian Federation, including a successful coup and maybe more than one. If instability is what President Biden sought to avoid, ironically, precisely that will ensue. There will be great costs. For America and its NATO allies, the costs will be enormous, particularly financial and, perhaps, political. For Ukraine, the cost will be dearer. Human lives cannot be monetized.

July 12, 2023

REFLECTIONS ON UKRAINIAN INDEPENDENCE

On August 24, Ukrainians throughout the world will celebrate thirty-two years of independence.

Independence anniversaries are celebrated annually in many countries with much fanfare but very often without spiritual content. This is not a criticism of these nations. Independence is routinely celebrated because people are self-confident about the future, and nothing threatens them. Their borders are safe, and although there are political opponents or even enemies, they are not threatening or dangerous, at least for the moment. In these countries, the celebration of the anniversary of independence is simply an occasion for a holiday with fireworks.

But not for Ukrainians. Ukrainians, perhaps like few others, view their independence as the basis of the nation's existence. If there is a danger to the independent state, the question of the existence of the nation also arises. This may be an emotional, but unfortunately, a very real feeling because the Ukrainian nation existed and persevered for centuries stateless. Ukrainians value state independence differently than other nations. The 32nd anniversary is the longest existence of our state since medieval times.

My late father, who passed away long before the declaration of Ukrainian state independence in 1991, wrote as follows in the early 1960's:

> *"The idealistic pillars, deeply rooted in the spirituality of the Ukrainian people from the earliest times, became the basis of an idealistic worldview with the central focus being the concept of nation, namely its independence and the free development of its strengths and values in a legal and political structure – known as a state Only a state can ensure freedom and equal*

justice for every person within the framework of the general good of the nation, which is an essential and inviolable law of all social existence. The state represents the (essential) good of the entire nation, encompassing all its generations, living, dead and unborn, bound by a common origin, language, history, culture, territory.... In a state of political enslavement, the prime postulate for the Ukrainian nation is the creation of an Independent Ukrainian State, and the duty of every person of Ukrainian blood, regardless of whether he has a second, chosen homeland or not, is to serve the Ukrainian nation, especially when it is engrossed in a struggle for its existence and freedom against a most heinous and barbaric enemy."

An independent state is the culmination of the aspirations of the people. It (the state), if it is both independent and democratic, is the best protector of the rights of its people and all residents of its territory, whether they are indigenous or not. Over time, all feel part of the country's culture. Whether it is such depends on the traditions and culture of the indigenous people.

This is clearly manifested in the tradition of building a state by the Ukrainian people in more than a thousand years of history, even in medieval times when the head of state (Kyivan) was not elected, but laws were implemented that ensured the rights of the population (Ruska Pravda) in the Cossack era of free people where the leaders were elected. This tradition was halted by the culturally authoritarian Moscow horde after the Treaty of Pereyaslav, but the basic principle and desire for choice and rights of the people was defined clearly in the Orlyk Constitution after Poltava in 1710. Ukrainian culture and traditions allow for the fact that the best president of Ukraine so far is a person of neither indigenous origin nor religion. There is no better Ukrainian in the world than today's president of Ukraine.

Here is the true understanding of our state independence in the 33rd year and the struggle for our existence in the second year of a very difficult war. The enemy challenged us. We accepted this challenge and managed to overcome it. But it remains for us to prevail ultimately, not just for the sake of victory but for our own existence. The whole world is assisting us, but only in a moderate relative manner. The decision in Vilnius at the NATO summit gave us a clear answer that only we are responsible for our future.

And that's probably how it should be. This is yet another lesson for us. We have had allies in our history who betrayed us, as well as our own traitors. We have learned that friends will come to help but not shed their own blood. Only our and our enemy's blood will be spilled on our lands.

In the 33rd year of independence, I have more faith in the spirit of my people than at any time in the past. The concept of "Little Russians" has been abandoned entirely; the Ukrainian language, which is the heart of the nation and the state, now resounds from the Carpathians all the way to Donbas. Ukraine is becoming stronger every day, even with bloodshed and physical destruction. Transcarpathian poet Ivan Irlyavskyi wrote that often, life blooms on the dead, which is born in the fire of an existential struggle. And so it is! Our nation and our state are built on the heroism of our people. All the more so today when this nation and state are the recognized champion and defender of its destiny and the future of all of Europe, perhaps, the world as well as of good over evil.

On this anniversary of our independence, each of us should remember today's heroes who gave their lives for all of us and resolve to do everything within our abilities and circumstances so that the Ukrainian people and their state persevere. Everyone should bear in mind that the fortune of millions rests upon each one of us, and we must answer for the fate of millions. So wrote our great poet, Ivan Franko, and this is how we should approach the anniversary of our national independence with love and selfless dedication to the greater good.

August 24, 2023

"I AM A UKRAINIAN- LET THEM COME TO UKRAINE."

In June 1963, sixty years ago, President John F. Kennedy traveled to Berlin, almost two years after the Communists had constructed the Berlin Wall separating the East from the West. He delivered a most memorable speech in which he expressed solidarity with the people of Berlin. "Today in the world of freedom, the proudest boast is 'Ich bin ein Berliner (I am a Berliner).'" For the next twenty-five years, the Berlin Wall was the symbol of Communist repression of its enslaved people and the hope of freedom, which was represented by the other side of the wall. No one was escaping to the East.

President Kennedy went on to say, "And there are some who say, in Europe and elsewhere, we can work with the Communists. Lass'sie nach Berlin kommen (Let them come to Berlin)."

These noteworthy words summed up my thoughts over the last week as Ukrainians all over the world celebrated the 32nd anniversary of the proclamation of renewed Ukrainian independence. I looked out at the dignitaries, guests, and general participants at these celebrations and noted that, indeed, we were all Ukrainian, at least for that day. This was a celebration, indeed, but marred in part by current events. We paid respects to more than one hundred thousand contemporary Ukrainian heroes, including civilians executed, among them women and children, yet still a celebration of the indomitable Ukrainian spirit.

When I hear of diplomatic channels to "provide an off-ramp" for the Russians in the current war against Ukrainians and Ukrainian independence, I become deeply indignant and hearken back to the words of President Kennedy, "Let them come to Berlin (Ukraine)." Let them come and see the devastation; the bombed-out targeted orphanages, maternity wards, hospitals, and residences. Let them speak then about "working with" the Russians.

Some global leaders have not heeded the words of President Kennedy as they apply to contemporary issues, in particular, the Russian aggression against Ukraine. Some, like the prime minister of Hungary or little-known Republican presidential aspirants, can be disregarded for lack of importance. However, the leader of the largest church in the world has been an embarrassment to the faithful and hierarchy of that Church. His latest glorification of the builders of the evil known as the Russian empire cannot be justified or even explained. It is the product of ignorance or a psychosis. Nevertheless, his ideological and moral, perhaps age-affected dysfunction, needs to be addressed. Inasmuch as there is no impeachment process in the Church, nor is its hierarchy in particular, those who defied the Holy Spirit by electing him of sufficient courage, significant prodding should ensue for him to follow the example of his predecessor. In the alternative, let him come to Ukraine to see what his "friends" have accomplished. God does work in mysterious ways.

President Biden has been a disappointment. How else can one explain the betrayal of Ukraine at the NATO Summit? Perhaps President Biden believes that Ukraine's invitation to NATO precludes talks with Russia. Frankly, where and how can such talks ensue? Vladimir Putin is a global pariah with an arrest warrant from the International Criminal Court. The only solution is the reestablishment of Ukraine's territorial integrity, compensation in hundreds of billions, and the decolonization of the Russian empire. Without the last, the next Russian aggression is only a matter of time.

Frankly, President Biden owes Ukraine much as Russia's land grab of Ukraine was precipitated by Vice President Biden's former superior's lack of foreign policy credentials and fecklessness. It is also important to note that much of the West's arms delivery to Ukraine is often preceded by an incongruous White House and Pentagon denial, then a period where America is proven wrong, and only then is the military support granted, sometimes because of the persuasive efforts of America's less than militarily proficient allies. The F-16s are a striking example of Holland and Norway stepping up and acting where America was not the leader but became a follower.

In the aftermath of celebration, but on the eve of another winter of war and devastation, it is important to focus on the good fight and the ultimate goal, as well as one's role, even if only auxiliary. Good can never reconcile with evil. Freedom cannot be compromised with repression. We must recognize what the Russian empire represents and resolve to rid the world of this scourge.

August 30, 2023

A CONVERSATION WITH A DISABLED UKRAINIAN SOLDIER

"The war will end for us when we enter Kuban." So said a disabled Ukrainian soldier with a missing left arm above the elbow. He is a Ukrainian soldier born in the Cherkasy region, serving as a soldier in the Luhansk region. He is almost two meters tall. He returned from working in Poznań in Poland to defend his native land, where he was born, baptized, married and baptized his child.

There are many like him. I paid attention to every word as if he were an icon of the Cossack brotherhood. By the way, he is similar to the Cossacks in bravery, only he is half bald instead of having a scalp herring. I met Oleksandr for the first time in the USA, where he came for a prosthesis. We met in my office in New York. We cooperated on the supply of drones and thermal imagers for his brigade.

In Lviv, we met as friends, that is, simply to talk. We agreed on helping his brigade with few words, but with a meaningful look. After all, we have been cooperating for three months. It seems to me that friendship ensues when you understand each other by looking.

Today, he is completing rehabilitation and says he plans to return to the front. He says he feels fine. But, since he is disabled, it is necessary not only to change his military category and role from an infantryman to a sniper, and also to retrain formally. The brigade has already submitted its approval and is waiting for him.

Why did he join the fight immediately, in March 2022, and now wants to return. "Because this is my land... I hate them and will never forgive them... I want my daughter to live in Ukraine without fear and in the European way."

Oleksandr speaks Ukrainian but with some Russian words peppered throughout. Well, I also peppered some Polish and English words. Enemies and influences on every side. East and West sang together during the Orange Revolution. I have never felt a stronger sense of unity. These phrases that this is my land and I will never forgive them are probably not unique. Ukraine is united even if diverse. Aren't there many Oleksandrs in the Armed Forces of Ukraine?

I didn't want to taint our conversation with negativity, but at one point, I couldn't resist when he praised the help of the diaspora. I brazenly acknowledged that we have Ukrainians in the diaspora who even call themselves nationalists who do not provide any help in our struggle. He explained, "They are Americans, and this is my country." He was being polite.

Oleksandr, for some reason, or so he says, is not afraid of death. He is only thirty-six years old. By my standards, he is a kid. He worries only about the fate of his twelve-year-old daughter, also Alexandra by name, and her future life on Ukrainian land. The wife and daughter are not to leave their native land. "There were no Muscovites in my village in Cherkashin; we spoke mostly in Russian, but only because we were used to it. In fact, we did not distinguish. Now I see the difference, because this is the language our enemies speak. They want to wipe us off the face of the earth. I will not allow it...I will try to erase them...they are not human..."

My interlocutor still has a long way to go. He must complete his rehabilitation, and only then can he be retrained before he returns to his brigade. We agreed that he would let us know what our soldiers needed most. And we, for our part, will help and monitor how our soldiers defend Ukraine and marvel at their bravery. We are a nation of heroes.

My conclusion is that we will not give up Ukraine. Our defenders are diverse and yet very similar. I need not be convinced about our role. The whole world is on our side. But the world gives us only funds and weapons. We give blood. Alexander gave his arm for the time being and only his left. He returns to the front.

We agreed that after the war, we would meet on Ukrainian land in the Kuban. Having met Oleksandr, I have no doubt. After all, Kuban is our land. Alexander is not the first and not the last such Ukrainian with such vision. Fortunately, we have many Alexanders.

Thank God!

Glory to Ukraine!

Glory to Alexander!

See you in Kuban!

October 21, 2023

A GUY NAMED NICK

Last Tuesday, my wife and I went to a German restaurant in Kyiv. Why? Perhaps in gratitude for those Leopard tanks. Frankly, The bratwurst was bad, and the sauerkraut was worse. But the beer was excellent. It was Czech, though.

The patrons were sparse, and the mood was not particularly upbeat. That was until Nick walked in. We noticed him only because he spoke English to the waiter. He *eh'd* several times, so we decided that he must be Canadian, probably a Ukrainian Canadian. I was about to pounce on him for neglecting his Ukrainian language. That's my routine in Ukraine when meeting people. He calmly responded that he was not Ukrainian at all but from the British Columbia province in Canada. I asked him hockey questions as a form of interrogation. Shamefully but apologetically, he acknowledged that he not only did not play ice hockey but had very little interest in it. He was more of a football (soccer) fan. I made a bad joke, something like, do your parents know, and we all laughed.

It turns out he was a Canadian with German roots. He had military training in Canada but was bored. When he learned about the war in Ukraine, he became excited. He came over, loved the people, and asked to join the war effort. I asked whether it was one of the Ukrainian girls that made this experience even more special. It turns out he does love one of the people even more than others.

It turned out that this was Nick's 21st birthday. We bought him a German beer, sang "Mnohaja Lita" (Happy Birthday), and began calling him "Mykola." We stayed only a bit longer. He told us he was due back by 10 PM and that he would be going out to the front very soon. At last, we said, "Goodbye, Nick, and good luck." He corrected us. "Mykola," he said.

For my wife and me, this was a very special meeting. We know that there are non-Ukrainians serving in Ukraine's armed forces. But meeting one, getting to know him, albeit briefly, was very personal and emotional. My wife cried.

Ukraine has made many friends during this almost two-year brutal ordeal. In fact, during the very first few days of Russia's invasion, as I recall, many throughout the world flocked to manifest support for Ukraine. As I live in New York City, I was astounded by the number of Ukrainian flags that were hung out from windows and fire escapes. In particular, I was highly encouraged by New York City's cultural elite, Broadway and Lincoln Center celebrities, and even the average New Yorker.

Over the course of almost two years, an element of fatigue has set in, fed in part by an acknowledgment by Ukraine's president and the military that the effort to save the civilized world from Russian barbarism would indeed be a marathon rather than a sprint.

The cost to Ukraine in terms of blood and infrastructure has been enormous. And still, Ukraine, its people, and Nick have resolved to go on. While fatigue in the West is understandable, it must be balanced by a recognition that war often provides an opportunity for the better.

On February 24, 2022, Russia was the single greatest threat to the security not only of Ukraine but the civilized and democratic world. The world is a much better place today because Russia has been exposed. Russia has perpetrated acts of aggression, war crimes, crimes against humanity, and attempted genocide as enumerated by the International Criminal Court, and yet it has accomplished nothing in terms of achieving its purpose, losing more than three hundred thousand of its own soldiers in the effort.

America and the West have spent money, not lives, to secure its own future and have reinvigorated its defense industry in the process. Ukrainians are fighting the world's battle to preclude a World War 3.

My meeting with Nick was a reason to rejoice as I saw in him reinforcements. Nick is only one man, yet he is symbolic of the very fact that Ukraine is not alone. With friends like Nick, Ukraine's victory is inevitable. Dear friends and allies, stay with Ukraine not merely for Ukraine but for the sake of all of us – people who love and cherish freedom. This is Nick's message.

November 4, 2023

LET'S NOT REPEAT OUR MISTAKES

There is a nation captive within the Russian Empire. The Erzya's number is less than one million. They predate Russians on their ethnographic territory partially in what is now known as Mordovia. On October 17, 2023, some twenty of their activists were arrested, interrogated, and robbed of their cell phones and computers. Ultimately, they were let go with a warning to support Russia in its current war against Ukraine. This is a part of the contemporary Russian aggression, which is a cause of concern for the whole world as it appears on our screens and troubles our lives.

On October 19, 2023, the Erzya leadership, with its chief elder, who is in exile in Ukraine, issued a statement. I met with him and an associate in Kyiv several days ago. We spoke in Ukrainian and English. The chief elder is also the current president of the Free Nations League, a network based in Europe of nations struggling within the Russian empire.

"We often hear voices advocating the preservation of the Russian Federation, which express concern that the collapse of this monster will lead to unnecessary trouble! You are "worried" about the fate of our executioner! But what about democratic, universal principles and values? What about the Universal Declaration of Human Rights? Russia will fall apart anyway, and it will be sooner rather than later. But we are aware that it will have enough time to destroy many of us. Your concern does not extend to the disenfranchised existence of millions of non-Russians. Over the past ten years, the number of Erzya alone has decreased by 200,000 people. The price for your "tranquillity" is the lives of our peoples, and it is growing rapidly! You can, you are strong, you are just, pay attention to our situation, unless your talk about principles and values is grandiloquent but empty declarations!"

I came away from our meeting with a renewed purpose and a much better understanding of the current war. It's about territory, but more importantly, about good and evil and the further duration of this Russian scourge. From my perspective as an American, it's also about America's role in ridding the world today and the future world of our children of this menace, which not only evokes fear, destroys our planet, and costs trillions of dollars that should be used to fight poverty and disease. Even in a **less-than-perfect** world, the Russian **Empire** should not exist. Russians could then become civilized and, perhaps, even democratic. Russian mothers and the Russian church would not be forces for evil.

War is an awful occurrence. History has proven that. However, it sometimes offers opportunities. The post-World War 2 history of our relationship with Communist Russia remains very relevant today. The USSR suffered great losses in World War 2. Were it not for the naivete of American leadership and Soviet infiltration of our own government, State, and Treasury of which there is no doubt, which led to incongruous appeasement, we could have prevented a Cold War.

America was in a position to secure a just and peaceful world without the Russian Communist menace that blighted the world for almost half a century thereafter. Yet we failed to act on behalf of the freedom-loving non-Russian people in the USSR and its satellites. People all over the world suffered, but mostly those captive nations that were persecuted, their culture repressed, and their activists incarcerated, tortured, and killed, all because of our American failure to act.

The Soviet-Russian regime and the Russian Empire are one scourge distinguished only by name and time. God, fate, and history are giving the freedom-loving and democratic world another chance. In particular this opportunity has been afforded us through the courage and because of the blood of the Ukrainian people. There are many such peoples and nations, albeit less populous, within the Russian empire. There are also those on the fringe of the empire, such as Belarusians, Georgians, Armenians, Kazakhs, and others, who continue to face fear on a daily basis lest they attempt to forge a truly independent existence free of the Russian scourge.

Similar to the Erzya, some tens of nations within the Empire itself have expressed their desire to be free. They include Tatars in Tatarstan, Chechens, Buryats, Bashkirs, Oirat-Kalmyks, Sakha-Yakuts and others. In order to keep their hope alive, they need an expression or manifestation of compassion, understanding, and support from us Americans. We turned our back on the people oppressed by Russia before. Let's not repeat our mistake!

November 6, 2023

RELIGION AS A WEAPON

The Ukrainian Orthodox Church Moscow Patriarchate (UOCMP) is a geographical appendage or branch of the Russian Orthodox Church, Moscow Patriarchate (ROCMP). It takes its directives from Moscow and pays subsidies to Moscow. In fact, for a long time, even after Ukraine's independence, the UOCMP was the largest contributor to the budget of the ROCMP. For the sake of credibility in Ukraine since the war started in 2014, over the last few years, it has often abbreviated its name, deleting the MP suffix for purposes of public relations as it began losing faithful and parishes. Nevertheless, its history and purpose have remained unaltered.

In 1685, the earlier version of ROCMP assumed control over the original Ukrainian Orthodox Church pursuant to Russian abuse of a military agreement with the Ukrainian Cossack state from 1654 and a specious accord with the Ecumenical Patriarch in Constantinople, who had been held hostage for purposes of consent. That accord was later disavowed by Constantinople. Nonetheless, since then, Russian Orthodoxy has imposed its will upon Ukrainian Christianity by force.

The Ukrainian faithful were somewhat vulnerable because of their deep belief in Christianity. In fact, as noted above, even after the demise of the USSR in 1991, the largest contingent of the ROC in terms of faithful and churches was in Ukraine. Such was the case in Russian czarist times as well. Religion, after all, is a very strong moral and communal factor in life.

A better understanding of this ROCMP can be deduced from history. While it functioned in Russian czarist times, for the Soviets intent on implementing atheism as a component of communism, the ROCMP was ineffective. The Soviet dictator Josef Stalin provided an imprimatur to his control of the ROCMP by reorganizing it within his own Ministry. Thus it became an agency of the special services. Stalin proceeded to abolish all other churches, including the Ukrainian Catholic and the ROCMP under his jurisdiction became the only avenue for religious expression.

For purposes of some perspective, however disproportionate, it may be interesting to note that the ROCMP operates in the United States pursuant to the religious freedom accorded by the non-Establishment clause of the Bill of Rights. Despite the fact that the ROCMP works directly with Moscow and has often retained highly paid lobbyists **who work** to influence American politics and legislation, the ROCMP has never registered as a foreign agent under the Foreign Agents Registration Act. That has often been commented upon at State.

This can be partially explained by the reluctance of the United States Department of State to address arguments or defenses by the ROCMP that other churches are subservient to foreign capitals, such as the Vatican or the Ecumenical Patriarch in Istanbul. Religious organizations are afforded the widest latitude in the United States because of the Establishment Clause to the point that, unlike other tax-exempt organizations, they are not required to file even annual tax returns.

In the United States, the role of the ROC, while certainly not benign, as evidenced by the recent recruitment of highly priced lobbyists, is certainly not as dangerous as its mission and work in Ukraine. Its purpose in the United States is largely disinformation, and its work often lacks credibility, particularly in today's Russia-sanctioned environment.

Ukraine is at war with Russia, a war which was instigated entirely by Russia for not only territorial enlargement but also historical enhancement. According to spokesmen for the ROC, this is a war "to wipe Ukrainians off the face of the earth."

Both the Constitution of Ukraine and the European Convention on Human Rights are circumspect in this regard, perhaps cognizant of their neighbor's historical and rhetorical proclivities.

Paragraph 35 of Ukraine's Constitution guarantees religious freedom. However, it goes on to specify that freedom may be limited in the interests of the public good. Well, certainly, stopping Russian aggression and saving the Ukrainian nation from extinction may be the public good.

The European Convention on Human Rights guarantees in Article 9 "Freedom of thought, conscience and religion" yet subject to such "limitations as are prescribed by law and are necessary in a democratic society in the interests of public safety, for the protection of public order, health or morals, or for the protection of the rights and freedoms of others."

Certainly, the right of Ukrainians to exist is one such limitation. The ROCMP has made itself clear in this regard - "to wipe Ukrainians off the face of the earth."

December 6, 2023

MIKE JOHNSON'S BIBLE

In the course of my personal Christmas introspection, which deals with both my Christian and Ukrainian sour, I recalled an interview with the then-just-elected new Speaker of the United States House of Representatives, Mike Johnson. He stated that in his political life as well as his personal, he is guided by the Bible. He probably should have made some reference to the United States Constitution as well. Be that as it may, over the first almost two months of his activities as speaker, I am convinced that the Bible to which Mike Johnson referred is the Donald Trump version, meaning the one, if any, on Donald Trump's nightstand. That version does not include many of the subjects commonly found in the regular Bible, including the parable about the Good Samaritan. Love for one's neighbor manifested through tangible assistance, is the focus of Christianity. Discerning between right and wrong, good and evil, is its essence.

There remains much hope that with or without the support of Speaker Johnson, military aid to Ukraine will be worked out. Unfortunately, much damage has accrued to date. The war in Ukraine is an existential one for Ukrainians. Ukrainians are defined as all residents of Ukraine as well as those residing abroad who consider themselves Ukrainian. Optimism is a factor in any war and very much a part of human nature as much as a legitimate cause for concern when that optimism is wounded. Ammunition is beginning to lack, and the current war is, at best, a stalemate, as seen by the Ukrainian military. One Ukrainian soldier pointed out that there are more Russian soldiers than Ukrainian bullets.

There is at least one billion dollars available and some four billion more in draw-down supplies as per the Pentagon, but the message received in Ukraine has been very concerning. The European Union's decision to begin Ukraine membership talks is being highlighted in Ukraine to support optimism, but the more tangible Hungarian veto of military and humanitarian aid has been put on the back pages.

The people of Ukraine, **the** military, volunteers, and the general civilian population have been heroic. Ukrainians abroad have been predominantly lethargic. Russia has been buoyed by the apparent indifference of Western support and has increased its barbaric behavior, even boasting of the use of chemical weapons and continuing to shell civilian targets, including residences, health facilities, and schools, indiscriminately killing women and children. Mike Johnson's Bible, however, does not consider these facts. In any event it is anticipated hopefully that aid to Ukraine will be revisited in both the United States and Europe this coming January.

If politics is an art of sometimes accomplishing creatively what is possible, then there are some alternatives to overcome or circumvent Speaker Johnson's "religious convictions." This includes other MAGAs in Congress, including such blind or simply dishonest politicians as Jim Jordan and Marjorie Taylor Greene in the House and a self-identified hillbilly such as J.D. Vance in the Senate.

Some ideas have come forward and are supported apparently by our allies: using frozen Russian assets throughout the world estimated at some three hundred billion dollars, suspending EU and NATO support for Prime Minister Viktor Orban and Hungary, which requires support from our European allies, transferring "Patriot" defense systems manufactured at Mitsubishi in Japan and to be sold at a great discount or even simply given to the United States. Japan has agreed to do so; the only remaining issue would be the compensation for Russian assets seized in the United States, which might require an act of Congress, but the lion's share of seized Russian assets are in Europe. Our allies in Europe certainly are guided by a different Bible than Mike Johnson or Donald Trump, for that matter, even if only because of proximity.

Anyone or all of these creative solutions would not only be a valuable temporary substitute for what Ukraine has been promised but would serve to encourage the Ukrainians who a willing to die for their own existence and to rid the world of the Russian imperialistic threat. The war against Russian aggression must be a global effort. President Biden has often referred to American assistance as an investment in a peaceful global community that is cost-effective. Apparently, Speaker Johnson and his fellow MAGAs not only rely upon an abridged, if not bizarre, version of the Bible but suffer from political shortsightedness. Merry Christmas, Speaker Johnson. This is a good time to pick up a real Bible.

December 24, 2023

2024? PREDICTIONS OR WISHES EITHER WAY!

Predictions for a new year are like resolutions, rarely measured by success or failure. Generally, no one remembers them. As a society, we have short-term recall at best, and most pundits purporting to have expertise dare to give answers to serious questions with much levity. I have lived for more than seventy years and have seen and heard almost everything imaginable, including the bravado of political scientists, pundits, and other experts who ought to be measured by their accuracy for their professional existence. But they are not. Henry Kissinger was a prime example. He got it wrong more times than not.

I am neither a political scientist nor a pundit. I have no pretended qualifications except for the ability to read, study, and reason, at least so far. I also have the luxury of listening to experts and laughing. I rarely cry. Experts abound! As a football NY Jets fan, I am reminded of this year's Super Bowl predictions. Oh, those experts!

Many years ago, I came to meet with Ukraine's fifth President, Victor Yushchenko, at his interim office on the grounds of the St Sophia Cathedral. This was a time between his premiership and his presidency. I was a strong supporter and headed the Ukrainian World Congress at that time. Victor was late. I waited for him relatively calmly, considering my inveterate impatience. His assistant was relatively uncomfortable because, despite my apparent patience, I kept approaching her and questioning when Victor Andriyovych would come.

After a quarter of one hour, a self-identified apiarist (beekeeper) came to the waiting room. By way of introduction, he began to boast of his abilities, which, by the way, was his only connection with Victor Andriyovych, who was distinguished in this field besides politics. The beekeeper stated that he had acquired the ability to predict the future. I am a cynic on most boasts and, therefore, listened to his predictions very superficially. Finally, I got over his dissertation on beekeeping and asked him, inasmuch as he saw the future, to tell me when Viktor Andriyovych would come. He did not know what to answer. Viktor came with Petro Poroshenko within a few minutes. However, the assistant had to convince the beekeeper that, despite his extraordinary prowess, I should go in first since I had preceded him.

My skills at foretelling what will happen in 2024 should be given as much credence as those of the beekeeper. That is to say that my prognostications can be reduced to wishes. However, my conclusions as to the gravity of events should be considered.

The war in Ukraine is a conundrum without a quick solution. For all the success of Ukraine's military, a war lasting almost two years requires much weaponry, quite ordinary and high-tech. Ukraine has a military strategy, but as with most matters, it depends on its allies and conditions.

America's President Biden has been Ukraine's best friend and largely responsible for Ukraine's military failures. Secretary of State Tony Blinkin and Secretary of Defense Lloyd Austin have urged greater resoluteness. Biden is by nature a very cautious person and not very sophisticated in foreign affairs, aside from almost forty years of experience in politics. The history of this two-year relationship has been Ukraine needing and requesting specific weapons and President Biden declining, arguing, strangely enough, that Ukraine needs other weapons. Shortly thereafter, as events proved that Ukraine was right, President Biden gave in, but only after Ukraine had lost both lives and opportunities.

Surprisingly, Ukraine's biggest successes were in the sea and in the air, where Ukraine should not be competitive. This is proof of the skill and creativity of the Armed Forces of Ukraine. When NATO declined Ukraine's invitation to NATO membership in Vilnius and instead promised a faster pace of implementation of membership without MAP, America also promised such a military relationship with Ukraine outside of NATO as with Israel. It is true that America is fighting with Israel in the air of Syria and Iraq and in the Red Sea. America has not fought together with Ukraine anywhere except for Afghanistan at the request of America.

My prediction or wish is that Ukraine will receive weapons from America and Europe in the shortest possible time, meaning early in 2024. This will repel the Russians and enhance a counter-offensive, but not in the style of the recent failed attempt, which involved large casualties. The strategy of Ukraine must be different since Ukraine does not have as many soldiers as Russia and because Ukraine values the life of every person and its own soldiers. The strategy should follow the aerial and maritime models, but now, with American F-16s and drones and missiles, they will be able to fire and bomb deeper into the territory of Russia as well as the occupied territories. This way of fighting gives Ukraine an opportunity to win. However, this does not mean that the war will end in 2024.

The elections in America in November 2024 are probably the most important elections for Ukraine during Ukraine's statehood. Not only the American president but all 435 members of the lower House of Congress and almost half of the members of the Senate will be elected. We have come to the point in America where democratic values and not the party line are important.

I would no longer appeal to Ukrainian members or simply registered Ukrainian American Republicans because if their own conscience has not reached them, then this deafness and blindness have become insurmountable moral issues. An elementary school child can count the friends of Ukraine from the Republican side. Representatives of this immoral and incoherent party preach and spread lies much like the Russians.

A genius from an extreme network recently argued that President Joe Biden should be impeached because, as VP, he demanded that Ukraine dismiss its Prosecutor General Viktor Shokin, who was intent on prosecuting a company in Ukraine that included the VP's son, Hunter. All of Europe was insisting on the removal of Shokin, who was very much corrupt. Another Republican genius stressed that Putin had never threatened to invade any other part of Europe other than Ukraine. There are many instances of Putin's, Medvedev's, Pskov's, and Nebenzya's threatening proclamations. The sad fact is that there have been so many threats, and they have been so blatant that the Republican's statement cannot be attributed simply to ignorance. Quite simply, the Republican Party is doing the work of the Kremlin.

To be honest, I abhor Ukrainians who call themselves Republicans. No longer do I urge them to examine their own conscience. Frankly, I know not a single Ukrainian Republican who continues to support the Republican Party today who has done anything tangible in terms of effort or money to aid the Ukrainian war effort. Am I surprised? No, we Ukrainians had had our share of "useful idiots" and "fence sitters" historically.

My prediction or wish is that Joe Biden will be reelected and Democrats will take both houses. The abortion issue (freedom to choose), rights and freedoms, and a fear of extremism and even dictatorship will decide this election. Support for democracy abroad will be a part of this platform. Immigration will not decide the election because America needs immigration reform, not suppression, and Republicans have not addressed this issue.

I'm not an absolute realist. I am a bit of a dreamer with a strong will and determination despite the odds, yet with the conviction of Polish or Jewish Ukrainians that all who live in Ukraine are Ukrainians, and such a mix, imbued with genuine love for Ukraine and its people is what today's Ukraine is all about. I look forward to 2024 with much hope yet anxiety. Either way, 2024 will be a very important year for American democracy and leadership and crucial for Ukraine's freedom. Those two issues are connected inherently.

December 31, 2023

MATTERS DIFFICULT TO COMPREHEND

For purposes of this analysis, I am presuming that Ukrainian missiles did indeed go down a Russian plane near Belgorod in Russia. There has not been nor will there be an international investigation either by the International Red Cross or the United Nations since Russia will not allow it. Russia asserted that it was conducting its own investigation. A Russian truth-finding investigation is an oxymoron.

Russia accused Ukraine of downing the Il-76, alleging that the transport carried 65 Ukrainian POW's for a swap at the border. To date, almost two weeks after the event, only the bodies of 5 crew members have been unearthed in the rubble. Ukraine has asked for the bodies of the POW's for burial. To date, Russia has not produced them.

What would have been the motive of the Ukrainian side in killing their own prisoners of war? None! The only possible answer would be that there was a mistake on the Ukrainian side. There does exist the probability that Ukraine was unaware of the Ukrainian POW's on board. Ukraine has stressed that it was not informed of the POW transport. The Russians, in their best defense, asserted that notice was given 15 minutes in advance. Questions persist about to whom the notice was provided and whether 15 minutes' notice is reasonable.

Russia would be highly motivated to kill Ukrainian soldiers by simply not informing Ukraine of the POW transport and then blaming Ukraine, which would result in internal discord within the population of Ukraine. While by Russian accounts, some eight Russians lost their lives, that would be deemed very minor collateral damage for the Russians as, according to Russian culture, manifested many times, people are treated as cannon fodder.

And so, in all probability, the truth will never be known.

In another story, Vladimir Putin is planning a visit to Turkey at the invitation of President Erdogan. Why is that of any interest? Turkey is a signatory of the Rome Treaty, which formed the International Criminal Court. Granted, the Turkish Parliament has not ratified the Treaty, but the Parliament of Turkey means relatively little in the Erdogan authoritarian regime. The ICC has issued a warrant for the arrest of Vladimir Putin. Will this become a test for the relevance of international law and its structures?

Ukraine's Foreign minister, Dmytro Kuleba, recently met with his counterpart from Hungary. Kuleba came away saying that Prime Minister Viktor Orban was not pro-Russian but a Hungarian patriot. Kuleba is the quintessential diplomat, often at the expense of his own country.

In any event, pressured by the EU, including not only withholding of funds earmarked for Hungary but also a loss of his veto power, Orban caved, and the EU allocated 50 billion euros to Ukraine on February 1, 2024. Nevertheless, questions remain as to the ability of Hungary and its Prime Minister, Viktor Orban, to hold both Ukraine and the EU hostage for a month and a half. Ukraine certainly suffered significant casualties as a result.

Hungary is a small country with a small population and a corrupt and authoritarian regime. It is currently under significant sanctions by the EU for its transgressions. It offers the EU or NATO very little. It is one tiny speck, even less than a proportionate part of the 27 countries that comprise the EU. Its benefits for the EU, much like its power in NATO, is an aberration.

Finally, despite Ukrainian Catholic insistence, the Pope of Rome is not a dear friend of the Ukrainian people. Ukrainian Catholics do pray for him at least four times at each Mass. He traveled to Mongolia in 2019. There are 1300 Catholics in Mongolia. Pope Francis named a Cardinal for the Mongolian

Catholics, albeit an Italian one. There are some 5 million Ukrainian Catholics, in fact, the largest Eastern Catholic Church. There is no Ukrainian Catholic Cardinal. Granted, Ukrainian Catholics would want one of their own nationality.

A recent compendium of the Popes' "Ten Prayers for a Future of Hope," published in 2023, sets aside one chapter to the "madness of war." Ukraine is mentioned twice but merely as a venue. A "humanitarian crisis" is referred to, but no sympathy is expressed for the people of Ukraine. Russia is never mentioned as the aggressor or perpetrator of the "madness."

The Pope, in his previous life as an Argentinian cleric, was a good friend of the current Ukrainian Catholic primate, Archbishop Swiatoslaw. Swiatoslaw is not a Cardinal. Russia's ban on the Ukrainian Catholic Church in Ukraine's occupied territories has not been condemned or even addressed by the Pope. He could have interceded with his diplomatic counterparts Vladimir and Kirill.

Perhaps Ukrainian Catholics should pray for the Pope more often. He certainly needs their prayers to approach simple humanity, let alone spiritual leadership.

February 3, 2024

WHAT DOES THE KILLING OF ALEXEI NAVALNY MEAN?

It means much. It means that Vladimir Putin is an arrogant barbarian with no regard for civility or humanity. It means that Russia considers the West feckless. It should be a wake-up call for America and Europe. It removes any illusions that Putin is yet another leader of a country that we simply do not understand. It confirms that Russia, democratic America, and Europe are at the crossroads of a conflagration unless we address this problem now.

The death of Russian opposition leader Alexei Navalny is significant because Navalny was the leading opponent to Russia's and Putin's regime, even though he was thousands of miles away from Moscow in the Arctic Circle in a prison camp. He was not a threat to Putin's presidential ambitions. In essence had he languished in the Russian prisons, he would have become irrelevant after a while. There was no way that the Kremlin would release him. He would have died eventually. Why did Putin kill him? Simply because he decided that he wanted to.

Three days before his demise, Navalny's mother met with him and later posthumously stressed that he was well and in good spirits. On the day before his death, he appeared before some Russian facsimile of a court and actually joked and ridiculed the judicial system. His immediate death was not anticipated. Yet Vladimir Putin decided to kill him on the eve of an upcoming presidential election, a farce in Russia and in the midst of fragile American resolve to help Ukraine.

For many, Alexei Navalny is difficult to understand. He was a man safe in exile by virtue of the fact that he was a medical patient in the West after the Kremlin tried to poison him. He could have decided to stay relatively by Russian standards, safe and become a leader of the opposition in Russia from exile. No, he decided that he had to die to make any significant difference in the Russia that he apparently loved and hoped to change.

Very few would have done what Navalny did. He went back to Russia, essentially, in order to be killed. There are few Navalnys in this world. To grasp the significance of his sacrifice, we need only to consider some alleged leaders in our own country: Tucker Carlson, Speaker Mike Johnson, and former President Donald J. Trump.

A comparison of these individuals with Navalny would not be laughable but disproportionate only because there is nothing laughable about Navalny's death. But this is what we have in America today: Carlson, Johnson, and Trump. All misplaced. Carlson has no business being a journalist. Johnson has none, being the Speaker of the House of Representatives of the United States of America, and Donald J. Trump is an aberration as former president of the United States and a candidate once again for America's highest office.

It is possible that Putin, in his arrogance, made a mistake. Thugs and strongmen do make mistakes. In democratic societies, we seem to think that the other side is exact in its evil. Putin has been emboldened recently by his poll numbers in a farcical election where all opposition has been essentially eliminated and what appears to him to be America's apparent betrayal of Ukraine with his friend looming in the near distance as America's president.

Aside from the tragedy of a human death, there is a huge political component to Navalny's death. Navalny, because of who he was and his courage, transcended simple humanity and normal human demise. He was a symbol and may become a martyr to future generations, although Russian culture is almost impervious to anything good or decent.

There has been a world reaction to Putin's killing of Navalny. World leaders have expressed their opprobrium against Putin. They have clearly accused Putin of murder. Even Speaker Johnson has addressed the killing. There may and should be a tangible reaction.

And so let's refrain from scoffing at people hiding fecklessness behind religious zealotry like Mike Johnson, who talk good Christianity and reverence to the Bible but are indifferent to their fellow human beings. Give Speaker Johnson a chance to do what is right. He has spoken, but the response from him should be putting the aid for Ukraine bill to a vote immediately. Mr. Speaker Johnson, consult the Bible. You must know what is wrong and be able to find it in Scripture. Killing is wrong.

In the interim and because of American fecklessness, another Ukrainian city has fallen, Avdiyivka. An immediate and overwhelming vote in favor of military aid to Ukraine by the House should be our American response to Putin's murder of Alexei Navalny. The best response to Putin's and Russia's killing machine is a military victory of democracy and good over evil in Ukraine.

February 19, 2024

THE NEED FOR A WAR STRATEGY

One of the most significant problems within the Ukrainian diaspora worldwide, and in particular the United States, where it matters most, is the lack of political sophistication. Intentions are mostly good, but they are not informed and aimed so as not to interfere with one's personal life, no matter how banal. The Ukraine issue is tangential or marginal, which suggests that it is not a priority. The bottom line is that there is no war strategy.

There are numerous examples of this characterization. Case in point is recognizing that the war in Ukraine is 10 years old, and the full-scale atrocities are 2 years old. Many organizations have spent time and even resources organizing events for this occasion. These events have taken myriad forms: demonstrations, vigils, conferences and, frankly, I have no idea how to characterize events organized by the Ukrainian Institute of America in New York City. Essentially, it was announced almost as an Institute touring exercise.

There was an interesting event that I attended at the Cooper Union Great Hall, historically the site of a speech by President Abraham Lincoln. It had possibilities for strategic success, meaning helping Ukraine because of the venue, myriad sponsorship by relatively important partners, including universities, at least one recognizable speaker, and the very acute problems facing Ukraine today.

The main speaker was Oleksandra Matviichuk, the president of the Center for Civil Liberties and a recent Ukrainian Nobel laureate. Her virtual presentation was eloquent, informative, moving, and emotional. She made a significant observation, albeit erroneous, that in recent history (the last one hundred years), the only case of punishment against an aggressor was through the Nuremberg Tribunal. She suggested the need for a similar tribunal to punish Russia for its war crimes today.

What she failed to mention was the need for victory in order for that or any existing tribunal to act and implement decisions or verdicts. She did mention support but failed to call specifically for ammunition in order for Ukraine to achieve that victory. That should have been the focus of her presentation.

There were other speakers and a round table discussion, which mostly bemoaned how much the Ukrainians had suffered during the war. The moderator did not focus on the strategic immediate needs of Ukraine. Towards the end, she did raise the issue of very little time remaining. The discussants merely touched upon this important and very complex topic where there are issues of jurisdiction, criminal intent, and evidence involving the United Nations Convention on the Prevention and Punishment of Genocide, the International Court of Justice and the International Criminal Court.

This was an opportunity to help Ukraine in the war. It turned into an academic discussion. Perhaps worse, it gave many in the audience the satisfaction that by attending, they had done their part in somehow assisting Ukraine's war effort.

Such events could have an important role in garnering support for Ukraine, particularly in the United States, which after all, is the strongest military and economic power in the world but has and continues to experience problems with its identity as a foundational NATO member and the leading democracy in the world today to the point that the future of NATO is questioned. Europeans are considering an alternative European defense structure, relying less and less upon American military capability. The focus has to be on strategic and tangible assistance, which is absolutely crucial today.

It should be stressed that Europe's contribution to NATO is increasing annually, and about two-thirds of NATO members are fulfilling their 2% GDP budgetary commitment. It should also be recognized that only once in its history has Article 5 of the NATO charter been invoked, and that was to benefit the United States. These facts are anathema to most of the primitives within the Republican party in America.

Ukraine needs to win the war. That must be the focus. It needs soldiers and ammunition. Lamentations, condemnations, and even international Court rulings are all important, but at the present time, Ukraine needs shells, Patriots, Abrams. HIMARS, F-16"s. Without victory, there will be no punishment for war crimes or genocide. Worse, there may not be a democratic Ukraine in the center of Europe.

That should be the paramount strategic concern for the entire democratic world.

February 25, 2024

A CRITICAL TIME FOR AMERICA AND UKRAINE

One would suggest that time is more critical for the latter. There appear to be more Russian soldiers than Ukrainian bullets. Ukraine is undergoing a very trying time, not because of a lack of will or resolve but because it feels betrayed.

But the case in America is equally critical; America is not in danger of ceasing to be a country or a nation. But certainly, its role as a democracy and a global leader is under question. Yet, there ought not to be pessimistic thoughts that Donald J. Trump, now clearly the Republican candidate for President Of the United States, will prevail in November. For most Republicans, the primaries were a resounding victory for the former president. For the rest of us, it was reassuring that forty percent of Republicans could not vote for Trump.

I am reminded of Diogenes' search for an honest man. The Greek philosopher would have been very much frustrated had he encountered the MAGA Republicans. The latest to join the roll is the old self-identified political expert Mitch McConnell, with nary a bone in his spine. He condemned Trump after January 6, 2020, and then voted against impeachment. There were personal issues as well. Trump disparaged the Senator's wife. Nonetheless, Senator McConnell voiced support for Trump. There could not be a need for reciprocal political support because McConnell has stated that he will not run for Republican Senate leadership in November. Furthermore, he has four years left in his Senate term. So why frankly diminish your career in history by being a sycophant? There are so many McConnells in today's American Republication party.

Nonetheless, this leads me to believe in America. Diogenes would be gratified. Independents today constitute the second-largest voting group in America. The Republican Party under the leadership of Donald Trump, under indictments on 91 counts, has garnered the support of the uneducated and the Evangelicals. The latter has assumed that he is their anti-abortion champion when, in actuality, Trump could not care less about that political or moral issue and, probably, has paid for more than one abortion during his less-than-Christian lifetime. The Evangelicals supporting Trump are certainly the most gullible electorate in America.

And so the victim of this American betrayal is Ukraine. Allowing for the benefit of the doubt, speaker Mike Johnson is a neophyte and gullible. The alternative is that he is simply evil.

Ukraine will survive this madness because the Ukrainian people are intrepid. Additionally, they are creative and inventive. They manufacture their own drones, both for land and sea. They are destroying Russian fighter jets and warships. They have taken the war with Russia to Africa. They may be losing ground temporarily, but they are garnering more support from Europe. France is beginning to talk about boots on the ground, as is Poland and other countries. Germany, **post-Angela,** has supplied more weapons to Ukraine than any country other than America. Supplying German Taurus missiles is only a matter of time. Europe understands that a Ukrainian counter-offensive has to involve the territory of the Russian Federation as deep as Moscow with European support.

No one in Europe wants to see Russians on their own territory. Ukraine is the European red line. Ukrainians are dying so that Europe may live as in the past. Please consider Ukrainian Cossacks defending Vienna. People like Prime Minister Viktor Orban of Hungary have been rebuked, and they will follow if they wish to remain and benefit from EU and NATO membership, and justifiably so. He has been an albatross to Europe.

The war will not conclude in 2024, but it will take a turn for the better. Europe will become much more involved. Ukraine will manifest even more resolve and courage, and finally, America will come around.

I sincerely hope that the Republican Party in America will undergo yet another transformation, but if it does not, it will become irrelevant in America. Not for any other reason except that the American people, whether they are educated or not, can only be fooled so many times. I feel for some of the good Evangelical supporters of the MAGA aberration. Donald J. Trump is a fraud. You will experience an epiphany. You will recognize your apostasy, and finally, you will do the right and moral thing. Interestingly enough, no country in Eastern Europe has as many Evangelicals as Ukraine. My message to the Evangelicals in America, reach out to your brethren in Ukraine. You have so much in common, including a deep and moral conviction in good triumphing over evil and the Christian mantra of helping your neighbor, something that Donald Trump does not share.

2024 may not be a bad year for America or Ukraine. It will be an awakening for America and a time of some difficulty with a very hopeful future for Ukraine. I believe in both the American and Ukrainian people.

March 7, 2024

A PORTRAIT OF HYPOCRISY

Senator Lindsey Graham, a sidekick for the late Senator John McCain and caddie for former president Donald J. Trump traveled to Ukraine to meet with President Volodymyr Zelensky. This happened only weeks after he voted against aid to Ukraine, despite the bi-partisan nature of the bill, supported by 20 Republicans and passed by an overwhelming majority. While President Zelensky was gracious, Senator Graham was hypocritical to the end, calling for Ukraine's accession to NATO membership and providing a lesson for the conscription of additional Ukrainian military. He was soundly rebuked by the courageous people of Ukraine for the latter as Graham went on a teaching moment regarding earlier mandatory military service for Ukraine's youth. (Graham did serve in the US military, but only as an attorney. He never saw any fighting.) Ukraine should probably deny him future entry, but Ukraine is much too civilized and democratic for that.

This most recent game by the Senator from South Carolina deserves some attention and much opprobrium. Graham is the chief clown of the Senate, but even so, his behavior here is embarrassing for the Senate, even by his standards. There are other clowns: McConnell, Cruz, and Vance. These are four of the worst U.S. Senators in terms of hypocrisy. Graham's and McConnell's records are lengthy, so they have a history of which no one could be proud.

Graham has served in the Senate for twenty-one years, assuming the seat vacated by Senator Strom Thurmond, a well-known racist. Graham's term is up in two years, so his duplicity can be explained since he sits in Trump's pocket and loyalty is core for Trump. There is a democratic solution for such scoundrels to be applied by the electorate. I would not get too excited about the chances of his removal since this is South Carolina, the first state to secede from the Union, which precipitated the Civil War.

Graham was a relatively unknown but respectable member of the United States Senate, particularly when he was in the company of the much-adulated war hero Senator from Arizona, John McCain. He always followed Senator McCain's lead. When Senator McCain passed away, Graham was left to his own devices. Having run for the Republican presidential nomination in 2015-16 and embarrassed himself, he sought the favor of then President Donald J. Trump, who had disparaged him during Graham's short-lived campaign. This was embarrassing but not unusual for other Republican pretenders such as Little Marco Rubio and Ted Cruz and quickly forgiven for the sake of politics. Trump not only disparaged Ted Cruz but called his wife unattractive and his father a co-conspirator in the President John F. Kennedy assassination.

All was forgiven apparently on the links of Mar-a-Lago. Graham chose to become and continues to be Trump's "caddie." But he insists on being an international player. His recent lesson on military conscription in Ukraine has been ridiculed in Ukraine as being "none of his business" and in the United States as being "not exactly the purview of a US Senator, particularly one who is not supporting Ukrainian defense."

So now Lindsey Graham is an international clown and a shameless one whose message to Ukraine is, "We are not giving you any weapons to defend yourself, but do send your children out to die." It is difficult to imagine a more despicable character.

This is meant to disparage Lindsey Graham and not only him. My purpose is to shame those who speak loudest about patriotism and democracy but serve as Russian assets. Poor John McCain must be turning over in his grave. Senator Graham, at the very least, please never mention that John McCain was your friend. The most appropriate term would be Chutzpah; I am not sure that arrogance or shamelessness is adequate. Ever since the beginning of Russia's full-scale war in Ukraine and American material support, America has been telling the Ukrainians what they ought to be doing. In most instances, when Ukraine requested sophisticated weaponry, America responded, you do not need that. Again, in most instances when America was proven wrong, it did comply with Ukraine's request, albeit belatedly and at the cost of Ukrainian lives. American weapons given to Ukraine were not gifts. After all, Ukraine was fighting NATO's war.

Ukraine's Deputy Prime Minister for European and Euro-Atlantic Integration, Olga Stefanishina, made a bold declaration at the "Kyiv Security Forum," affirming that oil refineries within Russia's borders are legitimate targets for Ukraine from a military standpoint. This statement, echoing amidst the ongoing conflict between Ukraine and Russia, underscores Ukraine's strategic positioning and adherence to NATO standards.

Addressing inquiries about Ukraine's reaction to the US pleading to stop attacks on Russian oil refineries, Stefanishina articulated a resolute stance, stating in Ukrainian, "The Ukrainian side responded, I think, precisely by achieving its goals and by very successful operations conducted on the territory of the Russian Federation."

In her direct speech, Stefanishina elucidated Ukraine's military rationale, highlighting that these strikes align with NATO standards. She emphasized the necessity of leveraging available capabilities, resources, and practices to defend Ukrainian interests effectively. Reflecting on a prior interaction with NATO officials in February 2022, she emphasized her urging for UN intervention, suggesting the capability to "close the sky" over Ukraine—an indicative strategy against potential aerial threats.

Stefanishina's exchange with NATO officials revealed a fundamental divergence in interpretation regarding NATO standards. While acknowledging the "appeals of our American partners," she underscored Ukraine's commitment to its defense strategies, mirroring NATO's focus on disrupting infrastructure within Russia to safeguard Ukrainian territories from aerial assaults, including missile production facilities.

Furthermore, Stefanishina provided insights into Ukraine's immediate needs amid escalating hostilities. Commenting on enemy attacks on March 22, she emphasized the imperative for international support, particularly in the provision of weaponry, stating, "Reaction is one thing; we expect weapons first and foremost."

"We do not encourage or enable attacks inside of Russia."

Stefanishina's remarks come in response to alleged calls from the United States to dissuade Ukraine from conducting strikes on Russian refineries. Citing concerns over potential repercussions, including global oil price hikes and retaliatory actions, the US administration has issued repeated warnings to Ukrainian officials.

According to sources familiar with the discussions, these warnings were conveyed directly to senior officials within Ukraine's state security service and its military intelligence directorate. The Financial Times reports that both intelligence units have significantly expanded their drone programs since Russia's full-scale invasion of Ukraine in February 2022.

The White House has reportedly expressed growing frustration over Ukrainian drone attacks targeting oil refineries, terminals, depots, and storage facilities in western Russia. These strikes have impacted Russia's oil production capacity, contributing to a rise in global oil prices, which currently stand at $85 a barrel.

March 21, 2024

THE IRONY OF AMERICAN
EXTREMISM

God Works in Mysterious Ways.

Ukraine, America, and the world await Speaker Mike Johnson to do what is right.

Congresswoman Marjorie Taylor Greene has done her part by putting the Speaker's position in jeopardy and uniting the Democrats behind the Speaker. Politics is the art of what is possible. And it certainly makes for strange bedfellows. More importantly, it is often very ironic. Marjorie Taylor 6Greene may unwittingly enable aid to Ukraine. "Unwittingly" is the magic word. Most of what she does is without wit.

In the meantime, and since the New Year, Ukraine is surviving, not with smoke and mirrors but with greater European help and its own innovation and creativity. President Zelensky is proving himself to be a magician as well as a first-class politician with nerves of steel. He has replaced his surrogates where needed without too much rancor and appeased the dismissed with alternative positions. In fact, without American assistance, Ukraine has inflicted many losses on Russia, including disabling some half of its naval and aerial power, limiting Russian unlawful occupation of international waters, and Russian threats to the world, including the hungry in Africa, with its full control of the Black Sea. Russia is now limited to the eastern part of the Black Sea. Still, Russia continues shelling Ukraine's large cities, such as Kharkiv and Odesa.

President Macron of France and Polish Prime Minister Tusk have stepped up, suggesting the possibility of their own countries' boots on Ukrainian ground. While other NATO members have disavowed that, the proposal remains in light of the very real likelihood that the United States will continue to provide mere band-aids for Ukraine's defense, including the use of the interest on the Russian assets, which are sanctioned repositories.

America continues to inhibit Ukraine's strategy, often embarrassing itself with red lines against Ukraine's legitimate attacks on Russian oil refineries. Even the Republican poster boy for hypocrisy, Senator Lindsey Graham, traveled to Ukraine, seemingly to make amends by proclaiming Ukraine's place in NATO and suggesting anachronistic lend lease alternatives as espoused by his boss, the witless Donald Trump. Furthermore, Graham brazenly encouraged a younger Ukrainian conscription, attempting to cover up his vote in the Senate against aid to Ukraine. Ukrainians were deeply offended by his pomposity.

While there is reason for optimism, there is pessimism as well, and that is being exploited by Russia. Ukrainian society feels betrayed by America. Russia is and will continue to exploit that feeling. The only argument that will entirely stem Ukraine's disillusionment in America's commitment would be immediate and tangible action.

President Biden recently scolded Speaker Johnson for his two-week Easter vacation while the world is in peril and needs American support. Two weeks with little or no ammunition to defend itself is a long time. Passing a bill on aid to Ukraine does not immediately deliver the much-needed ammunition, but it does immediately deliver equally needed moral support. Other steps must be taken in the interim so that the ammunition shells and missiles arrive at Ukraine's border. A previous break at Christmas and now this Easter hiatus simply underscores that Speaker Johnson is a neophyte. Unfortunately, there are few Republicans in the House who can influence Johnson in the right direction.

That influence must be convincing in explaining to Speaker Johnson that this is not a gift to Ukraine. This is an investment not only in the American defense industry but **also** in the jobs of ordinary Americans throughout the United States. Furthermore, it is an investment in global security. Providing old and outdated US weapons to Ukraine is cheaper than maintaining them or even destroying them, as they've outlived their usefulness to the US military. These outdated weapons have to be replenished by American industry and American workers, thus strengthening America's economy. Furthermore, a Ukrainian victory saves American lives because it precludes a war on NATO territory.

My suggestion here is a bipartisan coalition of the sane and moral. There have to be 218 sane and moral members in the House despite the debilitating cynicism and amorality in America today. The best example is the recent introduction by Donald J. Trump of his election campaign Bible at $60 per copy. When Speaker Johnson, a self-proclaimed student of the Holy Bible, saw this display and heard Trump say May America Pray Again, he should have expected Trump to be struck by a bolt of lightning. Fortunately for some and to the disappointment of others, that did not happen. Ultimately, the good in America will prevail. God works in mysterious ways!

"REDLINES"

By Askold S. Lozynskyj

"Chutzpah"

There is no better word to describe and encapsulate the behavior, nearsightedness, arrogance, and shameless rhetoric of the United States in providing assistance to the Ukrainian war effort. While the aid has stopped, the "chutzpah" persists. The current "redlines" coming out of the White House are simply more than the Ukrainians can take. Societal dismay to the point of anger has become pervasive in Ukraine. President Zelensky has been more diplomatic than his people.

There have been so many manifestations of American arrogance and ignorance during the more than two years of Russian aggression. The ignorance is a several generations old and almost inveterate affliction dating back to the 1940s known as appeasement. President Joe Biden is a nice guy, but his refrain, "This is not who we are," is tiresome and not convincing. The rude and abrasive Marjorie Taylor Greene, the hillbilly J. D. Vance and the hypocritical Lindsey Graham are all symptomatic representatives of their constituents. Donald J. Trump is more aberrational on a national level since Americans are generally good people. Judaeo-Christian values still predominate in America, although these so-called values often serve as excuses for hypocrisy. Another component of American malaise and selfishness is illiteracy.

In the contemporary situation, America could argue that it had the right to display arrogance and purported superior military acumen and experience because America was Ukraine's most important and benevolent benefactor and the leader of the Free World. As a result, America limited geographically and strategically the use by Ukraine of American weaponry. America often declined delivery of some specific and advanced weapons, instructing Ukraine that Ukraine did not need those weapons. In this instance, America was proven wrong more often than not. American military leadership often made strategic recommendations as to how Ukraine should conduct the war. Now, that is arrogance.

All of this was inappropriate but justifiable to the Ukrainians since the weapons were American and, especially since, most times, the Ukrainians paid little or no attention to American military strategy, knowing that they (the Ukrainians) certainly knew better. Nevertheless, the Ukrainians did respect one American redline - they did not use American weapons beyond Ukrainian territory.

More recently, Ukraine has increased its strategic bombing of Russian energy refineries and weapon manufacturing and storage facilities using Ukrainian-made weaponry. In view of a tremendous dearth of ammunition, Ukraine has developed greatly its own defense industry.

Nonetheless, America, specifically the White House and the State Department, have criticized these recent bombings, arguing that this will implode the scope of the war and, of more immediate concern, have the effect of increasing global energy prices. Ukraine has been silent instead of telling America to mind its own business.

America has fallen into governmental chaos mainly caused by Republicans in Congress but also due to the inability of the current Democratic administration to navigate through this chaos. Setting redlines for Ukraine without appreciable assistance under these circumstances is "chutzpah."

Ukraine has manifested an exemplary ability to work with what it has, as well as great creativity and wherewithal. Ukraine manufactures its own long-range air and sea drones reaching St. Petersburg, Moscow, and well into the Black Sea so that the western part of the sea has been open for grain transport. Europe has been of much assistance. The U.K. has helped the Ukrainians develop weaponry in Ukraine. Some European leaders have suggested European boots on Ukrainian ground, even if only for training or mine decommissioning purposes.

Psychotic former Russian president Dmitri Medvedev has stated that the Russians would kill those NATO auxiliaries first. That would certainly bring NATO into the war. America would then have to get involved, and so American soldiers would be dying on the Ukrainian steppes.

Ironically, this may prove to be the tragic cure for American governmental chaos, isolationism, and "chutzpah."

April 5, 2024

THE ENEMY WITHIN

Ukraine's NATO Membership is the Best Deterrence to Russian Aggression

"We understand that there's concern about the safety, security, and sovereignty of Ukraine, but the American people have those same concerns about our own domestic sovereignty."

Words spoken by House Speaker Mike Johnson in response to a reporter's inquiry as to why he was holding up aid for Ukraine, certainly a challenge to both his political and Christian "bona fides." I would submit that even a hundred thousand Central American asylum seekers, including women and children, at America's southern border do not measure up to one hundred fifty thousand Russian soldiers armed to the teeth at Ukraine's eastern border as was the case on the eve of Russia's vicious invasion of Ukraine on February 24, 2022.

The extremist Steve Bannon is not happy with Mike Johnson and offered his own tirade against the Speaker for negotiating with the White House, attacking his Christianity and suggesting it be replaced with Islam, thus forming for the Speaker a backbone made of titanium. This is the criminal Steve Bannon, who was charged with siphoning "wall money" for his own purposes, faced prison time, and was saved by a Trump pardon. I should refrain from further criticism of the Speaker despite his poor choice of similes and strange political reasoning. But Speaker Johnson has become unbearable in his fecklessness and hypocrisy.

President Zelensky appeared at the last Davos forum to a most cordial reception, including assurances that the European Union, with its 27 members or with 26 members without Hungary, would approve a 50 billion euro aid to Ukraine package. The EU did.

Separately, the United Kingdom, France, Germany, and Sweden have all stepped up.

However, the lack of American leadership had become a little less a problem for Ukraine as America appears to have reverted to a time not so long ago when Donald Trump was president and American global leadership was not only missing, but the President of the United States himself was ridiculed by most of America's allies. At a recent summit of Ukrainian diaspora global leaders in Bucharest, the prevailing mood was very negative toward America,

A full week has passed since the two-week break of the lower house of the US Congress regarding the implementation of Speaker Johnson's Easter promises. Apparently, with the inspiration of the Resurrection of the Son of God, the deeply religious Speaker promised during the break that he would consider the issue of aid to Ukraine, as he felt it was necessary from a moral point of view. And so, his morality has become dormant once again. After three days, Mr. Speaker decided to meet with his puppeteer. And so, a meeting between Johnson and Trump took place with the topic of aid to Ukraine a minor issue. Trump apparently agreed to give aid to Ukraine in the form of a loan.

What does that mean, and why is this an aberrational phenomenon? Because the person holding the Speaker hostage is Congresswoman Marjorie Taylor Greene whose interviews are often peppered with obscenities and who had been stripped of her committee assignments by her own party. This is not unusual as far as integrity is concerned within the ranks of the Republican party. It's almost as if the Republican party in America is following the script of the AfD in Germany, manifestly supporting Putin and the Kremlin.

President Zelensky often talks of the consequences and points out that Ukraine will lose the war without American help. Perhaps that is not quite so. Ukraine has opened new networks, producing its own weapons, in which Europe helps. Only time will tell if they are sufficient. America, on the other hand, has begun a process of losing its world leadership. Even Israel does not listen to American instructions or admonishments. The truth is that Israel perpetrates war crimes but is surrounded by enemies who refuse to recognize Israel's right to exist. The recent attack on Israeli territory by Iran with more than 300 missiles and drones was both a peril and a major show of strength for Israel. The Iron Dome prevailed, and there was no loss of life or serious damage. American support is an integral part of the of the Israel Defence Force.

We live in quasi-medieval times when power overwhelms what is right, and evil wins over good. Moscow is said to influence events and decisions in the US Congress not unlike Germany. There are many "useful idiots" in Congress, among them the feckless Mike Johnson (often referred to as Moscow Mike), a Ukrainian American neophyte Congresswoman Victoria Spartz who does not support aid to Ukraine now that she is running for re-election, and Senator Lindsey Graham who prefers playing golf with the former president to doing what is right. Congresswoman Marjorie Taylor Greene and Senator J.D. Vance have been so outrageous that they ought to be investigated for Russian contacts, much like some of the members of the AfD in Germany.

This is not a lamentation of a Ukrainian American. This is a direct challenge to honest people. For more than two years, Ukraine has shown extraordinary spiritual and physical strength. What happens next? Military and political setbacks due to a lack of ammunition should be considered temporary and neither fatal nor final. It is necessary to look at the entire perspective optimistically, but with the readiness to assist and there are myriad methods of doing so.

I believe that Americans will come to Ukraine's assistance. A bit of a wake-up call came when Iran bombed Israel unsuccessfully. Senator Vance stressed that Israel is a closer ally than Ukraine. What a ridiculous observation! They are both strategic allies in different theatres. Israel is also much better prepared to fight Iran than Ukraine to fight Russia. Both are equally important. Strategically, Europe is as important as the Middle East. Globally, Russia is certainly more dangerous than Iran.

With Republicans serving as "useful idiots" or even clandestine agents for the enemy, Democrats and the White House have to get creative. There is much flexibility with the Europeans, who are more perspicacious, perhaps because of their proximity to Russia. With some persuasion they will agree to loosen not only Russian sanctioned profits but capital as well. This must happen before the Washington Summit.

The White House needs to send a message that it is willing to offer Ukraine immediate NATO membership. Here President Biden has been so wrong for so long. Offering Ukraine NATO membership will enrage the bully but, at the same time, deter him. The appropriate strategy is not appeasement but deterrence. Ukraine, as a member of NATO, is the best deterrence. Championing that membership will restore American credibility and leadership.

PLAYING BOTH SIDES

Professor Francoise Thom teaches Soviet history and international relations at Paris Sorbonne. In September 2023, she wrote an article entitled 'The Second Front.' The annotation reads as follows:

"According to historian Francoise Thom, Russia has not renounced its original plan to install a pro-Russian government in Kyiv. In pursuit of this goal, not only Ukrainian people are the target of an operation of psychological war, but decision-makers circles in Washington and European capitals are being infiltrated and manipulated. Convincing the Ukrainians that Western support for Ukraine is shaky, discouraging Ukrainians from fighting to victory is now a priority for the Kremlin."

Thus, the "ride" offered to President Zelensky at the beginning of Russia's full-scale "special military operation" should be viewed as something less than a benevolent gesture. Further back in February 2014 the admonition by The White House (President Barrack Obama-AL) that Ukraine not confront the "little green men" in Crimea should be reconsidered as less than genuine concern for Ukrainian lives. Perhaps most importantly the current cooperation between American and Ukrainian intelligence should be a cause for alarm. America is not an honest broker. Russian Foreign Minister Sergei Lavrov communicates with the CIA's Director William Burns or his surrogates on a regular basis. Francoise Thom writes:

"We now understand why Putin chose the term 'special military operation' to designate the war of annihilation of the Ukrainian nation that he planned to wage in that country. The idea was to fool not only the Russians, but also the Americans. It is also clear why Putin literally grew wings after this meeting, to the point of issuing the infamous ultimatum to NATO. Burns had practically given him 'carte blanche' to attack Ukraine, provided he did not attack NATO countries. This disgraceful episode did not prevent the Americans from relaunching 'back-channel diplomacy'. Russian Foreign Minister Sergei Lavrov met for several hours in April (2023-AL) in New York with Richard Haas, a former diplomat and outgoing president of the Council on Foreign Relations, European expert Charles Kupchan and Russian expert Thomas Graham, both former White House and State Department officials and members of the Council on Foreign Relations."

There is a rationale, albeit misplaced, behind this manoeuvring – if Russia does not win the war in Ukraine, Putin's regime will collapse and there will be chaos in Russia, a country with the second largest nuclear arsenal. America does not want this. According to Professor Thom, "This theme had already worked admirably in 1991, when the West (President George H.W. Bush-AL) fearful of chaos, did everything in its power to keep Gorbachev's head above water and dissuade the nations of the USSR from proclaiming their independence."

This is known as the "blackmailing with chaos." With the fall of the Putin regime may come the demise of the Russian Federation and the inherent aspirations to freedom by the constituent currently enslaved nations. This equation has to be neutralized by a renewed tale of the good Russians. This is despite the fact that historically, "good Russians" such as Aleksandr Solzhenitsyn were, despite their dissent, Russian chauvinists. A deeper analysis of the Russian soul is never addressed. Putin's election, while certainly neither democratic nor free, was certainly an expression of the will of the Russian people. There is the representative of Christianity in Russia, Patriarch Kirill who is an agent of Russian Special Services. Much worse than that, there is the Russian mother who is willing to let her sons die so that the empire may live. We may find this bizarre, but it is very real. For some reason, we attribute democratic processes to Russia when they do not exist and never have.

Worse than that we fear Russia's demise and perhaps the Spring of the nations within Russia as apocalyptic.

"Lately, the theme of Russia's apocalyptic collapse in the event of military defeat has become the obligatory commonplace of all experts. Russians from the establishment, theoretically anti-Putin Russians from the diaspora, and Western observers with a propensity to be influenced by Russian analyses, especially when these observers are critical of Putin's policies."

And then there is the anachronistic notion of the good Russians. This notion prevails with American intelligence and such institutions as The New York Times and those dominated by American intelligence as the Jamestown Foundation, the Heritage Foundation, and, much more importantly, the Council on Foreign Relations. There are Ukrainian Americans affiliated with the Council and directly with American intelligence. Some have prominent roles in the Ukrainian American diaspora. They are involved in selling these ideas to the detriment of Ukraine. Wittingly or not is irrelevant. They are "useful idiots."

Professor Thom concludes:

" ...the plan is to demonstrate the power of the pro-Russian lobby and the party of Western appeasers mobilized by the Kremlin for this purpose in the West... In this vein, Pope Francis tops the list. He did not know better than to praise Russian imperialism before the young believers of Saint Petersburg: 'You are the heirs of Great Russia, never forget this heritage'. Such is the gigantic psychological war machine deployed in Russia that Westerners and Ukrainians alike must be aware of this. Once the Kremlin's objectives and "modus operandi" are understood, the game can be won. On the battlefield too."

I traveled to Ukraine immediately following American approval of 61 billion in war aid to Ukraine. The prevailing mood in Ukraine had changed dramatically. It had become almost euphoric and America had recaptured a good portion of its nearly completely lost respect and adulation. Ukrainians became much more confident as well, and this has been manifested most recently on the battlefield, stopping the Russian Kharkiv onslaught, holding off air assaults in major cities, and destroying yet another Russian behemoth in the Black Sea despite the fact that tangible assistance thus far has come only in trickles.

Generally, Ukrainians are fans of America, so the mood swings with each success or failure. It is true that for some time Ukrainian society had been down on America. President Biden's speech about expeditious deliverance was an added factor for optimism. Even in Poland, the feeling was palpable. Ukrainian-Polish friendship may prove to be long-term even on a societal level as long as Ukrainian grain is not an impediment to Polish farmers and the Poles recognize that Ukrainians are dying to defend themselves as well as to protect Europe from the scourge of Russian imperialism. Besides American aid, Prime Minister Tusk has been a major attribute of Polish goodwill.

Following the vote in the House, I wrote to Congresswoman Victoria Spartz, who had voted "nay" on Ukraine. I admonished her for her traitorous behavior towards her country of birth. She did write back, albeit disingenuously and by rote:

"The bill completely failed to include funding for border security, as promised. Additionally, the bill allocates $77B to Ukraine: of that, $61B in budget outlays and $16B in a blank check for drawdowns and loans for any foreign country or international organizations, only $13.8B is dedicated only somewhat to military aid. Further, the Spartz Amendment that would have eliminated the $16B blank check written to President Biden in this supplemental package ultimately failed... It is important to know exactly where every American taxpayer dollar is spent, and this bill's slush fund provides no ability to do so. Congress failed the American people yet again by failing to include any funding for border security in this package."

The Ukrainian American Congresswoman from Indiana failed to mention that she had manifestly and loudly opposed a bipartisan bill submitted by the Senate that did include border security and aid in one package. She did manage to win her Republic primary in her MAGA district.

Congresswoman Spartz is not the only problem in the U.S. Congress. There are members Greene, Jordan, Stefanik, Cruz, Vance, Rubio, and others. Some are disregarded because of their comedic effect, but others are taken seriously. Then there is the frightening specter of Trump in November unless he is incarcerated beforehand on state charges.

The sun came out in Lviv, which is a rare occurrence in April. The city's markets were preparing for Easter Week. Ukrainian baked goods and elaborate Easter eggs (Pysanky) were displayed prominently.

There is another very important factor that played out in Ukraine during the Republican six-month "useful idiocy" on behalf of Russia. Russia exploited the apparent American betrayal. Ukrainian society is very diverse which is a result of opportunity, normal immigration but also centuries of attempted genocide and resettlement. Thus, a family of a Ukrainian wife and a Russian husband or vice versa is quite susceptible to Russian disinformation and propaganda. Russia fed that anxiety in an effort to persuade at least some of the population that opposition is useless and very costly. And there are many elderly remnants of the Soviet past who can acclimate and, at this stage, not present any opposition but simply survive.

Certainly, many, if not most, Ukrainians are not slumbering, lulled into a false sense of security by American apparent goodwill and tangible support. They've learned a hard lesson not only over the last six months when American aid was not forthcoming but also from the past when American F-16s had been promised and not delivered for a year. Ukraine must rely upon itself essentially, producing its own ammunition, including drones. While the future is not bright, it is at least hopeful.

The single most potent weapon Ukraine possesses is the indomitable spirit of its own people. I received a hopeful text from a Ukrainian soldier, a one-arm amputee from the Cherkasy region, that he has been cleared for battle, this time not as infantry but as a sniper.

And so it goes. American military assistance to Ukraine has a two-pronged effect. The first is the weaponry, which can be measured in dollars, and the second is the spirit-lifting effect not only in Ukraine but throughout Europe, which is immeasurable. That is something that the members of the U.S. Congress who voted "nay" on Ukraine seem not to understand.

In the third week of May 2024, Secretary of State Blinken traveled to Kyiv to give Ukraine's President Zelensky a heads-up on the July NATO Summit in Washington. Lest President Zelensky have any illusions of receiving an invite to NATO at the Summit, the Secretary was diplomatic suggesting that Ukrainians will be provided not a timeline but, in essence, an action plan for future membership. Corruption will be the overwhelming, albeit disingenuous, message since Ukraine has certainly manifested its military capability, including arms production, particularly drones. This was not strictly speaking duplicity but political showmanship and a glaring message of President Biden's policy towards Ukraine.

Certainly no one except Blinken himself and his closest colleagues and perhaps President Biden know what is the Secretary's position on Ukraine's NATO membership. He is merely a messenger. Interestingly enough, but undoubtedly President Biden and U.S. intelligence are in charge, indeed. In an election based on an electoral college where one state and several hundred votes can be decisive, President Biden cannot stand to lose the Ukrainian American electorate, but he won't. He often points out that he is running against the alternative, not the Almighty, and the alternative is a narcissist under four indictments on 88 counts who fancies himself a friend and even an acolyte of the Russian thug Vladimir

Putin. Donald Trump is a thug wanna-be.

President Joe Biden's fecklessness should be addressed. Joe Biden owes Ukraine. His debt dates back to the presidency of his former boss, Barack Obama. President Obama will go down in history as the first American black president and father of the Affordable Care Act. He will not be remembered as a competent foreign policy president. You may recall his "off microphone" message to Dmitri Medvedev to "tell Putin."

This is America. Despite being the leader of the Western free world for more than a century, America's population is notoriously primitive when it comes to issues outside its borders. One of America's most respected presidents was Franklin Delano Roosevelt, properly lauded for his social programs but little criticized by history for his ineptness on foreign policy, even more so because his administration was riddled with Soviet agents and Roosevelt was not aware of this, even accompanied by one at the Yalta Summit where the President of the United State served as the ultimate appeaser to Josef Stalin, history's second biggest killer after Mao.

Two issues are quite clear. Firstly, that Ukraine will not be invited nor given a timeline to NATO membership in Washington in July. Ukraine will be given a consolation prize. Secondly, rational Americans may enable President Biden to serve a second term. A large segment of Americans are primitive in foreign affairs, but a larger segment are essentially good and moral people, which means that even if they do not understand foreign policy or Geo-strategic issues, they recognize that it is wrong for Ukrainian children to die as a result of Russian aggression.

These are some consolation suggestions, hopefully, interim substitutes for an actual NATO invite. Most importantly, America must allow Ukraine to formulate the war strategy, and America should simply respond to Ukrainian requests positively. Ukraine needs a quasi-iron dome as the United States provided for Israel. NATO missiles, as long as they are fired from NATO territory, should be used to bring down Russian missiles and drones fired at Ukrainian targets. An important part of this is the defensive "Patriots," which have been distributed much less than generously, while many remain in NATO countries, not under attack. President Zelensky has asked for only seven more. America should not prescribe where and what Ukrainians may attack, nor whether Ukrainians may use American weapons to hit Russian territories. Russian oil refineries on Russian territory are not only fair game but strategically important. World oil prices pale in comparison with Ukrainian lives. Even American generals are not prepared to tell Ukraine how to fight its war. So much less qualified is President Biden or anyone at the White House or State.

Moving forward it is important to recognize that this Ukraine-America relationship is an alliance of equals. There is a quid pro quo on each side. The Ukrainian side is defending all of Europe at the cost of its own human lives. America is supplying money, mostly arms, investing not only in global security but also enhancing its own defence industry. While President Biden has stressed this many times, his behavior often has been arrogant, particularly through his surrogates. Arrogance and fecklessness are mutually exclusive. Allies need to recognize their roles. Ukraine's mandate is to prevail against Russian aggression; America's is to supply what Ukraine needs. This would be so much clearer if Ukraine was invited to join NATO.

And so, America's political game with Russia continues. Remember the tale of the good Russians. Unfortunately, to borrow from the bard, "It is a tale told by an idiot, full of sound and fury, signifying nothing." More unfortunately, there are far too many innocent victims of both this game and tale.

April 20, 2024

PEARLS OF WISDOM MORE OF THE SAME

A friend of mine from Canada alerted me to yet another display of egregious ignorance by a Republican elected official, this time, as high as a Senator. His name is Tom Tuberville and this is what he said: "He (Putin-AL) didn't want Ukraine. He didn't want Europe. Hell, he's got enough land of his own. He just wants to make sure he does not have US weapons in Ukraine."

And so, I replied casually, perhaps jokingly, to my friend, "Hey, he is a football coach, probably has been hit in the head many times without a helmet. Frankly, elected officials at the Senate level should be required to take an IQ test before being permitted to run for such a high office."

One of the Republican party's senior representatives, Senator Lindsey Graham, attempted damage control by suggesting that the position of the Senator from Alabama was an outlier within the Party. I suspect that rational people in America and the world remember the Helsinki press conference in the Summer of 2018 with then-President Donald J. Trump and President Vladimir Putin at the podiums. President Trump was asked about Russia's interference in the U.S. 2016 elections, asserted unequivocally that he asked Putin whether this was true; Putin denied it, and then Trump acquiesced, "I do not see why that is not so."

Senator Tuberville is a creation of Donald Trump. He may be an embarrassment, but this is the Republican Party today.

Still, this is only part of the problem. The "extreme right," as often referred to in today's political jargon, is a danger not only within the United States but in Europe as well. The common denominator is often migration and, at the very least, appeasement towards Russia and Putin and, in many instances, an affinity. Why is that? Thugs support each other.

228

Adolf Hitler supported Mussolini and Franco and vice versa. Frankly, Stalin and Hitler were allies in 1939 pursuant to the Molotov-Ribbentrop pact. Had the Germans not betrayed the Soviets, who knows how long the alliance would have lasted? Hitler precipitated his own demise.

Donald Trump is in that same category. He is a narcissistic autocrat by training, in this case as a businessman and television celebrity. He has no political or intellectual skills. And yes, global domination is a regional concept, so the autocracy of others abroad can be accepted. Trump does not wish to rule the world. He does not even know it.

Recently, I wrote an article on a similar theme and sent it by email to almost one thousand addresses. Inadvertently, I exposed the emails of my addressees. There was an immediate reaction not to what I had written but to the exposure of email addresses. I soon realized that the reason for the volcanic disapproval by some was that I had exposed them as Trump supporters. I call them Trumsheviks in the vein of Bolsheviks.

I ended the brouhaha by apologizing without remorse and suggesting that each individual and, in particular, those who were apoplectic about my denouement, take some time to make of list of what they had done for Ukraine, particularly over the last two war years. Not surprisingly, that concluded the uproar.

Ukraine and Ukrainians are today in great peril. The war has turned a bit recently, and it appears that the city of Kharkiv is safe, America is delivering as promised, and so is Europe. Ukraine is making incredible strikes even on Russian territory. However, a long-term war, which this one undoubtedly will prove to be, like anything else of some duration, has its ebbs and flows. Long term, Ukraine can overcome Putin and the Russians for the moment, but it cannot survive a betrayal or lack of support from the West or its own diaspora.

Tommy Tuberville may be an Alabama football coach, something less than a rocket scientist, but there is no excuse for many members of the Ukrainian diaspora. My admonishment and simultaneous opprobrium rest on the fact that these Ukrainian Trumpsheviks are stubborn in their allegiances. The Republicans today are like Tommy Tuberville and not like Abraham Lincoln, Dwight D. Eisenhower, or Ronald Reagan, who decried isolationism in his speech forty years ago in Normandy on D-day. I have to say, wake up.

Finally, I would like to address the bulk of the Ukrainian diaspora community, which traditionally sits on the fence and often attends cultural events or even political discussions, which serve to feed a feeling of being involved. Every person in the diaspora has a role to play. No role consists of verbal support. Tangible support is mandatory. We are all very fortunate, by the grace of God, to live at a time when we matter.

June 11, 2024

GOOD NEWS ON THE UKRAINE FRONT

Recent events in and around Ukraine have improved substantially since America re-assumed its leadership role. In fact, on the battlefield, Ukraine has stopped the Russian onslaught in the Northeast near the city of Kharkiv, and Ukrainian defense systems most recently knocked out 29 out of 30 Russian drones and missiles. Ukraine was the primary subject of the G7 Summit in Italy, concluding with a ten-year Security Agreement signed between the United States and Ukraine. Ukraine was the main subject at a NATO convocation of defense leaders in Brussels. Internally, Ukraine stepped up, announcing further privatization of its state-owned assets, which not only may bring in valuable currency but diminish governmental corruption provided auctions are conducted in a uniform and transparent manner. Much of this may be difficult to evaluate at this stage but will be more prime for analysis in the near future.

These issues are not only about Ukraine. Europe and the United States are in focus very much. Europe because of the recently concluded European Union elections and imminent parliamentary elections in both the United Kingdom and France, and the United States, with elections not only for the president but both houses of Congress in November. These are all sobering factors.

Even the recently signed US-Ukraine Security Agreement is quite elusive as it depends on the November elections. Specific matters such as the use of profits from Russian-sanctioned capital for Ukraine's reconstruction have, at the very least, moved forward with all parties agreeing. China, with its duplicitous policies towards Russia, remains not so much a conundrum but more so a work in progress, which, hopefully, may be swayed for the sake of its economy.

America recently imposed new sanctions on China. Whether they work is mostly an issue of economic opportunity. China needs the West to buy its goods. It also needs Russia for energy supply and perhaps a politically strategic alliance against the United States. Strategic alliances between autocratic states are always ephemeral. In this case, America must be smart by not antagonizing the Chinese with additional tariffs yet maintaining its resolve towards Taiwan. There are plenty of differences between Russia and China that can be exploited.

In any event the symbolism of Ukraine's peril and its needs are very much apparent globally. Even some right-wingers within the European community have expressed their support in favor of Ukraine and much in opposition to Russia. Certainly, a democratic European continent united under the umbrella of the EU plus the United Kingdom is not only preferable to any form of autocracy, such as more than a decade of rule by one man, as in Hungary.

Ukraine, despite the accusations of corruption, has managed throughout little more than its 30-year history to excel in pursuing democratic processes, elections, and a peaceful transition of power. In two instances, there was a problem, but the people of Ukraine prevailed each time, and that is what democracy means.

Two matters need to be addressed when analyzing Ukraine. One is the nonsense that Ukraine is not ready for NATO. The second is that Ukraine is abnormally corrupt.

The first has been debunked seriously over the last two years. Ukraine is the paramount military force in Europe today. The war has not only manifested Ukrainian military resolve but wherewithal as well. Ukraine's soldiers are military-ready, and Ukraine's defense industry has stepped up, manufacturing much of what it needs, including cost-efficient weapons. Russia has proven to be somewhat of a paper tiger, primarily due to Ukraine's efficiency and the sacrifice of the entire population, as well as Western help with supplies, but not on the field of battle. Ukraine will not be invited to NATO at the Washington Summit in July, not because it is not ready, but because of politics, and in this case, misled politics.

Corruption is the other issue. Ukraine is a descendant of a Soviet society predicated entirely on corruption. In a Communist system boasting of equality there was an oligarchy known as the Communist party. All others had to fend for themselves. You could not survive unless you stole in one form or another. After only thirty years, and with much of the oligarchy remaining in place, Ukraine has made tremendous progress in this regard.

In 1997 I attended a Congress in Lviv of Ukrainian attorneys from all over the world. The biggest difference between former Soviet attorneys from Ukraine and those from the West was that the former insisted that the duty of attorneys was to protect the interests of the state, while the latter argued that the role was to protect the interests of the individual from the overreaching of the state. Such was a diametrically different understanding of the rule of law. That Soviet culture prevailed for a long time.

I am an American attorney. I am 72 years old. I remember that two hundred years after the Declaration of Independence, law enforcement and low-level government officials were susceptible to bribery. Even today members of the Supreme Court and the Senate of the United States are open to bribes. Let's not stop there. While Donald J. Trump was in the White House, his daughter accrued more than a few trademarks in China. His son-in-law has become a billionaire with Saudi money since his White House tenure. The President himself reaped the benefits of having a hotel close to the White House. My message to American detractors of Ukraine on the issue of corruption is to look at ourselves and then cast the first stone.

June 13, 2024

SEARCHING FOR SUBSTANCE

The NATO Summit in Washington had two purposes: to recognize the 75 years of NATO, strengthen the defensive alliance, and substantively help Ukraine. The first was fanfare although its purpose was to encourage the remaining one-third of NATO nations to spend on military more than 2% of its GDP. The remaining one-third includes some serious members, such as France and Germany, but also less serious members, such as Canada, Slovenia, Spain, Belgium, and extremely wealthy Luxembourg. Granted that Canada has an ocean as a buffer.

Nevertheless, with the Trump assassination attempt, NATO must take into account that the United States will be missing in action as to Europe's defense against Russia. Senator J.D. Vance, now a candidate for Vice President under Trump, posted about two hours after the incident: "Today is not just some isolated incident. The central premise of the Biden campaign is that President Donald Trump is an authoritarian fascist who must be stopped at all costs. That rhetoric led directly to President Trump's attempted assassination."

It is interesting that the shooter was a Republican and clearly an advocate for the Second Amendment, more so because he used an automatic weapon. For Senator Vance, an original hillbilly from Kentucky, that type of refutation of his assertion would be clouding the issues with facts. The Senator is not very cognitive when dealing with that type of argument despite his age.

This is clearly not what America is about, and the election is certainly not over, but for the next three and a half months, that will be the MAGA message. Senator Vance is so clearly an extremist, but his message will resound.

And so it's relevant to consider NATO without the United States or, at the very least, without tangible American support.

The Washington Summit NATO statement was strong on Ukraine, but did it have substance? What exactly does "irreversible" mean?

"Taken forward the establishment of the NATO-Ukraine Joint Analysis, Training, and Education Centre (JATEC), an important pillar of practical coop. We fully support Ukraine's right to choose its own security arrangements and decide its own future, free from outside interference. Ukraine's future is in NATO. Ukraine has become increasingly interoperable and politically integrated with the Alliance. We welcome the concrete progress Ukraine has made since the Vilnius Summit on its required democratic, economic, and security reforms. As Ukraine continues this vital work, we will continue to support it on its irreversible path to full Euro-Atlantic integration, including NATO membership. We reaffirm that we will be in a position to extend an invitation to Ukraine to join the Alliance when the Allies agree and conditions are met. The Summit decisions by NATO and the NATO-Ukraine Council, combined with Allies' ongoing work, constitute a bridge to Ukraine's membership in NATO. Allies will continue to support Ukraine's progress on interoperability as well as additional democratic and security sector reforms, which NATO Foreign Ministers will continue to assess through the adapted Annual National Programme."

Frankly, within the NATO Charter, probably, no member state can explain what "irreversible" means. In addition or subtraction, the limitation on the range of armaments delivered by the United States and Germany was not removed. And so, Russia is relatively safe from NATO weapons.

It was a bad week. NATO gave Ukraine no substance, Donald J. Trump became a martyr, and J.D. Vance became a candidate for VP under Trump, a Kremlin Dream Team. Perhaps my callousness as to the assassination attempt is palpable, although I am very sensitive to the fact that a human being died and several were injured in the attack.

There is a tremendous irony in all of this. There was a Summit, essentially for Ukraine, giving Ukraine little, if any, substantial relief. There was a tragic assassination attempt by a Republican who was an advocate of the 2nd Amendment and utilized automatic weapons, a vignette of America under Trump. The pictures are bizarre: Ukraine is no better off, and Donald Trump will run for office as a martyr of the movement that he created with a VP that must have been toasted in Moscow.

July 16, 2024

PRESIDENT KAMALA HARRIS

Kamala Harris, the most likely Democratic candidate for the Presidency of the United States in November 2024, presents the following qualifications: current Vice President under President Joe Biden, formerly a four-year Senator from the State of California and six years the Attorney General of the State of California. Aside from these qualifications, these are some of her attributes: she is a Black and Asian woman. Her election would be historic for the United States the minute she is elected and as soon as she is sworn in. America has never had a woman president, white or otherwise. It is long overdue.

Philip H. Gordon is the National Security Adviser for Kamala Harris. He is certain to play a significant role in the upcoming Administration of President Kamala Harris. In a recent interview with the President of the Council on Foreign Relations, he characterized the Russian invasion of Ukraine over two years ago as the biggest land war in Europe that we've faced since World War II with tremendous geopolitical consequences—threatening other close allies in Europe and NATO; driving up energy prices, food prices; disrupting supply chains. He went on to say:

"I mean, first I would...take a step back...going back to...February '22, or even before that when we had intelligence that Russia was going to invade that many doubted, and we shared with our allies, we shared with the Ukrainians, and we put the world on notice that this was going to happen, it did happen. And then we immediately kicked into gear and helped the Ukrainians prevent, essentially, a Russian takeover of all of Ukraine. That was their plan. That was their assumption, that they would be able to do it. Many people thought they were right. But we were determined to prove them wrong, surged in military assistance and political assistance, put a huge coalition together, hit the Russian economy hard with sanctions... I give the most credit to the Ukrainian people for their valiant fight against Russia, but far from taking Kyiv, they got stopped. They not only got stopped, they pushed—they got pushed back. They ended up taking some territory in the east, but even that the following year—in large part thanks to our assistance, and no one has provided more assistance than the United States—we helped the Ukrainians prevent a Russian takeover of Kyiv, put together a coalition of some fifty countries who are all involved in supporting Ukraine. And, you know, almost two and a half years after this Russian invasion with the intent to occupy Kyiv, Ukraine is a democratic country with support and solidarity from around the world that is standing tall and proud in the face of Russian aggression. So I think, again, first credit goes to the Ukrainians for their fight. But I think the United States and our allies around the world have also done a remarkable job in providing support to Ukraine...And with aid flowing in to come to the rescue and make clear to Putin that he may have thought he was able to wait us out, but he is not going to be able to. Last point,... what about the criticism that you haven't done enough? We have very few restrictions on what Ukraine can do or on what we provide to Ukraine. It's true that some of this has evolved over time as battlefield needs have changed, as our available resources have changed, and as things have become available that couldn't have been provided earlier that we're able to provide now. To the point that you know, whatever category of weapon you might be interested in, we're essentially providing it to Ukraine now. So I don't think—I don't think it's right to suggest that somehow our policy or what we are doing is preventing Ukraine from doing what it needs to do, which is to continue to stand up in the face of this Russian aggression."

The question that Mr. Gordon both answered and avoided was: "There's been some critique from some quarters of the administration that, you know, restrictions on Ukrainian use of U.S.-

supplied arms maybe should be lifted. There's been some questions... that too little, too late. Does the administration need to rethink its strategy on Ukraine?"

Well, that's to be expected, and it's both good and bad news. Granted that if Gordon had suggested a waiver of restrictions or even, at the very least, a timetable for Ukraine's membership in NATO, he would have been critical of Biden's policies. Lack of timely delivery of weapons was not a policy issue but a logistical, nevertheless, often a very costly one for Ukraine and Ukrainians. Nonetheless, Gordon was diplomatic.

The paradigm very often repeated by President Joe Biden is that he was not running against the Almighty but against Trump. Trump was and remains a buffoon and a charlatan. Prosecuting the case against Trump should result in a tremendous windfall for candidate Harris as a former prosecutor.

In any event, what Ukraine needs from the Harris administration is the removal of any geographic and other restrictions on the use of American weaponry, timely delivery, a reasonable response to Ukraine's requests for various weapons, recognizing that Ukraine understands its strategic military needs better than all of America's top generals put together and finally a timeline for Ukraine's NATO membership. NATO membership must be accorded even if that includes that membership will not be granted for the duration of the current war or in the alternative with a provision that Ukraine's NATO membership would not allow it to invoke Article 5 during the current war. "Irreversible" cannot be defined.

Finally, President Joe Biden deserves much praise not only for withdrawing from the presidential race, which he probably could not win but also for his more than half a century of public service. Every human has flaws. But Joe Biden was and is essentially a good and honest man, ambitious but with an unselfish personality and a giving nature. As far as I am concerned his only flaw was a level of politeness or even fecklessness. As a VP, he was not able to steer American foreign policy via a junior senator who historically became America's first black president. History will never denounce, much less criticize, Barrack Obama, but in foreign policy, he was a disaster. He simply had no knowledge or expertise. Biden was too polite to tell him so or President Obama was too sure of himself without the necessary acumen and experience. As a result, the world suffered. Ukraine lost 17% of its territory. That aside, Joe Biden will go down in American and World history as one of its greatest leaders.

Looking towards the future, President Kamala Harris will be a historic figure when elected. Her mission is to work hard, take advice, be tough on principles, but be compassionate. If she does that, then she will become historical not only because of her chromosomes and the color of her skin but because of her legacy for America and the world.

July 25, 2024

NEGLIGENCE AND ITS CONSEQUENCES

As the world knows, Moscow rockets recently hit a children's hospital in the capital of Ukraine, Kyiv. Two people died, and almost fifty were injured. The New York Times reported a few days later that among the components of those missiles were American parts purchased through Hong Kong. This was supported by the fact that although America has imposed significant sanctions on trading with the Kremlin or its surrogates, America and many in the West continue to trade with countries such as China, India, and others. In this case, these American parts were sold to an international firm in Hong Kong, and upon closer inspection, it turned out that the human components of those firms were Russians.

This may be just an American lack of attention and implementation. America and Americans of capitalist view are much intoxicated by the concept of economic profit and such cases often occur, in particular in government circles, which are not only not the most competent, but are also very accommodating in accepting money for personal largesse. Obviously, business has little principles or morals, even when it comes to the consequences on children.

Even more so this can be said about such buyers as China and India, the two most populous countries in the world. The Paramount Leader of China recently held meetings with both the President of the United States and the President of the Russian Federation. In China, human and national rights are not respected, and in fact, the Chinese regime is actively committing genocide against the Uighurs of the Islamic faith. True, at the last session of NATO, China was recognized as a belligerent state, but those were just words.

Regarding India and its Prime Minister Modi, who also recently visited Putin in the Kremlin, and only a month earlier, he visited

Washington not on a working visit but on a state visit with all the parade fanfare. Prime Minister Modi is a popular Hindu leader of India who unabashedly carries out genocide on people of the Islamic faith in his territory and adjacent locations. This is incongruous since many Indians are of the Islamic faith.

Politics rarely possesses moral attributes. But the situation with a disregard for sanctions resulting in even a modicum of contribution by America in killing Ukrainians, and Ukrainian children among them, is a very serious problem. The New York Times, based on its research, goes on to show that the Kyiv Children's Hospital was not an aberration but that American military components found a place in the Russian Federation and later in Ukraine in the amount of billions of dollars.

Perhaps for a simple but less awful understanding of this problem, I give a local example. In the state of New Jersey, where I live, I noticed at least three places where the Moscow gasoline company Lukoil still stands and trades. True, I did not go there due to laziness, but I saw a few buyers, albeit rarely, because the price was high. This probably means that there is a gap between the sanctions where Moscow gasoline goes. I don't know if anyone is following this, and that's why I'm setting for myself a mission against Lukoil in New Jersey. I urge all Ukrainian Americans to follow.

And so here is another recent example, albeit less devastating, where Ukraine fought against extraordinary obstacles. It's more for personal respite; although I was so stressed, I thought I was on the verge of a heart attack. We Ukrainians are truly unconquered or indomitable. This is evident every day on the battlefield, where we repel Moscow missiles with Ukrainian and Western weapons.

I was extremely impressed by the Ukrainian junior football team at the Olympic Games against the Arab country of Morocco. Ukraine finally won 2 to 1. But what a competition it was! No highlight film can measure the greatness of this victory. The stadium was filled with the red colors of the Arabs. Ukrainians in Europe, wake up! Ukraine led 1 to 0 at halftime. The referee added 5 minutes to the first half as if to give Morocco an opportunity since the Ukrainians were killing time. At the beginning of the second half, a player from Morocco found himself with the ball in front of the goal of Ukraine. He was stopped by a Ukrainian competitor grabbing him from behind. Not only was Morocco awarded a penalty, but the Ukrainian player received a red card, which meant that the Ukrainian team would play the second half without one player, i.e., 10 v 11. Morocco pressed after a successful penalty, but the Ukrainians held on. Such was the pressure from the Moroccan side that the referee gave them an unheard-of 12 more minutes added to the second half. Ironically, it was not Morocco who scored the second goal in those 12 minutes, but the Ukrainians. In the end, even though this was completely prejudiced by my perception referee had to end the competition. Ukraine won despite all obstacles.

This is the history of the Ukrainian people. They survive. A soccer competition is a levity for the most part, but a children's hospital in Kyiv or anywhere is a grave matter. Ukrainians appear indomitable, but failure to implement directives or recklessness in this regard on the part of not only the world but also Ukraine's allies and friends, especially America, must be considered, investigated, and remediated.

July 27, 2024
Askold S. Lozynskyi

THE CASE AGAINST A DIPLOMATIC SOLUTION TO THE WAR IN UKRAINE

History has shown that there is no diplomatic solution because Russia and Vladimir Putin are not partners in diplomacy.

War is hell! Peace is clearly the preferred alternative. Those are axioms. Surprisingly, in view of the aggressor, peace without victory is no peace at all. Lasting peace depends on many factors. A temporary ceasefire or a temporary peace is an illusion when the aggressor partner is an uncivilized and criminal side with a history of not only aggression but brutality, war crimes, and no regard for international institutions or the rule of a just law. A lasting peace is clearly the preferred alternative. But what does that mean and how do you attain that?

How many lasting peace agreements have we had in history? Hitler and the West engineered one whereby Hitler was accommodated, took Sudetenland, and then simply pursued his aggression. And another whereby both authoritarians took territory pursuant to Molotov-Ribbentrop resulting in no peace but occupation for many. Then Hitler attacked his counterpart. Is that ancient history? Maybe history does indeed repeat itself, but only because people, particularly of good faith, simply repeat mistakes of history, naively or for the sake of short-term solutions that have an effect only on the next political election.

America's peace with the Taliban and withdrawal from Afghanistan was a fiasco, not only because of the way it went about but because America negotiated with the Taliban and not a legitimate good-faith side. Aside from the sacrifices during the withdrawal, Afghanistan is no better off today than it was before America went in following September 11, 2001.

Even in the most recent prisoner exchange, the terms of the deal were bizarre. Russia released human rights activists and journalists, while the West released killers. This does not mean that the exchange was not the way to go for the sake of the prisoners themselves and their families. Unfortunately, this emboldens tyrants and criminals. In Putin's mind, send out assassins; if they get caught, arrest the innocent and arrange for a prisoner exchange. Thus, long term this was a bad deal. Yet, we live in the present.

Peace attained by accommodation is an ephemeral one replete with anxiety because war may erupt again at any minute. This is probably to be expected and worse relatively than the tragic certainties of war. Why would anyone sign on to a peace agreement knowing that the other side is definite to violate the terms of the agreement?

Such is the current reality in Ukraine with a ruthless, totally inhuman, and uncivilized Russian Empire as Ukraine's neighbor and concurrently forever an aggressor. The regime in Russia is brutal even towards its own people, including Russians and, in particular, the non-Russians on its ill-gotten territory.

Anna Politkovskaya, the highly regarded Russian journalist (she was actually Ukrainian with a maiden surname of Mazepa) was critical of Putin's regime in particular since the regime slaughtered indiscriminately the Chechen people during the two wars. She was murdered in 2006 without regard to public opinion in Russia or the West's opprobrium. Frankly, public opinion in Russia is not relevant. The dark Russian soul, if there is one (yes, the soul of Dostoevsky and Raskolnikov), has historically and continues to be a peril to freedom-loving people everywhere. When learning of Politkovskaya's death, Vladimir Putin said that she had no effect on Russian politics but that her killing would be investigated thoroughly. And so we wait for the results of that investigation. But what results can be expected when the order comes from the Kremlin itself?

Politkovskaya recognized that Russians themselves within the Russian Federation are essentially slaves of the governing regime similar to Czarist and Soviet times. What she did not see was that such is Russian culture. Even worse, there are some 150 other nationalities in the RF who are below that level. Politkovskaya wrote extensively about the Chechens, but the same would apply to the Bashkirs, Buryats, Sakha, Tatars, Erzya, and many others. In the current war, these nationalities are mostly on the front lines, essentially canon fodder. But their national identity is becoming palpable and more clearly defined. Those Chechens, and now the Bashkirs, Buryats, Sakhas, Tatars, Erzya, and others, are creating structures such as the Free Nations' League, availing themselves of America's Captive Nations' legislation to tell their story. They wish to be free. For that to happen, there is no room for a Russian Empire. This is not a story for another time. This is the current reality.

The supreme leader of Russia, Vladimir Putin, has suggested negotiations for settlement of the war, prefacing his offer with self-imposed red lines that, in addition to Crimea, the regions of Luhansk, Donetsk, Kherson, and Zaporizzhia be ceded to Russia, that Ukrainians withdraw their troops from those regions and Ukraine renounce any ambition to join NATO. Naturally, no one has or would take this proposal seriously.

However, consider an alternative proposal more towards Ukraine's side but nonetheless bizarre: a cessation of hostilities, a return of all occupied Ukrainian territory, including Crimea, but with a Ukrainian renunciation of NATO membership. Why is this not a serious option? Because Russia would continue to be a threat to Ukraine, but now even more so because of Ukraine's NATO renunciation. In the interim, Russia and Putin would cease to be pariahs, sanctions would be lifted, and perhaps even the arrest warrant of the International Criminal Court against Putin rescinded. Business would begin to go on as usual.

Except for the fact that at least one hundred thousand Ukrainians have died, and Ukrainian reconstruction costs are in the vicinity of several hundred billion dollars. Ukraine would not be able to rely on NATO membership or assistance from NATO member countries. Russia, irrespective of any promises not to attack, would certainly attack again because that is the nature of Russia. Agreements or treaties are not worth the paper on which they are written. Putin should take this deal if only to rehabilitate Russia himself and forge a path for an easier genocide against the Ukrainian people only a few months from now.

Two and a half years is a long time, especially when you are living with constant sirens in your ears and loved ones dying. I suppose that living in America, it is easy for me to say that there is no diplomatic solution ultimately.

But there is not. Russia is beyond diplomacy. The entire world needs victory. The Russian Empire has to be dismantled with independent countries like Chechnya, Bashkortostan, Tatarstan, Erzya, Sakha, and others in its place. Sure, there is room for a Russian country, but not an empire. Ukraine has to join NATO and, in fact, become one of its leading members, given its experience. Resolute action is the only rational solution to the peril the entire world faces: Russian aggression.

The world has to be more compassionate, meaning cognizant of the suffering of others, but less tolerant of Russian crimes. People are not born evil, whether you believe they are simply a result of procreation and gene transference or God's creativity. It is important to recognize that Vladimir Putin did not make Russia evil. Russian history and culture made Putin so. After Putin will come another Putin or Stalin or Czar Peter or Ivan the Terrible. A civilized world cannot allow for such a global affliction and its perpetuation.

War is hell, but often an opportunity to cleanse. World War 2 cleansed the world of Hitler and Nazism, unfortunately leaving behind an equally heinous counterpart. But it did rid the world of one scourge, and Germany is a very different country today. The opportunities presented by the current war in Ukraine are very similar: to rid the world of the Russian imperialistic scourge. A diplomatic solution is not only dangerous but also irrational.

POST SCRIPTUM NOTES

Adolph Hitler entered into two major agreements, one with the West and the other with the Soviet Union, before commencing his all-out aggression against his neighbors: the Munich Agreement of 1938 and the Molotov–Ribbentrop Pact of 1939.

The Munich Agreement was an agreement reached in Munich on September 30, 1938, by Nazi Germany, the United Kingdom, the French Republic, and Fascist Italy. The agreement provided for the German annexation of part of Czechoslovakia called the Sudetenland, where more than three million people, mainly ethnic Germans, lived.

The Molotov–Ribbentrop Pact, officially the Treaty of Non-Aggression between Germany and the Union of Soviet Socialist Republics, was a non-aggression pact between Nazi Germany and the USSR with a secret protocol that partitioned between them Central and Eastern Europe. This resulted in the occupation of Poland, the Baltic states—Lithuania, Latvia, Estonia—and Finland and Romania. The pact was signed in Moscow on August 23, 1939, by German Foreign Minister Joachim von Ribbentrop and Soviet Foreign Minister Vyacheslav Molotov.

A portion of Poland was Western Ukraine. The Soviets came into Western Ukraine and slaughtered and arrested people indiscriminately. According to witnesses, the Soviet occupation of Western Ukraine was a display of brutality never before witnessed by the inhabitants, Ukrainian and Polish. On June 19, 1941, the Nazis entered Western Ukraine. Their occupation was considered initially by many to be a brief respite from the Soviets.

Anna Politkovskaya was born to a Soviet Ukrainian diplomat and his wife in New York City in 1958. Her birth ethnicity was not very important to her apparently, as in her writings, she refers to herself as Russian. She was the child of a Soviet bureaucrat since there was no Ukrainian foreign policy or diplomacy. The Ukrainian SSR Mission to the United Nations was merely a prop to increase the number of votes of the USSR at the UN General Assembly and other UN bodies.

In fact, in her writings, she refers to Ukraine only in geographic references. It would appear that, by choice, she was Russian. This does not detract from her courage and integrity, as the USSR was not a melting pot but a cauldron intended to make all of the nationalities Russian.

The particular irony here is that her birth surname was Mazepa. There are few, if any, Russians with that surname. Hetman Ivan Mazepa was the leader of the Ukrainian Cossacks in the late XVII and early XVIII centuries who rose up against Czar Peter I of the Muscovite state and, together with the Swedish King Charles, was defeated by the Muscovites at the Battle of Poltava in 1709.

The Muscovite Orthodox Church issued a condemnation of Mazepa which stands until today. Prior to the Poltava battle in 1708, the Ukrainian Hetman's capital, Baturyn, was destroyed and leveled. This event is considered the first attempt at Ukrainian genocide by the Muscovites. Czar Peter then assumed the name Russia from the ancient Ukrainian capital Kyiv Rus as the name of his empire, the Russian Empire.

Hetman Mazepa became a legendary figure in world poetry. English poet Lord Byron glorified Mazepa in his poem entitled "Mazeppa."

Since the proclamation of an independent Ukraine, Ukraine has signed many agreements with Russia, most recently the two Minsk Agreements signed after Russia's initial incursion into Crimea and the Donetsk and Luhansk regions. Russia never adhered to either Minsk treaty.

In April 2010, two months after he took office and swore

allegiance to Ukraine's Constitution, Ukrainian President Victor Yanukovych signed an extension of a lease agreement for the Russian Black Sea Fleet in Sevastopol, Crimea. Russia did not adhere to this most favorable-to-Russia agreement when they occupied all of Crimea in February 2014 and annexed it by a specious referendum in March 2014.

The two most significant agreements signed between Ukraine and Russia were the Budapest Memorandum and the Ukraine–Russia Friendship Treaty, as both guaranteed sovereignty and inviolability of borders. The Budapest Memorandum was signed by Russia, the United Kingdom, and the United States in December 1994.

It held that none of the signatories would threaten or use force against Ukraine's territorial integrity or political independence. It also pledged that none of them would use economic coercion to subordinate Ukraine to their own interest. The memorandum was a result (quid pro quo) of Ukraine's agreement to give up its nuclear weapons and transfer them to Russia for dismantlement.

The Treaty on Friendship, Cooperation, and Partnership between Ukraine and the Russian Federation was an agreement between Ukraine and Russia, signed in 1997, which fixed the principle of strategic partnership, the recognition of the inviolability of existing borders, and respect for territorial integrity and mutual commitment not to harm the security of each other.

Budapest and the Friendship were striking examples of both Ukraine's early naivete and Russia's historic and persevering mendacity.

Select Sources:

The Munich Agreement of 1938.

The Molotov Ribbentrop Pact of 1939.

Budapest Memorandum, 1994.

Treaty on Friendship, Cooperation and Partnership between Ukraine and the Russian Federation.

Dissolution of the Russian Empire, Ed. By Y. Syrotyuk, Y. Olinyk, O. Chupak, Kyiv, Ukrainian Publishing Activity, 2024, 328 p.

Politkovskaya, Anna, Putin's Russia: Life in a Fading Democracy, Owl Books, Henry Holland Company, Translation Edition2004.

Politkovskaya, Anna, Is Journalism Worth Dying For? Final Dispatches, Melville House, Translation Edition, March 16, 2011, 480p.

THE SIGNIFICANCE OF UKRAINIAN STRIKES WITHIN RUSSIA

The Russian Belgorod or the Kursk regions are ethnically and historically Ukrainian regions. Most recently, the residents accepted the Ukrainian flag with the words, "Whatever, as long as we are safe." Ukraine has downplayed the event. Russia has manifested some concern, but with customary bravado and threats. The United States has approved the incursion as being within the limitations imposed on U.S. arms. What are the short and long-term implications?

Frankly, who knows? Anyone who suggests that he/she knows is simply guessing. This is the second or third of many such attacks to come. Or perhaps Russia will better defend its territory. In any event the obvious consensus would have to be that Russia is very vulnerable.

The myth about Russia is much greater than reality. It is, in part, based on Russian arrogant behavior internationally as well as fear that Russia is the world's second-largest nuclear power. The question that must be asked is whether those matter. Any answer would be a guess. Would Russia solicit a nuclear Armageddon with initial use?

In any event, the only solution to the current war is the dissolution of the Russian Empire, leaving behind only a Russian state with clearly defined borders. That Russia would not be a global threat. It would be surrounded by many nations that, in the past, had experienced Russian brutality and, therefore, would impose a mandate upon their new governments to arm to the teeth against any possible Russian revenge.

"Realpolitik" is the real issue here because that concept has an entirely new meaning. Nothing is possible unless you have tried it. On February 24, 2022, the global community gave Ukraine, at most, a week to stand up to Russia. We are now two and a half years beyond this week, and Russia has achieved only a little new territory, with missiles and drones raining over Crimea.

Aside from the Ukrainian resistance, a number of other phenomena have manifested themselves. NATO has expanded and become stronger, at the very least in the sense that at least twice as many members of NATO are now expanding more than 2% of their GDP on military matters.

Germany, a traditionally friendly country to Russia under Angela Merkle, albeit not an ally, has experienced an epiphany with a leadership consisting of a left-wing coalition of Social democrats and Greens. France, traditionally, at best often an isolated country until it hurts French interests, has been at the forefront of resistance to Russian aggression, suggesting even boots on Ukrainian ground. The only two NATO members resisting full support for Ukraine are essentially irrelevant Hungary, with a madman at the helm, and Slovakia, with a budding madman. Similarly to the European Union, NATO motions will fly to disenfranchise Prime Ministers Orban and Fifo.

Then there is a budding movement of enslaved nations within the Russian Federation itself, organizing structures and united in their efforts to bring down the Russian empire: the Free Nations League, the Anti-Imperialism Bloc of Nations, the Americans Against Russian Imperialism, and others. These nations include, in part, the Bashkirs, the Buryats, the Tatars, the Kalmyks, the Erzya, the Circassians, and others. In their manifestos, these nations no longer speak of autonomy within some type of federation with the Russians. They speak only of independence.

It is a different world. "Realpolitik," as we know it, has become an anachronism or has acquired a different meaning. Seeking a lasting diplomatic solution with the Russian Empire is the furthest removed from being a realistic solution to the current war. All empires eventually fall because people in general, perhaps even the

Russians, want individual freedoms. Maintaining an empire is a difficult chore, requiring sacrifice not only from oneself but one's dear ones, including the sacrifice of life.

The strongest weapon on the side of freedom is transparency (that term was called "glasnost" in the ebbing days of Soviet Russia under Gorbachev) via the Internet, cell phones, etc. Almost everything can be viewed on-screen globally. The Czar or the Commissar never had to address those realities. What about Russian presidents? That title "president" in a real sense is entirely foreign to Russians but they will have to adjust. Czar, commissar, or emperor are anachronisms.

August 10, 2024

HE WAS ALWAYS AN ENIGMA – NOW HE IS AN EXISTENTIAL THREAT.

Pope Francis was an enigma during his Argentinian days. Still, Catholic Cardinals worldwide believed that with the help of the Holy Spirit who hovered over the College of Cardinals, somehow they got it right when they voted him in as the Primate of the Universal Catholic Church.

But after the election, eventually a new period saw renewed puzzlement when Pope Francis chose to entertain criminals at the Vatican in the persons of Putin and Kirill. His lack of humanity for the long-suffering people of Ukraine, particularly at a time of great peril for them, and his bizarre affection for Russian history and its criminal leaders was very disturbing.

Perhaps, now, his support for an agency of the Kremlin's criminal regime is not surprising. The Catholic Church, using its own terminology, appears to have been taken over by the Devil. Perhaps this is a Biblical realization. The ramifications may have been forecast, but nevertheless, to the average believer, the Apocalypse is now, and there cannot be anything more frightening. Given his age biologically the situation with the Pope will only get worse. Physically, he will become more frail, and mentally, he will be even more cognitively challenged.

The Russian or Ukrainian (as it now calls itself in Ukraine) Orthodox Churches belonging to the Moscow Patriarchate are "de iure" and "de facto" creations of one of the most heinous killers in history, Josef Stalin. It is not a religious institution but an agency of the Kremlin's special services. The Moscow Church, in fact, was installed in Ukraine to create a false impression and an alternative to the liquidated Ukrainian Christian churches. Even after Ukraine's proclamation of renewed independence, the Moscow Church in Ukraine never registered as a foreign agent. That in and of itself was sufficient to have it banned in Ukraine and its leadership brought before the courts. That did not happen because of Ukrainian tolerance.

That Church's predecessor was not a religious institution either, but an agency of the czarist regime. The criminality has extended for some four centuries and includes the establishment of the Moscow Patriarchy in the late 16th century, contrived through criminal kidnapping and holding hostage of the Ecumenical Patriarch. Every significant leader of the Church had to be a member of the Muscovite secret service.

Is Pope Francis familiar with history? Frankly, it's not relevant. He does have advisers. His behavior while bizarre, is the product of his unhinged mind. There may be more to it than that, unfortunately.

The Vatican News provided:

> *"In his words following the Sunday Angelus, Pope Francis expresses his fears over Kyiv's decision to ban the Orthodox church linked to the Moscow Patriarchate. He appeals 'Let no Christian Church abolished directly or indirectly."*

Perhaps the problem is with the Catholic concept of Papal infallibility. It is often misplaced and, too often, extended to areas where the Pope's mind cannot reach because of frankly limited exposure to fields of education. No human being is even astute, much less infallible, on every issue. Even more so when the possessor of this trait bestowed upon him gratuitously is reaching his nineties and is not educated in the first place, especially on matters other than theology, such as history and politics. We are all with great many flaws so we should learn to forgive. However, the biography of this Pope is so abysmal that there is no room for forgiveness or even Christian consideration.

This, perhaps, is both funny and sad. Naturally, the Vatican News report concludes with, "Your contribution to a great mission. Support us in bringing the Pope's words into every home."

The words of the Pope came a day after Ukraine's Parliament had enacted legislation later signed by the President to forbid the Moscow Patriarchate Orthodox Church in Ukraine. The legislation was a result of at least a year long active discussion by the Parliament and Ukrainian society as to the propriety and even Constitutionality of such legislation. During the course of the war, many criminal cases had been brought against the hierarchy of the Church for treason, among other crimes. The patience and tolerance of both the Ukrainian authorities and society had been exemplary/ bordering on ridiculously excessive. Two of the three holiest places of Ukrainian Christianity belonged to the Moscow Church.

As the discussion ensued, the Moscow Patriarchate Church in Ukraine reached out to the Ecumenical Orthodox Patriarch in Istanbul to lend its legitimacy to the Church. Only several days before the legislation, representatives of the legitimate Orthodox Church of Ukraine under Metropolitan Theophany met with the Ecumenical Patriarch, who stated unequivocally that he would not be lending legitimacy to the Moscow Church in Ukraine.

Both the decision of the Ecumenical Patriarch and Ukraine's Parliament and President sparked outrage in the Kremlin surprisingly. The Kremlin has not commented on the condemnation by the Pope as of now.

As a Catholic, I suspect that, once again, the role of the Catholic Church and Pope Francis in particular cannot get any more outrageous than this. The Universal Catholic Church now carries the same mantra as the Kremlin and the "Representative of Jesus Christ on Earth" Pope Francis, and the war criminal under a warrant by the International Criminal Court for kidnapping children Vladimir Putin, speak with one voice. How bizarre!

August 26, 2024

UKRAINIAN GENOCIDES

Criminal intent ("mens rea") is the keystone of any crime, especially the most serious crime of Genocide. Evidence of criminal intent is required by any criminal court. Accordingly, it underlies the UN Convention on the Prevention and Punishment of the Crime of Genocide and is clearly a requirement of the International Court in The Hague.

However, that court, as well as other courts that arose after such crimes were perpetrated, do not consider historical crimes, meaning those that predated them or the Convention.

Historically, there are many crimes that are suitable for global public condemnation, particularly serious crimes such as genocides. The last 100 years witnessed at least three separate crimes of attempted Genocide perpetrated against the Ukrainian nation: the "Holodomor" (The Ukrainian Famine-Genocide of 1932-33) more than 90 years ago with some 7-10 million deaths; Operation "Vistula" on ethnographic Ukrainian lands over 75 years ago in Communist Poland with only several thousand deaths but almost 150,000 forcibly displaced into areas of total assimilation; and the current and ongoing genocide of Ukrainians by Moscow and Vladimir Putin and his acolytes, including the Moscow Church which to date numbers tens of thousands killed and millions displaced.

Two of the above predated the UN Genocide Convention. Two major Genocides against other nations were attempted prior to the Convention (The Armenian Genocide by the Turks of 1915 and the Jewish Holocaust perpetrated by the Germans during World War 2. Together with the Ukrainian Holodomor of 1932-32. The Holocaust constituted the motivation for the Convention's draftsmen. Among them, perhaps the best known was Raphael Lemkin, a Polish-Jewish attorney who studied law in Lviv, Ukraine.

To date and essentially forever, the only Genocide prior to the Convention ever punished was the Holocaust through a Special Tribunal set up by the victors known as the Nuremberg Tribunal. Individual perpetrators were punished, and Germany was compelled to pay remuneration. Since the adoption of the Conventions, several Genocides have been recognized and punished, but only where the perpetrators were not the eventual victors in the conflict.

It is important in each case of an alleged Genocide to consider the elements of the crime by evaluating the establishment of criminal intent directly or indirectly. It is equally necessary to realize that criminal intent manifested directly is very difficult to establish. To do so would require oral proclamations before witnesses, admissions, and declarations against interest, all in the presence of corroborating witnesses or written documents consisting of orders or commands or written confessions, especially when it comes to crimes in history where witnesses are all deceased. The burden of proof is overwhelming and is obviously so because criminals mostly act covertly and do not declare their intentions.

In establishing criminal intent, particularly with reference to Genocide, key components of criminal law as they are currently defined by the International Criminal Court are very helpful. The number of victims, when it happens in peace or in war, and whether the entire or only a part of a group is affected are not relevant components.

While Genocides have existed for centuries, the terminology was established and defined only in the XX century with the UN Convention, which was adopted in 1949 and ratified by most member states over the next few years. The International Court of Justice (ICJ) in the Hague, which deals with member states, was established in 1945 when the UN was set up. The International Criminal Court (ICC), which addresses individual crimes, came into effect only in 2002 as a belated follow-up to the Rome Treaty of 1998.

The Russian Federation signed the Treaty of Rome of 1998, creating the court, but later withdrew its signature. Ukraine signed the treaty, however, and has ratified it only recently. Accepting jurisdiction remains an issue. A crime of Genocide that takes place on the territory of Ukraine is subject to the ICC, which considers four types of crimes: crimes of aggression, against humanity, war cries, and the most serious crime of Genocide.

This obviously makes it impossible for the ICC to consider the "Holodomor" or Operation "Vistula." Of the above-mentioned genocides, the ICC may only consider and rule on the current Genocide in Ukraine, and the defendants may be Putin, Lavrov, Kirill, or any Russian soldier but not the Kremlin or Russia. Obviously, there is still the UN Convention, but neither the "Holodomor" nor Operation "Vistula" can be considered, investigated, condemned, and then punished because they took place before the Convention. In any event, the Convention lacks a serious practical methodology for prevention and punishment, as will be noted below. Nonetheless, the guidelines of both the ICC and the UN Convention are not only relevant but indispensable for a serious discussion of the very crime of Genocide, contemporary or historical.

The UN Convention imposes an obligation on UN member states to act to prevent Genocide, but because prevention, security, and protection are within the purview of the UN Security Council, which Russia has the right to veto, the issue has little practical viability. Therefore, as noted above, it is necessary to resort to another forum besides the Convention or the ICC, and this is the court of public and global assessment and opinion. In fact, this can and should be a legitimate exercise because of the frailties of international law where sovereign states act or consider only such topics as are politically opportune for them.

As noted above, evidence of criminal intent is a "sine qua non" to establish the crime of Genocide. When we consider the cases raised, perhaps the most striking direct evidence comes from a review of historical documents on Operation "Vistula." A document dated April 16, 1947, from Warsaw, entitled Project of the Organization of Operation "East" prepared by the Ministry of National Defense and the Ministry of Public Security and stamped "Top Secret," sets forth a program to achieve the following objective: "The final solution to the Ukrainian problem in Poland." There are five points that define the operation's plan of action to destroy the Ukrainian ethnicity in Poland by forcing relocation and resettlement in conditions that would result in total destruction by way of assimilation. A review of the actual operations follows those five points. Thus, Communist Poland wrote a script that it then followed, which, in retrospect, damned the perpetrators historically. The motive was a final solution to the Ukrainian problem on their ethnographic territories and the creation of an almost 100% Polish Poland, a homogeneous country of which the regime bragged. The events follow almost literally Article II, paragraph (c) of the subsequent UN Convention on Genocide. Today, Poland is quite different, Ukraine's ally and the issue of responsibility and compensation is essentially dormant.

This is an entirely different Poland from the one in 1947.

Criminal intent to commit genocide is manifested in most cases indirectly through the following actions or declarations: devaluing a group as not a nation, accusing a group of mythical crimes, dehumanizing (denazifying) a group, identifying a group as a danger to humanity, preparing one's own population for a crime through propaganda and disinformation, mass murders in particular, the civilian population, specific attacks on shelters, humanitarian corridors, the bombing of inhabited neighborhoods, specific destruction of infrastructure and services essential to life, attacks on hospitals, clinics, orphanages, rape, and forced resettlement.

When looking at the materials related to the Holodomor of 1932-33, there is no direct document declaring a Genocide. The Soviet government acted in a very secretive manner, and Stalin himself had a paranoid psychosis. He kept everything secret. During the entire existence of the USSR, the authorities and the press denied the Genocide. The same position was taken by the authorities of the Russian Federation, in particular Vladimir Putin, its strongman since 2000.

A brief review of the Holodomor shows the following: the Law on Five Ears of Corn from August 7, 1932, Stalin's letter to Lazar Kaganovich, his henchman in Ukraine from August 11, 1932, resolutions of December 14 and 15, 1932 signed by Stalin and Molotov on the cessation of Ukrainization, in particular, outside of Ukraine, which doomed the Ukrainians of the Kuban, Lower Podolia, Slobozhanshchyna, Volga, Kazakhstan, Siberia, the Far East, Turkestan, Azerbaijan, Belarus to disappear as a nation, because everything Ukrainian was banned there. Stalin's telegram, dated January 1, 1933, was about the seizure of products from the population of Ukraine for failure to fulfill the ambitious plans for grain distribution and the Decree from January 22, 1933, on closing the borders of Ukraine and the Ukrainian concentrated Russian region of Kuban to prevent migration in search of bread. No other borders were closed.

The joint resolution of the Central Executive Committee and the Council of People's Commissars of the USSR, "On the protection of the property of state-owned enterprises, collective farms and cooperatives for the strengthening of public (socialist) property," was published, popularly known as the law "about five ears of corn." The authorship of the resolution is attributed to Stalin personally. Stalin's letter to Kaganovich contains the following words: "The most important thing now is Ukraine." The borders of Ukraine and the Kuban are closed because Ukrainians are most densely populated there. There were laws, decrees, and orders along with Stalin's scolding of everyone in Ukraine, including even the spokesmen of the Communist Party. All decrees and measures constitute an indisputable indirect document of genocidal intent.

In 1926, there were 1,412,276 Ukrainians in the Kuban alone and 3,107,000 in the whole North Caucasus Territory. Many Ukrainian schools were established. In 1932-33, accusations of 'local nationalism' were freely made (as in Ukraine) in the local paper 'Molot.' Early in 1933, a number of cultural and political figures in the Kuban were arrested, including most of the professors at the two Ukrainian Institutes. Russian replaced Ukrainian as the language of instruction. Between 1933 and 1937, all the 746 Ukrainian primary schools in the Kuban were turned into Russian schools.

These documents and the numbers, totaling the number of Ukrainian victims from 7-10 million, when all others numbered one million, indirectly indicate that there was a Genocide and it was directed against Ukrainians.

It was the same with the "Holocaust." In that case, Hitler and his surrogates acted with genocidal intent. They even instructed every Jew to sew an inscription label for identification. At each stop by the Germans, Jews were organized for execution at the very beginning of their invasion of Eastern Europe. They even held a conference on January 20, 1942, in Wansee with the participation of Hitler's underlings, led by Reinhard Heydrich, stating the final solution regarding the Jews. Still, there was not one document signed by the Führer to destroy the Jews as a nation.

Punishment for the crime of past genocides was manifested only in relation to Germans and Germany, and even then, not in relation to genocide, but only as to war crimes. Condemnation and criminal punishment of individuals took place through the Nuremberg Trials, and the German state, under pressure, accepted responsibility and financial compensation, which in some cases continues to this day. It is unlikely that the Russian Federation, Poland, or Turkey will ever agree to punishment in any form, let alone compensation. Surprisingly, Israel, with its own Genocide, stubbornly does not recognize any other genocides. No one can be forced to be humane or display sympathy.

Nonetheless, when commemorating genocides of the past is important, if only, to honor the memory of the victims. Calculating the number of victims is very important for a better understanding of a nation's present and future. The number of victims is not for establishing genocide as defined by the Convention but for the moral and historical context. Although morality is unfortunately not a big component in international politics, it should be an attribute of human beings.

Research on historical genocides, including the "Holodomor," should continue, and all efforts of self-identified, politically motivated experts to establish the framework and set limits on research should be rejected.

In considering the elements of the current war crimes and attempted Genocide in Ukraine, the following should be considered in particular: attacks on civilian targets, specific attacks on shelters and humanitarian corridors, the bombing of residential neighborhoods, destruction of infrastructure necessary-for-life services such as water supply; attacks on hospitals, clinics, and in particular maternity wards, children's hospitals, orphanages; rape and kidnapping including forced relocation. All of these are manifested in the current Genocide against Ukrainians.

On January 31, 2024, the ICJ ruled that Russia had violated global anti-terrorism and anti-racial discrimination treaties stemming from its annexation of parts of Ukraine in 2014.

The current Russian aggression is today's attempt at Genocide against Ukrainians. It raises numerous legal issues of war crimes and yet another attempted genocide. The intent of Putin, his associates Lavrov, Medvedev, Kirill, and even ordinary soldiers and their mothers is undoubtedly quite transparent: "Erase the Ukrainian nation from the face of the earth." This is criminal genocidal intent expressed directly by the Moscow Church, official statements of the Kremlin by individuals and publications.

The current Genocide against Ukrainians raises many legal issues currently allegedly under review by the ICJ, the ICC, and many member states of the global civilized community. The intentions of Putin, his spokesmen Lavrov, Kirill, Pskovand even many soldiers and their mothers are clear: "Erase the Ukrainian nation from the face of the earth." There is direct evidence of criminal genocidal intent expressed directly by the Moscow so-called Church, which is, in essence, a state church. There are official statements by Kremlin figures, and there are publications promoting this mindset.

The shooting of civilians with their hands tied, as witnessed in Bucha, is proof of the criminal genocidal intent indirectly. However, these acts, it may be argued, may be simply the criminal intent of an individual soldier or of several soldiers. However, aiming a missile at an orphanage, a maternity ward, or a children's hospital can only be a manifestation of the criminal intent of those who give the orders. In Russia, ultimately, only one person gives the orders. This is clear evidence of criminal intent to perpetrate Genocide by Vladimir Putin, a person who must be under investigation by the ICC regardless of whether Russia withdrew its signature under the Treaty of Rome. This Genocide takes place on the territory of Ukraine, a signatory state.

And even though the ICC arm of implementation or execution is not able to operate in Russia, it should establish the complete isolation of the individual criminals. Putin, Lavrov, and Kirill should not be able to leave Russia and travel abroad, even to the UN in New York or Vienna, if the wheels of justice begin to spin more rapidly.

In July 2021, Putin published a lengthy essay, "On the Historical Unity of Russians and Ukrainians," claiming that Ukraine is an artificial entity that occupies historically Russian lands. Numerous legal experts and historians cited Putin's essay as part of laying the groundwork for incitement to Genocide.

The shooting of civilians with their hands tied is indirect evidence of criminal genocidal intent. It may simply be the criminal intent of the soldier or soldiers, the immediate perpetrators. However, targeting a missile or drone at an orphanage can only be a manifestation of the criminal intent of the one or those who give the orders. In Russia, ultimately, only one person gives the orders. This is conclusive evidence of the criminal intent of genocide by Vladimir Putin, a person who was and is the subject of investigations by the International Criminal Court, regardless of whether Russia withdrew its signature from the Rome Treaty. This genocide is taking place on the territory of a state that signed the treaty and did not withdraw its signature.

On March 17, 2023, the ICC issued arrest warrants for Vladimir Putin and his surrogate Maria Lvova-Belova, the Russian commissioner for Children's rights, alleging responsibility for the war crime of unlawful deportation and transfer of children during the Russian aggression in Ukraine. If a country agrees to host Vladimir Putin, it must be condemned by the world, isolated, and deemed a pariah. Thus far, at least two countries deserve such treatment: Azerbaijan and Mongolia. Mongolia did sign the Rome Treaty. Although the arm of the International Criminal Court cannot reach the territory of the Russian Federation, the decision suggests the isolation of this criminal at least by the 123 countries that abide. This is the law. Reality may be different.

In addition to the ICC, there is also the ICJ at the Hague, which deliberates disputes between states. Here, Russia itself is a defendant in an action brought by Ukraine in February 2022. However, the wheels of justice here have moved very slowly.

Today's Genocide against the Ukrainian people is happening on the television screen and other forms of media. There are many witnesses and much evidence. The actions of the world community and international institutions, in addition to the ICJ, the ICC, the United Nations General Assembly, and the UN Human Rights

Council, are very much before the eyes of the world. The UN Security Council is well beyond the bounds of justice and the rule of law and, frankly, an oxymoron on the subject of security.

On February 28, 2022, four days after the full-scale invasion, the prosecutor of the ICC opened an investigation for war crimes and crimes against humanity. On March 2, 2022, the UN GA adopted a resolution deploring the "aggression" committed by Russia against Ukraine. Two days later, the UN Human Rights Council called for a "swift and verifiable" withdrawal of Russian troops. On March 16, 2022 the ICC ordered Russia to immediately suspend its military operation.

I traveled to Irpin, a city near Kyiv, in September 2022. I saw the devastation of residential areas. I saw simple motor vehicles riddled with bullet holes on all sides. There was no doubt that Russia was targeting civilians. This was a very important observation of war crimes. Not far from Irpin, in the City of Bucha, bodies of civilians had been discovered with their hands tied behind their backs. They were shot execution style. There is no doubt that these were war crimes and circumstantial evidence of an attempted Genocide. Targeting civilian residential areas, maternity wards, children, and kidnapping children are all war crimes. The question presents itself: does this rise to the level of genocide?

Why are the Russians targeting civilian objects and even maternity wards and children? In view of the blatant language beginning with Putin's rewriting of Ukrainian history in July 2021, pilfering the history of Kyivan Rus and stating that Ukrainians are not a nation, the intent is clear.

If Kyivan Rus is the history of Russia and Ukrainians are not a nation, then the intent to bomb maternity wards, kidnap children, and target the civilian population is to eliminate Ukrainians. For Ukrainians, this is an existential war.

Existential in its very meaning signifies the existence of the country Ukraine and its people. The characterization of the war as Genocide is very real and substantiated by the facts which serve as evidence. Why did the Russians invade Ukraine? By the Russians' own assertions, it was because the Ukrainians were not even a nation. That is what Putin stated in his bizarre version of history. What does that mean? The city of Kyiv, which is the capitol of Ukraine, was founded in the 5th century, while the village of Muscovy, which is the capitol of today's Russia, was founded in the 12th century. The sovereign Kyivan state was in existence in the 9th century/ Muscovy became a sovereign state in the 16th century. Muscovite history is very sparse, short, and replete with barbaric aggression.

Destroying an independent and democratic Ukraine is essential to obliterating people who not only live there but also refer to it as their motherland. That is why a majority of all Russian targets are civilian, maternal, life-giving, providing energy, and representing cultural treasures. Russia needs the Ukrainian identity. In order to achieve that, it needs to destroy the Ukrainian people. It has been tried in the past without success. Consider the Holodomor of 1932-33 when 7-10 million Ukrainians were starved to death by the Kremlin. Today's invasion of Ukraine is yet another attempt at Genocide. The big difference is that today, the Ukrainians are fighting back.

In an interview with his "useful idiot" Tucker Carlson, Vladimir Putin repeated his perverse view of Ukrainian and Russian history. In fact, there was no Russia until the 18th century when it was artificially forged and named by Czar Peter following his victory against the combined forces of the Swedes and Ukrainian Cossacks in the battle of Poltava in 1709. Czar Peter had commenced his criminal genocide against Ukrainians a year earlier by indiscriminately razing the city and slaughtering the inhabitants of Baturyn, the capitol of his nemesis, the Ukrainian Hetman Ivan Mazepa. Mazepa's courage was glorified a century later by the English poet Lord Byron.

Thus, for more than three hundred years, the Russians have been attempting the Genocide of the Ukrainian people. The current war is the latest example and a severe test requiring the resolve of the global community. Ukrainians have always persevered but never overcome this dreaded evil. Today is the best opportunity to bring an end to the evil Russian empire. This requires the will of the good people of Ukraine and good people everywhere.

Bibliography

"An Independent Legal Analysis of the Russian Federation's Breaches of the Genocide Convention in Ukraine and the Duty to Prevent," New Lines Institute for Strategy and Policy, Raoul Wallenberg Centre for Human Rights, May 2022

Conquest, Robert, "The Harvest of Sorrow," Oxford University Press, 1986

"Convention on the Prevention and Punishment of the Crime of Genocide," United Nations, December 9, 1948

"Final Solution: Overview," Holocaust Encyclopedia

Hilberg, Raul, "The Destruction of the European Jews," Quadrangle Books, Chicago, 1961

International Criminal Court, "Trying individuals for genocide, war crimes, crimes against humanity and aggression," ICC.org

"Projekt orhanizaciji Operaciji 'Schid'," April 16, 1947, Ukrainian Institute of National Memory

Snyder, Timothy, "Bloodlands," Basic Books, New York, 2020

"Zakon pro pyat koloskiw," Wikipedia

September, 2024

BACK TO UKRAINE: AN EYEWITNESS ACCOUNT

The first night in Lviv was replete with sirens of various categories and lengths. This had been preceded several days earlier by an unprecedented missile attack resulting in serious fatalities, including that of a family of four, with the remaining father hospitalized. Once again, this target bore no proximity to any military targets, energy grid, or anything remotely connected with the war and Ukrainian resistance. It was simply a grotesque message from the Russians to Ukrainians: we will wipe you off the face of the earth.

Today, Friday, September 6, 2024, the people of Lviv paid their respects to the young woman and her three children who perished. Amazingly, the war crimes charges against Russia dating back to the early months of the war are still being investigated as evidence continues to mount. The wheels of justice move so slowly that there is no justice.

Ukraine's request to the United States for permission to use US weapons deep into Russian territory to prevent such attacks remains unrequited. Patriot defense missiles continue to sit in European warehouses, gathering dust and playing no role as innocents in Ukraine die. Ukraine continues to be grateful for Western assistance, but the logical mind is confused.

And so, Russia has intensified its brutality. Still, the West, seemingly supportive of Ukraine in word and deed, somehow continues to sit on the fence and play both sides, allegedly fearing Armageddon. The specter of an anti-Ukraine America and a less supportive Germany looms on next year's horizon. Yet,, frankly, the friends of Ukraine have not done nor are they doing enough, actually inhibiting Ukraine's valiant efforts and sacrifice.

Many in the West have expressed support with an addendum; how long can this support continue? What is very often lost in this discussion is the very real fact that scenes of young people being laid to rest as a result of war crimes are a sight reoccurring only in Ukraine. Sure, young people are dying everywhere, but mostly because of cultural and political stupidity. More people die from automatic weapons wielded by civilians in America than in any other country. No country is more misguided than America on this score, but that is a whole different issue.

As an American witness to the requiem events in Lviv, (there was a procession of cars, a church service, then thousands walked to the cemetery). As I watched, I was sad and angry, sad for my fellow Ukrainians, but perhaps angrier at the murdering Russians and accommodating Americans, the latter aided and abetted through their lack of resolve. President Biden is a friend of Ukraine but a very flawed one.

The specter of great evil in November cannot whitewash the fecklessness of the current administration. The legacy of Joe Biden will be tarnished in my mind by the requiem events of today. There are so many to blame: the international courts, even Mongolia, for harboring a war criminal. Perhaps, most important, is a misunderstanding of the war.

Ukrainians should be grateful for Western support. What is lacking is reciprocal gratefulness from the West. Ukraine has taken on, albeit not voluntarily, the greatest evil in the world today. This evil has been enhanced largely by Western appeasement for at least a century. Sure, this war is costing Western money. Much more importantly, it is costing Ukrainian lives. Every Ukrainian who dies is a tremendous loss. People are not resources such as weapons and money. President Zelensky recently stressed this at a press conference. No human being is replaceable. Who can replace the young mother with her three children buried today in Lviv because of Russian criminal aggression and Western lack of resolve?

September 6, 2024

INTROSPECTIVE THROUGH OTHER EYES

I asked a friend of mine in Lviv what will it take to end this war in favor of Ukraine. What surprised me more than his answer was the rapidity and confidence. No, he is not the mayor of Lviv nor a high-level politician or military. He is an intellectual, once a television personality journalist, and for a long time, and currently a website master. He said that the Russian empire had to be brought down to its knees economically. As an example, he cited the Russian ability to purchase American chips despite American sanctions. Once Russia suffers severe economic distress, even the Russian population will revolt in favor of their personal well-being, forsaking the empire, which will make political turmoil by the other nationalities much more impact full.

Given the current political scene, that opinion seemed to make some, if not much, sense. American economic sanctions against Russia are not monitored. Its arms assistance is outdated and delayed, and even then, it is restricted. I began to think how Russia has for years outmaneuvered the United States and Europe in many areas and how negligent America and Europe have been in oversight. One example would be the Russian Orthodox Church Moscow Patriarchate, which, pursuant to American law, should have its U.S. leadership register as foreign agents. Yet they do not, and there are no consequences. Many within that Church are much more than foreign agents. They are spies.

Recently, a fellow Ukrainian American, totally immersed in the Trump swamp, wrote that Trump will be good for Ukraine precisely because of his ego, which will not permit him to play a subordinate role to Putin. This person clearly did not see the Trump-Putin Helsinki press conference from 2018, and granted, this individual is very primitive intellectually, but even so, such declarations are dangerous because they are aimed at the poorly educated and come right out of the Russian playbook for misinforming the Ukrainian American electorate.

A question arises as to whether this person is simply primitive or an agent.

Russia relies on disinformation, careless disregard, boredom, and even abusing Christian values such as that man is made in the image of God or that all Christian churches, even fake ones, must be protected. That is why the Pope is so dangerous in his irresponsibility. The vulnerable are all that lack any level of reason. Or, as President Ronald Reagan stated regarding Mikhail Gorbachev, "overlay ale provincial."

That is only part of the problem. We live in a world where Russia is able to find fertile ground. We somehow mix up the China variable, suggesting that the demise of one authoritarian regime enhances another. If the Russian empire is dismantled, China's hegemony will not be enhanced. Who is the greater threat to Western democracy and values: Russia or China? For countries such as India, South Korea, Japan, Philippines, Taiwan, and even Australia, clearly the enemy at the gate is China. How immediate is the threat? That is a topic for another time. Immediately, China is invested in production and export.

Russia is invested in war crimes and Genocide. Russia produces nothing. It simply exhausts its natural resources. Oil and gas are not renewable energy sources. Russia is a time bomb, and for that reason, it has to be an empire appeasing the masses.

Russia started as Muscovy and moved to expand its territory both West and East. It was much more successful in the East. It cannot go any further East, stymied by the Pacific Ocean. The possibilities in the West are quite fertile and tangible.

The fear of nuclear Armageddon is often suggested as a reason for appeasement, limitations on arming Ukraine, and restraint on

Ukrainian inclusion in European structures is misplaced if only because if Russia takes over Ukraine, Armageddon will be at hand. Victory in Ukraine is the only solution.

September 8, 2024

THE END OF THE EMPIRE

Several questions have been raised in the course of the Ukraine-Russia war, some provoked by threats that have come from the Kremlin. Will Russia resort to nuclear weapons? In what scenario would the Russian empire collapse? What happens to the nuclear arsenal in that case?

There are many schools of thought purporting to answer these questions, the predominant one in the United States and many countries in the West being the now-aged response of appeasement. The only accurate answer has been that appeasement of Russia has never worked in the past. And so why would it now?

An integral component of the appeasement approach has been denial of weapons requested, delay in delivery, and restrictions on use. A carefree approach to sanctions has resulted in Russia building new weapons with American chips. This is no way to fight a war. As a result, neither side is winning, and a diplomatic settlement seems to be the only logical conclusion. A diplomatic settlement serves only Russia as Russia is entrenched on 18 percent of Ukrainian territory, and Ukraine is no closer to actual NATO membership than prior to the war.

Nevertheless, the war has exposed some of Russia's weaknesses. On the morning of February 24, 2022, when Russia invaded full force, many Western experts, political and military, gave Ukraine a week. That certainly has changed two and one-half years later. Russia continues to bark about its power, but its bite has been significantly lesser. In fact, if Russia were to fight according to generally accepted rules of international law, meaning without war crimes, targeting civilian sites, women and children, kidnapping, raping, and pillaging, its success, and Ukraine's casualties would be significantly lesser.

Two days after Russia's invasion, Ukraine brought its case for Genocide before the International Court of Justice in the Hague. Two and one-half years later, the Court has considered only procedural matters. Wheels of justice spinning slowly has been the mantra of the international community. In the interim, Ukrainian children are being killed or kidnapped, women are being raped, civilians are murdered execution style, infrastructure is destroyed, and military casualties are mounting.

Ukraine's incursion onto Russian territory is difficult to assess since there has not been much opposition, and the local population appears mostly peaceful, offering little resistance, if any, but only time will tell. The lack of resistance may be very telling. There are only ten thousand Ukrainian troops involved. Further incursion in Bryansk and Belgorod regions is expected. Missile and drone attacks at the gates of Moscow are currently inexplicable but real.

No one will offer an opinion as to a timeline for the war, but many will opine with a war-end scenario. Much of this is predicated on extensive Western support, which is substantial, unrestricted, and timely. So far, the last two factors have been lacking. One other condition predominates. I have never met anyone in Ukraine among the political or military leadership or even the cabdriver that does not fear a Trump victory in November. To the rational mind, a Trump victory is unthinkable, but the polls show otherwise. Moscow is certainly doing its part to advance the Trump agenda. "Useful idiots" abound. Additionally, Germany has already announced a 50 percent cut in aid to Ukraine in the next year.

Traveling throughout Ukraine, in Kyiv, I met up with a Ukrainian citizen of Erzya descent and one of the major leaders of the Erzya people not only in Ukraine, where there are more than thirty thousand but of the Erzya in Mordovia, that number close to one half million, much vilified by the Kremlin and a former leader of the Free Nations League, Boljaenj Syresj. I posed these questions to him, and this was his response:

"Why is the disintegration of the Russian Federation inevitable? During the 20th century, the Russian state already disintegrated twice (1917 and 1991), but it never became a stable country capable of support democratic system of society. Authoritarianism and targeting of Russia's external expansion is not an anomaly Putinism, and the only option for the operation of the "Russian model" for the North Eurasia. This is a model of the colonial rule of the capital over the rest of the territories, and it became obsolete already in the 20th century. After all, societies in the middle of Russian Federations have modern requests for self-government and cultural self-realization. Further attempts to preserve the integrity of the Russian Federation encourage Kremlin to the escalation of internal and external violence. From the outside, Russia often looks deceptively monolithic, but this is the result of temporary efficiency repressive apparatus and state propaganda. Every serious crisis in Moscow leads to the weakening of its control over the regions and to the attempts of regional elites and national movements to acquire subjectivity. A truly stable and predictable situation in Northern Eurasia will come, when the fair requests of regional societies will be realized, and Moscow will not be able to subjugate the regions again. It can be said that the disintegration of the Russian Federation is historically inevitable - regardless of whether it is desirable or not for external actors. It's out of control the USA and the West as a whole. Instead, the US and the West are able to show leadership and to influence that this disintegration takes place in a peaceful and civilized manner scenario, instead of uncontrolled chaos, rivalry and struggle. 2. Why the disintegration of the Russian Federation is beneficial to the USA In its foreign policy, the United States is guided by pragmatic interests

279

support for security and prosperity, as well as idealistic motives spread of democracy and freedom. The USA has not given up on its principles even in relation to the closest ally, contributing in the mid-20th century decolonization of the British Empire. Modern Russia is definitely not a friend and ally USA. Moscow poses an ideological and geopolitical challenge to Washington, and determined to harm long-term American interests. Periodic "discharges" and "reboots" with Moscow are not allowed long-term effect. Instead, new post-Russian states are capable of becoming sincere friends and reliable partners of the USA, as happened with Ukraine after 1991. Moscow is deprived of the resources of the regions currently under its control will no longer be able to become a serious opponent for Washington. Yes, there is a Beijing factor that worries the US and even gives an excuse for illusions regarding the Russian Federation as a certain counterweight to the PRC. Recent events show that that Russia, in its desire to confront the West, is ready to become even younger partner of China. In the long term, a complete Russian Federation, at best, will be a poorly predicted player and a constant "defector" between the West and the East. Instead, the transformation of Northern Eurasia into a conglomerate of states more clearly structures the boundaries of the influence of the West and the East in this macro-region. Most of the potential post-Russian countries, among which there will be Turkic and Muslim, will have no reason to be friends with the PRC, which is itself a "second publication" of the anti-Muslim and Turkophobic empire, the yoke of which is over them countries just got rid of. 3. Why does the disintegration of the Russian Federation not threaten the spread of nuclear weapons? Fear of nuclear proliferation deterred the US from providing support independence of Ukraine and other

Soviet republics in 1991. It turned out a regrettable mistake, because the newly independent states declared without controversy its intention to become nuclear-free. Nuclear safety did not decrease after 1991, but on the contrary, it increased many nuclear weapons, their carriers and infrastructure were eliminated in the process nuclear disarmament of Ukraine, Belarus and Kazakhstan. These countries have stopped to be advanced bridgeheads for a nuclear attack on NATO. They are natural resources and scientific and technical potential no longer serve the interests of the nuclear industry Moscow races. There is every reason to hope for a repeat of this success in the event of an appearance now already post-Russian states. The new states will not just become nuclear-free – they will the appearance will reduce the nuclear potential of the nuclear successor state arsenal of the Russian Federation (unless we are talking about the complete denuclearization of the North Eurasia). Russian nuclear weapons pose a real threat only in orders of the Kremlin regime. The experience of Ukraine shows that the only a possible motive for the preservation of nuclear weapons by states that have left power Moscow, there is protection from Moscow itself. If as a result of the disintegration of the Russian Federation, Moscow will be objectively unable to threaten the new states, then this motive is also will cease to be relevant."

Why is this explanation important? Because it clearly points to a more suitable option than business as usual, that is, appeasing an empire that cannot be appeased, only further entices its appetite since its criminality has resulted in some gains.

September 14, 2024

A LONG AND GLORIOUS HISTORY, OFTEN TRAGIC

I am in Kyiv, the capital of Ukraine. It has been said that the Apostle Andrew visited the hills of Kyiv and blessed them for Christ, planting a wooden cross. The City of Kyiv was actually founded in the late 5th century. It flourished as a commercial center since it was located on a major waterway running from what is now the middle of Belarus to the Black Sea, the Dnipro River. From the Black Sea, you could travel and trade almost anywhere.

By the middle of the 9th century, Kyiv had grown into a state with adjacent lands and rulers, initially two brothers, Askold and Dyr, who, during one of their forays to Constantinople, took on Christianity and spared the City, protected by the Holy Mother. The State of Kyiv and its people did not officially become Christian until the reign of Prince Volodymyr the Great in 988 who himself was baptized in Crimea. The Kyiv empire stretched as far south as parts of Crimea.

Whenever I am in Kyiv, I observe Sunday service at a Ukrainian Orthodox Cathedral named after Prince Volodymyr, who is recognized as a saint by all the Ukrainian Christian denominations. The prelate of the Church is Patriarch Filaret, not of the Orthodox Church of Ukraine, blessed by the Ecumenical Patriarch Bartholomew. Kyiv, like the rest of Ukraine, is panoramic and diverse in its religions, including a variety of Christians, Jews, and Muslims. The people were very religious and managed to endure communist atheism, retaining their belief in God. It has been said that in Ukraine during Soviet times, the Communist Party of the Soviet Union was unable to deal effectively with this opiate as Lenin referred to religion, so his successor Stalin created his own Church, the Russian Orthodox Church, Moscow Patriarchate. That institution has been an agency of the Russian government ever since.

This Sunday, September 15, 2024, was no different. The service was long by my Catholic standards, but notwithstanding the duration, Patriarch Filaret, 95 years old, con-celebrated throughout. The Church was packed. There were many children and soldiers on leave. The choir, as usual in Ukrainian culture, was very moving. There was much audience participation. Unfortunately, of course, there were no women priests, only elderly women commanding the front rows.

Several days earlier, I witnessed the unveiling of a sculpture honoring Ukraine's preeminent film screenwriter and director, of global acclaim, on the 130th anniversary of his birth. Oleksandr Dovzhenko's best works were "Zvenyhora," "Arsenal" and "Zemlya" (Earth). The film "Zemlya" is considered one of the best silent films of all time in the entire world. The Dovzhenko film studio, where the sculpture sits, is located one mile up the hill from the St. Volodymyr Cathedral. Such cinematic gems as "Shadows of Forgotten Ancestors," "The White Bird Marked with Black," and "Famine 33" were produced by that Studio.

These two venues and events serve as magnificent reminders of the length and breadth of Ukrainian culture and, unfortunately, serve as tragic motivations for Russian aggression, war crimes, and ongoing genocide. "Ukrainians have to be wiped off the face of the earth," said one Russian religious leader.

It is that history that Russian strongman Vladimir Putin referred to in his perverse account of Russian and Ukrainian history in July 2021. There is so much more, but in microcosm, the Kyivan Prince Saint Volodymyr and the much persecuted by the Soviets Ukrainian film genius Oleksandr Dovzhenko manifest the long and glorious, albeit tragic history of the Ukrainian nation which is at the heart of Russian hatred and evil. Muscovy as a village in the swamps dates to the 12th century, and the Russian Empire came into existence only in the 18th century. That will never change and Ukrainian history and culture will go on.

September 15, 2024

INTERNATIONAL LAW IN THE TESTING STAGE

Regardless of how historians, lawyers, or politicians date international law, this field is currently in a testing phase. Some date it from 1920, when the Treaty of Paris was concluded and the League of Nations was formed.

In 1922, in his work "The Theory of the Nation," a well-known Ukrainian lawyer and legal scholar, Wolodymyr Starosolsky, wrote:

> *"This is the question. The evolution that takes place in the realm of state and interstate relations, and the creations of which are all kinds of relations between states on the one hand, and on the other hand, the idea of international or interstate law. works of a higher type — unions of states and allied states. Regarding the birth of international law, doubts are still raised about its real possibility, but for the impartial eye of the people of this law, it must be an undoubted fact... A state, subject to the orders of a supranational legal society, loses its sovereignty, but together with this, it gains some guarantee of its independence to the extent that foreign interests that would threaten its existence can be appeased without violating it. Thus, the development of international law contains a factor that preserves existing states."*

One hundred years later, there are three bodies of international law that should ensure world peace and security: the Security Council of the United Nations, the International Court of Justice, and the International Criminal Court. All institutions were formalized after the unsuccessful existence of the League of Nations. UNSC and ICJ in 1945 and ICC in 2002. Unfortunately, all institutions appear to be only in the process of evolution because none of them meet the needs of today.

284

In relation to today's aggression of Moscow in Ukraine, the inability of each is so tragic that it can be considered a mockery of the civilized world. This is not said for criticism itself but rather for constructive discussion. Moscow invaded the territory of Ukraine back in 2014 and with full force in 2022. It not only violated the laws of territorial integrity and sovereignty, but it also manifested all four crimes specified in the statutes, the last one in the ICC: aggression, war crimes, crimes against humanity, and genocide.

The subject institutions have provided only one tangible decision that can be considered significant, namely the arrest warrant of the International Criminal Court against Vladimir Putin in 2023 for kidnapping and abusing Ukrainian children. That this arrest warrant is not carried out is one of the fundamental problems of international law, but it was and is predictable and depends on the evolution of international law and how seriously the world community will interpret and adhere to it.

True, in March 2022, the ICJ issued a temporary preventive measure (injunction) instructing the Russians to stop the aggression. Moscow defiantly accepted the court's decision by publicly announcing that it would ignore it. On the same day, as if confirming its audacity, Moscow blasted the drama theatre in Mariupol with rockets, killing 600 civilians, including women and children who were sheltering there.

Two and a half years later, the ICJ continues to deal with procedural issues in the Genocide case, which was brought to the court by Ukraine on February 26, 2022. The Russian Federation illegally and defiantly assumed the seats of the USSR in the UN and the UNSC. Moscow has vetoed every attempt to implement security in Ukraine. Ukraine was powerless on this issue but also inactive.

So, this is an assessment of the activity and efficacy of international law as it serves today's largest global war. Clearly international law today is in a state of evolution. This is a big problem for the entire civilized world.

September 18, 2024.

FUTILITY

Vitaly Churkin was a successful child Soviet cinema actor. He was convincing in his roles, so the Soviet KGB wrote a new script for him and gave him a new role. One part of his new training was to learn the English language. Another part was learning "world history according to the KGB." Churkin memorized it well, and so he was sent out into the world with the Soviet diplomatic corps.

Once again, Churkin was persuasive in his new role, so after myriad smaller roles, he became an actor on the biggest global stage, taking on the role of the Permanent Representative of the Russian Federation at the United Nations in New York from 2006 until February 20, 2017, when he suddenly died.

On 21 February 2017, the New York Medical Examiner released the preliminary results of an autopsy performed on Churkin, which stated that the cause of death needed further study, which often indicates the need for toxicology tests. A gag order pursuant to a request of the U.S. State Department and the United States Mission to the United Nations suppressed public disclosure of the cause and manner of death, citing Churkin's posthumous diplomatic immunity. Russia maintained that the information was private and that disclosing details of the autopsy results could hurt his reputation. Churkin was posthumously awarded numerous Russian awards.

I met Mr. Churkin several times at the UN in my role as the Ukrainian World Congress's main representative at the UN. Impressed I wasn't. I was astounded. Astounded by Churkin's uncanny ability to lie without any betrayal in visage, body language, or voice timbre. Some of his best lies were: there was no famine, but more Russians died in the famine of 1932-33 than Ukrainians; Russia was asked to help the Baltic states in 1940, and so it intervened; Kyiv is the mother of all of Russia and has no relationship to Ukraine which came into existence initially as a Soviet state.

I specifically recall one press conference convened by Churkin and the Russian Mission in 2008 in essence to thwart any attempt by the Ukrainian Mission to pass a resolution declaring the Holodmor of 1932-33 a Genocide of the Ukrainian people. Churkin spouted his Soviet Russian propaganda. There was no time designated for questions, but I managed to overwhelm Churkin's microphone by asking why Russia was so adamant in refusing to honor the 7-10 million Ukrainians, including women and children, who perished. I was immediately surrounded by Russian and UN security. Nevertheless, a composed Ambassador Churkin told the security to stand back and that he would answer. And so he did, repeating his disinformation and propaganda, thanking all, and leaving. I said to myself, "Now, there is an actor."

In any event, the most recent UN General Assembly week was more of the same. It was an exercise in futility. Russian foreign minister Sergei Lavrov spoke for Russia. He was no Churkin. In his speech, as by his nature, he was the personification of a madman, threatening a nuclear Armageddon. U.S. President Joe Biden was strong in his rhetoric but feckless as usual in his meeting with Ukraine's President Zelensky.

President Zelensky spent a week in the United States accomplishing little. The nadir of his visit was an embarrassing trip to Trump Tower in New York, where Donald J. Trump boasted of his friendship with a criminal who runs Russia, imperils the entire world, has an outstanding warrant for his arrest from the International Criminal Court. Yet apparently, none of that matters; being Putin's friend is an attribute.

Next year, the UN will observe 80 years of its lack of efficacy. In that time the world has made little progress in terms of security, and even minimally as to world hunger. Big nations threaten smaller nations all the time. Most disputes are resolved by wars. Famines continue to exist. Women and children die unnaturally. Genocide and war crimes are never punished unless the victim is also the victor or an ally.

I noted above that I was not impressed by the likes of Vitaly Churkin. I stressed that I was astounded. Churkins come and go. He was a talented liar. Putin and Lavrov are much less talented actors, but the results are the same. Even allies are, more often than not, liars or, at the very least, disingenuous, except that they are called players or diplomats. Religious leaders mostly belong to the same category. The Pope is a farcical figure.

There has to be a solution. I do not know what it is, and so I offer none.

September 28, 2024

RESPECT

Certainly, one of the most egregious lies emanating from Trump and the MAGA campaign is that Trump and America were respected by the global democratic community while he was president. There is so much evidence to the contrary that the Trump campaign should relinquish this boast. Many considered Trump a buffoon; others simply winced at his behavior. And there was a prevailing fear of what may ensue in global security.

I should like to point to two nothing less than disgraceful Trump Summer of 2018 events during which the world not only did not respect the American leader but was appalled by his behaviour. At the Quebec G-7, Trump insisted that Russian President Vladimir Putin should have been included. The other members disagreed in view of his invasion and annexation of Ukrainian territory. They then agreed together with Trump upon a final communique. Trump left the Summit without signing it. The Canadian press took a baseball bat to Trump. But inasmuch as Trump had offended the host, Prime Minister Trudeau, I will defer to the Europeans.

The German "Der Spiegel" reported:

> *"The G-7 debacle shows the real problem with Donald Trump's politics is Donald Trump. His behaviour follows no order, no logic, instead just the desire to be the best, most important and biggest. The collapse of the West, the destruction of decades of friendship is simply a product of his unprecedented ego trips."*

The editorial board of one of France's biggest daily, "Le Monde" wrote:

> *"One thing is clear: the president of the United States, Donald Trump, is better disposed to the North Korean dictator Kim Jong-un, a man whose dynasty has locked his country and his people into a megalomaniac*

madness, than to his European, Japanese and Canadian allies [...] This kind of behavior has no precedent in the practice of diplomacy between allies. The Europeans must learn lessons from it now."

Trump then went to a Summit with Putin in Helsinki, Finland. This was the nadir of American global leadership as at the press conference, Trump acted as Putin's surrogate, acknowledging that Russia did not interfere in the 2016 American election and stressing his and Putin's "friendship."

"I hold both countries responsible, I think that the United States has been foolish. We've all been foolish. We're all to blame.

He later added that Putin "was extremely strong and powerful in his denials" of election meddling. And this: "My people came to me, [former Director of National Intelligence] Dan Coats came to me and some others, they said they think it's Russia. I have President Putin; he just said it's not Russia. I will say this: I don't see any reason why it would be."

Much more recently, in July of this year, with the specter of a Trump return as president quite real, the 2024 NATO Summit in Washington was a Summit of fear. The BBC reported:

"Camille Grand, a French former official who was one of Nato's deputy leaders throughout the Trump administration, described himself as "much more worried" than colleagues who think a second term may be "Trump [term] one on steroids" but ultimately workable for the alliance.'He doesn't have the same sort of guardrails, he doesn't have the same sort of adults in the room. And he has around him a team that is trying to turn his instinct into policy,' said Mr Grand, who is now a fellow at the European Council

on Foreign Relations. Four members of visiting delegations, who asked to remain anonymous, told the BBC their concern was not necessarily that a Trump administration would withdraw entirely from Nato, as he has threatened before. Rather it is a fear that the US commitment to the alliance's core principle of collective security - 'all for one and one for all', meaning any ally under attack can expect defence from the others - could wane. Trump's positions on Nato have veered erratically from outright hostility - portraying the alliance as a bunch of freeloading Europeans surviving off protection paid for by US taxpayers..."

I recently visited three countries in Europe on my way to and from Ukraine. In Frankfurt, at the Airport, an assistant volunteered her fear that Trump might be elected president. In Zurich, on the way back, another assistant looking over our passports voiced the same concern. In Krakow, Poland, where we stayed for two days, a guide and a hotel receptionist voiced their disapproval. Hearing that, an Irish group of tourists piled on.

In Ukraine, a representative of the Orthodox Church of Ukraine and an elderly lady just leaving services at a Ukrainian Catholic Church both told me that they were praying that Trump not be re-elected. Their spontaneous comments were peppered with such words as "very bad for Ukraine" and "an embarrassment for America as a global leader. A television interviewer who stated that Ukrainians are very much concerned with the American November elections sighed with relief when I tried to assure him that the American people, while often not well informed in the area of foreign affairs, are usually astute in recognizing a con man and that Trump will most assuredly lose the popular vote, but the electoral system is somewhat tricky. Nevertheless, I offered my opinion that the American people are conscious of history and the election of a black

Asian woman as president would be not only historic for America but overdue.

I remember watching the 2018 Helsinki Summit press conference. Aside from the pompadour and height difference, Trump and Putin were very much alike. Every time they opened their mouths, they lied. Current Republican Vice Presidential candidate J.D. Vance in 2015 compared Trump to Hitler. He has since remorsefully recanted for the sake of a political career. Senator, consider the similarities between Trump and Putin. Take your time. Granted, Trump does not kill his political opponents, kidnap children, commit war crimes, or perpetrate genocide. At least not yet. But he really has not had the chance. Let's not give him that chance.

October 3, 2024

A NECESSARY BUT NOT ENTIRELY TRANSPARENT MOVE BY POPE FRANCIS

There is probably no Ukrainian Catholic who is not happy about the new appointment of the Ukrainian bishop from Melbourne, Australia, Mykola Bychok, as Cardinal of the Ecumenical Catholic Church. The Ukrainian Catholic Church is the largest in Eastern Europe and has long deserved the appointment of a cardinal. Therefore, even the harshest critics of Pope Francis should not only rejoice but also praise the appointment of Cardinal Bychok and pray for him. He has a long and difficult road ahead of him because of his youth and the obvious fact that his choice was a political one.

The subject of the appointment itself is more than a little unexpected. Bishop Mykola Bychok will be the youngest Cardinal in the Church. He will also probably be the furthest removed geographically from the Vatican, even though communication networks are extraordinary today. He was born in Ukraine (Ternopil), served as a pastor in Ukraine and in America, and recently served as bishop for Ukrainian Catholics in Australia. He will be the only Cardinal from Australia, and as the Supreme Archbishop of the Ukrainian Catholic Church, nominally referred to as Patriarch Sviatoslav Shevchuk, said, Cardinal Mykola Bychok will represent the interests of Australia and also promote the interests of our UCC in the Vatican. Patriarch Sviatoslav obediently provided a diplomatic explanation of the geographical need of the Vatican.

But beyond the euphoria, even if artificial, many questions hang in the air and probably require a somewhat less diplomatic but real response. Why was the primate of the Ukrainian Catholic Church not nominated as Cardinal? After all, he is clearly the head of the Ukrainian Catholic Synod of Bishops. But that is the point. Pope

Francis does not want this. This would be a recognition of the autonomy of the Ukrainian Catholic Church or, God forbid, its Patriarchal state.

Pope Francis is not a friend of Ukrainians. In addition, as a person, he is very weak emotionally, subject to normal human weaknesses. These weaknesses are apparent in his behavior, including his delusions of a historic achievement of unity of Christian churches. For this reason, he even patronizes bandits Russian Strongman Putin and his lackey, so-called Patriarch Kiril. Religion is often an opiate, sometimes very useful for establishing a moral way of life, but very often it provides confusion such that the clergy is somehow above people, and blindness regarding the person of the Pope, that he acts under the influence of the Holy Spirit and therefore cannot make mistakes.

I ask why is the Ukrainian Catholic Church so disliked in the Vatican. This is a very difficult question, but one that has a logical and obvious answer.

A martyr for the Church after 17 years of Soviet camps, Patriarch Josif Slipyj, was not only respected in the whole world because of his martyrdom but also feared because he raised questions that undermined the authority of the Vatican when he posed the right of the Patriarchate of the Eastern rite Catholic Church according to Vatican II. Even spokesmen of the Ukrainian Church treated him with some trepidation because Joseph Slipyj was firm and principled in his convictions. This personality was greater than anyone in the Vatican, including the Holy Father, the Pope. Those who came after Patriarch Josyf were and are far from his greatness and even ceased to prolong his efforts, albeit mindlessly. Nevertheless, the concept of the autonomy of the Ukrainian Catholic Church is particularly disturbing for people like Pope Francis, both as pontiff and human.

There is also a second argument. The connections and deals between the Vatican and Moscow are quite old, and they also have to do with financial matters. The Vatican is not only the capital of the Universal Catholic Church but also the State and one of the largest capitalist real estate owners in the whole world. The Vatican Bank is at the service of investors, including Moscow, and this happens without transparency. The Catholic Church in America does not file tax returns.

In September 2023, the office of Ukraine's President Zelensky himself called Pope Francis a Russophile and accused him of financial cooperation with the Kremlin and Russian oligarchs to bypass Western sanctions imposed in view of the war. The Vatican routinely denied it but obviously did not open its books for investigation.

The discussion surrounding the finances of the Vatican is a very difficult matter, particularly because there is no mechanism to impose transparency. The emotions and perhaps jealousy of Pope Francis as a person, in particular, taking into account his past back in Argentina and as a Jesuit, are also not easy to unravel. One thing that can be said with certainty is that even for the most devoted faithful of the Catholic Church, during the election of Francis as Pope, the Holy Spirit was absent.

Besides all that, Ukrainian Catholics have their Cardinal to share with Australia. And they should rejoice.

October 10, 2024

POST SCRIPT BUT NOT THE EPILOGUE

And so, the war in Ukraine continues. There may be a settlement, a ceasefire, or even a temporary Ukrainian victory, but Russian aggression in Ukraine will continue so long as an Epilogue cannot be written on Russian imperialism. Russian aggression, at a first shortsighted glance, may be against Ukrainians and the persecuted nationalities within the Russian Federation, but the repercussions are felt across the globe.

I recently wrote about the Pope of Rome appointing a Ukrainian bishop from Australia as a Cardinal of the Ecumenical Catholic Church to some degree demeaning the Ukrainian Catholic Church, its faithful, and its Synod. I refer to it because, to a large degree, it manifests the reluctance of the Free World and, in this case, even the Religious Free World, to recognize and address tangibly a centuries-old and ever-contemporary scourge of evil known as the Russian Empire. Whatever the reason for this reluctance or passivity, including economic gain or fear of a potential Armageddon, this passivity is what keeps the evil empire alive, if not flourishing.

American President Ronald Reagan coined the term "Evil Empire". Unfortunately, he had only a passing idea of what that meant historically. The Soviet Union was indeed evil, but its worst atrocities had been equaled or even surpassed by Russia's czarist regime. They may be surpassed now by the successor to the USSR, the Russian Federation, as the Russian Empire is referred to today. From Ivan the Terrible to Peter I, to Josef Stalin to Vladimir Putin, all of these strongmen have common characteristics. In at least one case, that of Stalin, who was ethnically Georgian, all were exposed to Russian culture, literature, and even religion, always under state control. Stalin became a Russian. Dostoyevsky's Raskolnikov was the resolute product of a culture that was and is a symbol of everything that is dark and wrong with human beings when exposed to a contagious disease known as imperialism.

While today, there are many proposals, some even sincere, which have been made to end the current war, optimistic or not, there is only one solution to Russian aggression. Complete victory for Ukraine on the battlefield is, unfortunately, wishful thinking. Many other factors are at play.

The only valid conclusion is that Russia ceases to be an aggressor/ but that can happen only when it stops being an empire. There is no reason to fool oneself. A contemporary Russian democrat, if I may employ an oxymoron, recently opined on what is needed: the formation of a truly federal state based on a treaty among those regions that will include both Russian areas and non-Russian ones, which may then decide to work together. Further, this Russian democrat stressed that all these regions must be equal in status and have the right of exit, and they must be able to define their own borders instead of relying on Soviet ones.

For the benefit of the well-meaning but awfully naive proponent of such a solution, I will not expose her name or credentials except to credit or blame "Window on Eurasia – New Series" that published this insanity. I could not find a disclaimer on behalf of the publisher, but given the naivete (hopefully not intentional disinformation), this proposition is precisely what cannot be supported. This was the crux of the USSR as well as the Russian Federation. A treaty with Russians! What a concept. Ask the Ukrainians.

Ask the Chechens, the Tatars, the Kalmyks, the Bashkirs, the Buryats, the Sakhas, the Erzya, the Circassians, and many others with the Russian Federation how successful in terms of national self-determination or even simple cultural freedom that formula has proven to be. Non-Russians represent perhaps 30-40% of the Russian Federation in terms of population but a majority of its territory. The non-Russians have no rights culturally or otherwise.

Another part of this war's temporary postscript for purposes of a negotiated settlement is a very strong argument for the further enlargement of NATO. Stop playing games with Ukraine's obvious qualifications and need for NATO membership. Currently, the settlement considerations by the Russians appear to be a reward for Russian bad behavior in the form of illegally begotten territory as well as Ukrainian forbearance from NATO membership.

An immediate invitation to NATO membership for Ukraine eliminates that negotiating issue and chips in Russia's possession. While NATO countries are reluctant to send boots to free invaded Ukrainian territory, it is entirely within their power to offer Ukraine membership in NATO immediately. The result of such an invitation would not be World War 3 but an immediate diminution of the Russian bargaining position. Too bad President Biden does not understand.

In the long run, even with a docile Russia (not the Russian Federation, aka Empire) within its own more or less Russian borders (whatever that may be), NATO must be enlarged further to prevent any possibility of future Russian aggression. Russians have to be weaned slowly, like a drug addict, from their imperialistic affliction. Unfortunately, there are no drugs that may be beneficial, but fear is a strong deterrent. For the first time, perhaps, Russians must experience fear of dismantling their aggression or lack of their own sovereignty should aggression against their neighbors continue.

Ordinary Russians must be imbued with the idea that life is so much better in a democratic, market-oriented society where they may criticize with impunity their own leaders and yet have a television in every room of their house and a car for every member of their household.

Many good people have died. But there will be many more trials and tribulations and more victims. We are only at the beginning of hopefully the end of the Russian empire and Russian aggression, which is the ultimate goal and quite distant.

October 15, 2024

INDEX

www.ingramcontent.com/pod-product-compliance
Lightning Source LLC
Chambersburg PA
CBHW052109030426
42335CB00025B/2900

www.ingramcontent.com/pod-product-compliance
Lightning Source LLC
Chambersburg PA
CBHW052109030426
42335CB00025B/2900